P9-CNI-256

OUTDOOR COOKBOOK

WITHDRAWN

THE
SCOUT'S
OUTDOOR COOKBOOK

Christine and Tim Conners

FALCONGUIDES ®

GUILFORD, CONNECTICUT
HELENA, MONTANA
AN IMPRINT OF THE GLOBE PEQUOT PRESS

South Sioux City Public Library
2121 Dakota Avenue
South Sioux City, NE 68776

To buy books in quantity for corporate use
or incentives, call **(800) 962–0973**
or e-mail **premiums@GlobePequot.com.**

FALCONGUIDES®

Copyright © 2008 by Tim and Christine Conners

ALL RIGHTS RESERVED. No part of this book may be reproduced or transmitted in any form by any means, electronic or mechanical, including photocopying and recording, or by any information storage and retrieval system, except as may be expressly permitted in writing from the publisher. Requests for permission should be addressed to The Globe Pequot Press, Attn: Rights and Permissions Department, P.O. Box 480, Guilford CT 06437.

Falcon and FalconGuides are registered trademarks of Morris Book Publishing, LLC.

Text design by Sheryl P. Kober

Photo well credits: pp. i (top), vii (bottom) www.troop195greece.com; p. i (bottom) Julia Whiteneck, Bedford Hanscom Girl Scouts, Massachusetts; pp. ii (top left), iii (bottom right), iv (top); vi (botttom); Ed Bedford, SM Troop 820, Chapel Hill, North Carolina; p. iii (top) Al Direnzi and Anthony Catalano, BSA Troop 138, Rochester, New York; p. ii (top right) Judy Harbison; pp. ii (bottom), v (top), viii (top, middle, and bottom) Tim Conners, Statesboro, Georgia; pp. iii (bottom left), vi (top) Dave Morgan, ASM Troop 820, Chapel Hill, North Carolina; pp. v (bottom), vii (top) Gregg Shupe; and p. iv (bottom) Ken Harbison.

Library of Congress Cataloging-in-Publication Data is available on file.

ISBN 978-0-7627-4067-3

Printed in the United States of America

10 9 8 7 6 5 4 3

Contents

DEDICATION

To our children,

James, Michael, Maria, and David—

for the happiness you bring . . .

BENEDICTION

Those who hope in the Lord will renew their strength.

They will soar on wings like eagles; they will run and not

grow weary, they will walk and not be faint.

—ISAIAH 40:31 (NIV)

Acknowledgments

This book wouldn't have been possible without the recipes, recommendations, and critiques provided by the hundreds of outdoor camp cooking experts who assisted us along the way. Your positive attitude, limitless patience, and genuine enthusiasm in this project were the stimuli that kept us going. In retrospect, a simple expression of gratitude seems entirely inadequate. To all of you who taught us the wonders of scout cooking, please accept our heartfelt appreciation.

We couldn't use every recipe from the many hundreds that we reviewed and tested. Nevertheless, all the input received helped us to mold and strengthen the book in some fashion. For those who provided material that was not included in the end product, we are indebted to you as well.

Piece by piece, this book came together through the effort of all our contributors. But certain individuals played leading roles. Ken and Judy Harbison not only furnished a host of great recipes but also helped extensively with testing. The Harbisons combine a love of outdoor cooking with a deep interest in the science behind food preparation. Their attention to detail helped secure victory on many occasions as we worked through serious kinks in the testing process. In addition, Katie Cox, Ed Bedford, Millie Hutchison, Jamison Yardley, Sherry Bennett, and Kathleen Kirby collectively provided a multitude of awesome recipes and tips used throughout the book. Thanks so much to all of you. And a special note of gratitude to Will Satak, Chip Reinhardt, Georgia Bosse, and Bob Ballou, each of whom provided material critical to the appendices.

Scott Daniels, Managing Editor of *Scouting* magazine, played an essential role in kick-starting this project by providing information for hundreds of recipes from a national outdoor cooking competition sponsored by Boy Scouts of America. Through this treasure trove of data, we were able to make contact with dozens of experienced camp cooks. Their recipes and advice became an invaluable foundation and springboard. This book wouldn't have been the same without your help, Scott.

Special thanks to our Aussie friend and Scoutmaster, Max Coles, who contributed valuable material for the prefatory sections. Aware of our burgeoning interest in camp cooking, Max introduced us several years ago to a local camp Dutch oven expert who provided us with a rundown of the basics. With that, we

were launched into the world of cast iron, gaining a hands-on appreciation for the sizable differences between trail and camp cookery. Cheers, Max, for helping two backpackers learn that all that is heavy is not necessarily evil!

From the time they published our first outdoor cookbook, *Lipsmackin' Backpackin'*, the folks at Globe Pequot Press have impressed us with their support and professionalism. In particular, we are indebted to the efforts of Jeff Serena, Associate Publisher, and Max Phelps, Director of Sales and Marketing, who believed in this project and made it a reality. And special thanks to our editor, Heather Carreiro, project manager, Gia C. Manalio, and production manager, Melissa Evarts, for their thoroughness and patience as they ran out of red ink and hard drive space polishing the mother of all outdoor cookbooks.

By design, camp cooking produces a lot of grub; and our testing process resulted in thousands of pounds of food that even our family of six couldn't keep up with. We quickly realized that this dilemma presented a perfect opportunity to share our meals with acquaintances. But our actions weren't completely altruistic: We asked for their opinions and suggestions in exchange for the food! So here's to the many friends, neighbors, scouts, coworkers, and family members who helped us make the often difficult decision as to which recipes would remain on the list of the best of the best.

Introduction

We weren't certain what we were witnessing. Before us lay a large platform, knee-high, lined with long rows of large iron containers, all buried in a searing bed of coals. The crew was hard at work, quickly and quietly executing their tasks in the sweltering evening air. Using heavy gloves for protection, one worker carefully pulled coal-covered vessels from the red-hot bed while another prepared fresh containers to take the place of the ones that had just been carried off. Hot coals were shoveled onto the bare lids of the replacements. With assembly-line efficiency, the process continued in the same manner as it had all day. But it wasn't the operations of a foundry we were observing. We were watching Boy Scouts make Dutch oven peach cobbler!

And that was our introduction to camp cookery. Our forte was trail cooking, and we had already authored two successful books in the genre, *Lipsmackin' Backpackin'* and *Lipsmackin' Vegetarian Backpackin'*. Perhaps not surprisingly then, our preference had been to forgo traditional camp life, with its large and heavy equipment load typically based out of a nearby car, for the simpler life on the trail, living instead out of a backpack.

Now with four children of our own, two of whom were Cub Scouts, traditional car-based camping in established sites was becoming a more practical option for us. But along with it came a desire to expand our cooking options. We were experts at using a backpacking stove, but we didn't know a Dutch oven from a pie iron. Standing squarely between trail and camp was a dense material called cast iron, and the thought of piling coals on and around a heavy cook pot was a completely alien proposition.

Introduced to Scoutmaster Brad Thompson through a mutual acquaintance, we observed Thompson's scouts creating cobbler with magical precision that evening. The wonderful aroma belied the dusty and dingy scene. It was a brand-new experience as we watched hot, gritty, ash-covered lids lifted to reveal steaming wholesome treasures within: fresh Georgia peaches intermingled with golden brown pie dough, subsequently heaped into bowls and covered with ice cream.

We were witnessing an award-winning performance by Boy Scout Troop 400 at the annual Seafood Festival in Richmond Hill, Georgia. The judges would once again give Thompson and his boys top honors for their very popular dish. And having had this preview of camp cookery magic, we wanted to explore further. That is what we did, and you'll find what we learned in this book—yes, even the recipe for Troop 400 Peach Cobbler.

The Lost Art of Cooking

Food quickly heated, thrown on a plate, and rapidly devoured is not worthy to be compared with a meal carefully planned in advance, thoughtfully prepared through teamwork and camaraderie, slowly cooked in growing anticipation within a heady aromatic cloud, then shared together around the table or campfire. Scouting is one of few remaining venues in which the joy and art of cooking find a natural and welcome place within the order of the day.

The importance of food in scouting is famously well known. The sequence of daily events hinges upon the schedule of the meals. Scout camps are often constructed and arranged around chow halls. Cooking competitions flourish. A skilled chef is revered. But don't think that cookery falls in priority when scouts travel on expeditions to points far away. In fact, once scouts roam from their base camps and chow halls, the creativity found in real camp cooking blossoms. Out come the cook pots, Dutch ovens, and skillets. Over coals and campfires, in any locale and through all kinds of weather, scouts gather together, taking the time to create something truly special through a shared meal outdoors.

Beyond its obvious value of providing sustenance, cooking teaches thoughtfulness, cooperation, and gratitude. It emphasizes the need for careful planning, while requiring thoroughness, cleanliness, and caution in execution. It values creativity, patience, and resourcefulness. And, in the end, it rewards its apprentices with a wonderful bounty that brings people together in an atmosphere of friendship. The art of cookery wraps together a host of valuable skills that are worthy of learning, retaining, and passing along to our posterity.

But cooking skills are fast disappearing in an age when preprocessed and precooked food products increasingly dominate the options found at the grocery store. The many positive attributes associated with skillful cookery are languishing and becoming lost. Most younger people don't have any idea how to prepare a meal using individual ingredients, let alone outdoors away from the microwave. But even with modern society progressively valuing convenience, within scouting are bastions that preserve and celebrate the art of cooking. As any seasoned scout cook can testify, leaders and their charges wanting to fully explore the wonder of outdoor cooking will find a welcoming environment that generously rewards their aspirations and effort.

For those new to outdoor cooking, this book will help you acquire a full set of basic skills while building a solid foundation for future creativity and exploration. Dozens of skilled "camp cookies" from across the United States provided material for our book, so even experienced chefs will find plenty of new recipes and techniques that will add additional dimension and enjoyment to their outdoor cooking.

Concerned that you aren't up to the task of learning what might seem to be a daunting new skill? Don't be. A few years ago, with our knowledge of outdoor cooking limited to backpacking, we would have been lost creating a hot meal in camp without a backpack stove or grill. But our first Dutch oven dish turned out fantastic despite ourselves. And in no time at all, camp cooking became second nature. Now we could probably prepare corn bread in a hurricane. We've written this book to make it hard to mess up. So turn to a recipe, jump right in, and your scouts will be calling you camp cookie before the end of your next outing!

How Is This Cookbook Unique?

Many cookbooks are composed of material from only a handful of contributors. This can be a positive attribute should the reader favor a particular cooking style. But outdoor cooking for scouts is a significant problem requiring very creative solutions. To satisfactorily solve this problem for our readers, we sought counsel from nearly two hundred outdoor chefs from across the United States. Having captured the skill, creativity, and diversity of these many contributors, we're confident that we've met our objective: providing the scouting world with a wide variety of unambiguous and trustworthy recipes that will consistently produce excellent meals in the outdoors.

The camp recipes in this book are favorites of leaders from the Boy Scouts of America and the Girl Scouts of the USA. Many of these contributors have exceptional scouting credentials. Some have served as outdoor cooking trainers. And a large number have won impressive culinary awards. Several leaders contributed recipes with historical significance. Applying the same techniques we used in creating *Lipsmackin' Backpackin'* and *Lipsmackin' Vegetarian Backpackin'*, we've tested and refined every recipe, carefully gleaning each from a much larger original collection.

Many interesting camp cooking methods have been used by scouts over the years. Planks, foil, pie irons, and, of course, pots, skillets, and Dutch ovens are some of the more common devices employed to cook food. Sources of heat include charcoal briquettes, campfires, grills, camp stoves, box ovens, reflector ovens, solar collectors, vagabond stoves, and buddy burners. The history of scout cooking is a study in creativity and resourcefulness. But not all tools and methods listed remain equally popular. This book emphasizes the best cooking techniques currently used in scouting.

Different outdoor cooking situations present different challenges. For instance, long-distance backpackers require light and durable meals loaded with nutrition and flavor. Camp cooking for scouts presents its own very unique problem, with the emphasis placed less on the food's performance and more on the leader's need to entertain, teach, cheer, and nourish young scouts at mealtime. Leaders are challenged by the requirement to cook large quantities of food in a cost-efficient, no-nonsense manner while creating a mealtime environment that scouts find educational and enjoyable. When cooking outdoors for scouts, the characteristics that are valued are those that assist or streamline the end-to-end process, from planning and purchasing to preparation and presentation. This book was built exclusively upon recipes and techniques that emphasize those characteristics valued by scout leaders.

We've worked hard to make each recipe easy to follow using reliable and objective instructions that eliminate guesswork and variability. We eliminated opportunities for confusion and avoided cluttering the main body of the recipe with information not directly applicable to the instructions. Ingredient lists are clean and consistent in format from recipe to recipe. Preparation steps are sequentially numbered for smooth workflow that provides opportunity for leaders to clearly delegate tasks. We've also included interesting anecdotes from our contributors that add personality and shed colorful light on many of the recipes.

Breakfast, lunch, and dinner are thoroughly covered in this cookbook. And say goodbye to that sweet tooth: Our collection of snacks and desserts will keep it happy for years. A sizeable assortment of bread and drink recipes round out the list. Classic favorites and many excellent surprises are found throughout. And there are plenty of unconventional recipes that scouts, young and old, will cherish. Spanning over three hundred recipes, this book captures a large variety of cooking methods, food types, and cultural influence. Inside these pages, we are confident you will find the most comprehensive, delicious, and scout-friendly collection of outdoor recipes ever brought together in one book.

We'd love to hear from you. Stop by www.booksbyconners.com with any comments or suggestions or just to say howdy.

Using This Book

Our cookbook doesn't require an instruction manual to get started, but there are many organizational considerations worth knowing that will make the book easier and more enjoyable to use.

Recipe Categories

Categorizing recipes is never a straightforward process for a cookbook author. As personalities would have it, some enjoy pancakes for dinner and others prefer their largest meals at noontime. There are breads that make a meal all by themselves, and one person's dessert is another's between-meal snack. It's a subjective business when grouping recipes into categories. There is no single answer that everyone agrees with. But, as we found with our backpack cookbooks, it's possible to use an approach that satisfies most. So going with what we know, we've applied the same philosophy for organizing this book: Chapters are arranged by the three main meals—Breakfast, Lunch, and Dinner. They are further organized by the three most popular non-meal categories: Breads, Snacks and Desserts, and Drinks.

You'll recognize that we used a more traditional approach for grouping recipes into the breakfast and dinner chapters, building those sections around dishes typically prepared in the morning and evening hours. Bread recipes are fairly straightforward and stand apart by themselves, as do drinks. Light snacks are grouped with heavier after-meal desserts. Non-meat side dishes are a popular subcategory in some circles. But for this cookbook, the line between entree and side dish was thoroughly blurred by the hearty nature of our non-meat dishes. The creation of a dedicated side dish chapter would have appeared artificial and forced, and so we refrained from doing so. That left us with the category of lunch, always a tricky prospect for the outdoor cookbook author.

The lunch section was constructed on several premises, the most important being that the camp cook will usually seek easier meals so scouts can rapidly move on to their scheduled activities in the early afternoon. We suspect that a scout leader preparing a more involved meal at midday would naturally consult the recipes in the dinner section. We also avoided providing instructions for the obvious: simple cold sandwiches and the like. Instead, we built this section using unique and tasty recipes that can be quickly prepared, served, and cleaned up. Many of our lunch recipes are no-cook. Only a grill, camp stove, or a leftover campfire from breakfast is necessary for those recipes that require heat. Dutch oven cooking is far from difficult, but it can require added preparation and cleanup compared to other methods. So this technique was reserved for morning and evening, when the pace is often more leisurely.

Servings

Scouting demands a lot of food. The recipes in this book are generally designed to feed a hungry patrol or small troop. It's a straightforward task to multiply recipes as required to meet the needs of a larger group size, especially when using Dutch ovens. It's often less easy to scale down a dish; and so you'll also find an assortment of recipes developed specifically for smaller companies. Several recipes indicate only one serving. These have been designed to be fully scalable to the exact needs of your group simply by multiplying the recipe as required.

This book endeavors to satisfy the taste buds of a very diverse population: young, finicky Tiger Cubs and Daisies; famished teenaged scouts and young adult Eagles; and senior leaders with more refined palates. As if that wasn't enough, we attempted to compute each recipe's serving potential. Age, gender, activity level, richness of the meal, food preferences, snacking, even altitude—these all influence how many servings you'll obtain from each recipe. For consistency, our estimates generally assume the target audience to be hungry teenagers. Adjust your estimates according to your specific situation.

Challenge Level

Using a simple three-tier system, we've selected a challenge level for each recipe, basing our decision on the amount of preparation and cleanup required, the sensitivity of the cooking technique to variation, and the attention to care necessary to avoid injury.

This isn't an exact science, and it wasn't always immediately obvious to which challenge category each recipe should be assigned. Nevertheless, tagged as "easy" were those requiring less preparation and fewer ingredients, using only a few cooking utensils or one primary heating method, and which have brief and objective cooking instructions. Most of the recipes in the book belong to this category. When the ingredient list grew longer and required more cutting, chopping, and preparation, or once additional heat sources and major cooking instruments were introduced, then the challenge level became "moderate." About one-third of the recipes were labeled as such.

When a large amount of preparation or many cooking instruments became necessary, once the chances of success became highly dependent on finesse, or when considerable caution was required, the challenge became "difficult." We didn't want to frustrate our readers by including an excessive number of these recipes, so they are purposely few in number. But those that remain are valuable for two reasons: First, they are absolutely superb dishes worthy of the attempt, and second, they are meant to serve as exercises for scout leaders to further hone their skills and creativity. Reach for the next level and challenge yourselves. You and your scouts will enjoy the results!

Preparation Instructions

Instructions for each recipe include a list of ingredients along with step-by-step directions, each logically grouped and presented in numerical sequence. The use of numerical sequencing in the preparation steps is intended to not only help the chef stay focused but also to assist leaders in quickly identifying and assigning appropriate food preparation tasks to their scouts. The vast majority of recipes are prepared completely in camp, but some require at-home preparation steps. Those that do clearly indicate so. Note that ingredient lists have been adjusted to create less waste of key items.

Heating instructions are clear and consistent and provide high probability of success under a wide range of cooking conditions. Recipes requiring campfires, cookstoves, or grills as their heat source are generally more tolerant to deviation from the cooking directions. However, under conditions of potentially significant variability, be ready to use a food thermometer to ensure that the meal has been warmed to an adequately safe temperature before serving.

Compared to other methods, Dutch oven cooking generally requires additional attention to managing the heat source. Because some recipes are more sensitive to cooking temperature, a range in baking time is often provided and the end objective is also clearly stated. As an example, a recipe might also state that a cake is ready when an inserted fork comes out clean, irrespective of elapsed time.

To help avoid confusion, we always specify an exact number of briquettes (coals) to use on the lid and under the oven. In lieu of a coal count, many contributors originally specified a cooking temperature for their Dutch oven recipes. In practice, it's difficult to accurately read the temperature within a Dutch oven because the process requires removing the lid, which, in turn, quickly vents the heat you're trying to measure. So we transformed these notional baking temperatures into more-practical equivalent coal counts using widely available conversion data provided by Lodge Manufacturing Company. This information is replicated in the following table.

Coal-Temperature Conversion Chart

Dutch Oven Diameter		Oven Temperature					
		325°F	350°F	375°F	400°F	425°F	450°F
8"	Total Briquettes	15	16	17	18	19	20
	On Lid	10	11	11	12	13	14
	Underneath Oven	5	5	6	6	6	6
10"	Total Briquettes	19	21	23	25	27	29
	On Lid	13	14	16	17	18	19
	Underneath Oven	6	7	7	8	9	10
12"	Total Briquettes	23	25	27	29	31	33
	On Lid	16	17	18	19	21	22
	Underneath Oven	7	8	9	10	10	11
14"	Total Briquettes	30	32	34	36	38	40
	On Lid	20	21	22	24	25	26
	Underneath Oven	10	11	12	12	13	14
16"	Total Briquettes	37	39	41	43	45	47
	On Lid	25	26	27	28	29	30
	Underneath Oven	12	13	14	15	16	17

If you require an actual baking temperature, say, for instance, to modify the recipe or to adapt it to a larger or smaller oven, the conversion chart can be used to make the transformation by converting the specified coal count and Dutch oven size back into a temperature value.

We've found this conversion chart to be very reliable when baking with cast-iron stoves under pleasant Georgia weather using standard size, high-quality briquettes, fresh from the charcoal starter. But outdoor cooking is often performed in non-ideal conditions, and your Dutch oven cooking results will vary based on the size and condition of the coals as well as your weather conditions. In particular, pay close attention to coal size. If the hot briquettes have significantly eroded, increase the number of coals to compensate.

Options and Tips

Our contributors often provided interesting cooking options germane to their recipes. Options deviate from the main instructions, producing wonderful alternate endings to the recipe or adding additional dimension to the dish. We felt that embedding these options within the main body of the preparation steps would have been distracting to the camp chef, especially when using the recipe for the first time or when delegating cooking tasks to others. Therefore, options included with a recipe are grouped separately from the main preparation steps.

Likewise, contributors occasionally offered helpful tips that would assist the camp cook with purchasing ingredients or preparing the recipe in some way. As with options, tips not directly applicable to the preparation steps were listed separately from the main body of the recipe. In addition, recommendations and tips of a more generic nature, or applicable to a wider range of recipes and situations, are presented separately in the next chapter.

Required Equipment

To assist scout leaders with planning and preparation, a list of cooking equipment required at camp follows each set of instructions. For reasons of practicality and space, not every item required to prepare a recipe is listed. For example, a cooler or refrigeration device is obviously essential for keeping perishable foods safe. It is assumed that one is always available for use. In addition, a food thermometer, measuring devices, can opener, cutting knives, cutting board, long-handle wooden spoons, ladles, plates, cups, utensils, and a greasing agent such as vegetable oil are all presumed to be basic equipment residing in any scout cook's outdoor kitchen.

It is also assumed you'll have the necessary tools and equipment available for preparing the heat source required for the recipe, be it campfire, grill, camp stove, or briquettes for the Dutch oven. However, once a recipe's equipment necessities went beyond the list of these basics, we captured the requirements to help head off any meal-time surprises in the field. To keep the focus on camp, equipment required for any at-home preparation steps is not included in the list.

If you're a new camp chef, perhaps you're thinking you'll need to break the bank to get started in some serious outdoor cooking. You may be surprised to learn we prepared nearly every recipe in this book using only a handful of primary cooking utensils, most of which we already had in our modest kitchen. We used standard sundry pots and pans, including a 10-quart stock pot, our largest. For roasting hot sandwiches and goodies over the campfire, we put to occasional use a simple pie iron made of cast metal.

The real workhorses were our Lodge cast-iron heavyweights. But even then, we only needed a few items: a pair of camp Dutch ovens and a skillet. Our Dutch ovens cover two capacities: one at 12 inches diameter and 3¾ inches deep (6-quart), and the other at 14 inches diameter and 5 inches deep (10-quart). The skillet is a behemoth at 15¼ inches in diameter. A huge fry pan is certainly awe-inspiring. Ours could probably qualify as the Eighth Wonder of the World.

The large majority of Dutch oven recipes in this book were prepared using our 12-inch/6-quart oven, one of the more popular sizes available, but on the low side of the capacity range for an oven of this diameter. Because we used this lower capacity 12-incher for testing, nearly any model of this diameter is likely to provide adequate capacity when a 12-inch oven is called for. On occasion, our 14-inch/10-quart monster became a necessity, especially when roasting large cuts of meat or baking tall tube cakes. When a deep 14-inch oven is required by a recipe, the equipment list explicitly states so.

When skillets, cook pots, and mixing bowls are specified, we've opted to use the tags "small," "medium," and "large" to identify the required capacity. We believe that over-specifying the size requirements for these items is unnecessary and tiring for the user. Most folks already carry an assortment of sizes for each of these kinds of cooking utensils. By having several sizes available at camp, you'll never find yourself in a pickle during food preparation. If ever in doubt on utensil size requirements, simply err on the side of larger capacity.

Contributor Information

Rounding out each recipe, you'll find information about the contributor. These are the stars of our book: the scouts and scout leaders who made it all possible. In addition to their names and location of current residence, biographical data include their scouting title, troop, and council information. Nearly every state in the Union is represented by our contributors, about four-fifths of whom are associated with Boy Scouts of America and the remaining one-fifth with Girl Scouts of the USA.

Appendices

Each of the appendices at the back of the book covers a distinct and specific topic that the camp cook should find useful or educational. Much of the material has been provided by noted experts in their respective fields.

Measurement Conversions are provided in Appendix A. Customary in any cookbook, this information is included to help the chef with common conversion tasks and to assist international readers with the transformation from U.S. to metric kitchen measurements.

Cast-Iron Essentials are covered in Appendix B. If you've read through the remainder of the preface material, it will already be clear that cast iron in general, and the camp Dutch oven in particular, make for extremely versatile cookware worthy of a prominent role in any camp chef's repertoire. If you're new to camp cookery or have been hesitant to jump into cast-iron cooking, this section will provide encouragement along with a rundown of the basics.

Cooking in Cardboard, Appendix C, explains box oven essentials. The home-made box oven remains a popular cooking device within scouting. A properly constructed box oven holds an advantage over a Dutch oven for heating foods that are awkwardly large or which require finesse in controlling oven temperature. We never found it necessary to use a box oven for the recipes in this book. But because the cooking method is well-established in some circles, many of our recipes note where a box oven could serve as an alternate to the Dutch oven. Instructions for building a simple box oven are included.

Zero impact Cooking practices are discussed in Appendix D. Outdoor cooking can be messy business, especially when preparing food for a large group of scouts. Scraps, packaging waste, and discarded leftovers all detract from the beauty of our wild places and can harm local flora and fauna if not properly disposed of. When applying zero impact cooking principles, extra consideration is given to the planning and preparation process, resulting in less impact and a more enjoyable environment. Refer to this appendix for recommendations on how to leave the outdoors in better condition than you found it.

Find Your Path on the National Trails, Appendix E, is presented to inspire scouts and leaders. This information provides a portal to an America that many may not realize exists: regions rich in adventure, places that challenge and motivate, wilderness and history that can change lives forever. Look beyond the formal camp environment by learning more about the work of the Partnership for the National Trails System and the more than 43,000 miles of trails that this group is helping to create, preserve, and protect.

Recipe Icons

Large cookbooks are often bewildering at first glance. We designed an icon-based category system, employed at the top of each page, to help readers quickly narrow their search for recipes of interest.

Recipe Icons Category System

Dutch oven with coals

Cook pot on camp stove

Skillet on camp stove or fire

Foil, pie iron, or skewer over flames or in fire pit

Foil, skewer, or other direct heating on grill

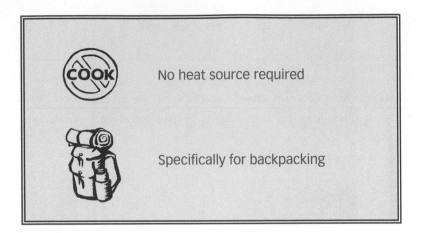

Any recipe can be categorized in many different ways: by required cooking tools, heat source, ingredients, and so on. The best method to apply to a scout outdoor cookbook wasn't immediately obvious to us, but after reviewing and testing all the recipes from our contributors, we saw that each could be readily identified by one of the following techniques: Dutch oven with coals, cook pot on a camp stove, skillet over stove or fire, direct heating in or over a campfire, direct heating on a grill, or no heating required in camp. Some recipes were developed specifically for the backpack. All backpacking recipes could have been identified by one of the previous techniques, but their intended application is so unique that a special identification seemed appropriate. The result was a total of seven icons as indicated in the legend above.

With one glance, our icon system provides you with a rapid introduction to the primary tools and heat sources required for each recipe. Will a grill or fire pit not be available on your next camp out? The icon system quickly moves you past the recipes that won't be an option for you. Don't have a Dutch oven? The remaining icons immediately point you to your many alternatives.

No simple system can perfectly categorize every recipe, especially those that are more involved. For example, some recipes call for the use of a cook pot and a Dutch oven. In cases like these, where more than one icon was an option, we identified the recipe by the technique most critical to the recipe's success.

Recommendations and Tips

Bona fide cooking is hardly effortless. Awash in convenience food options, it's easy to forget how long it actually takes to prepare a real meal. We unconsciously grab the box of lasagna out of the freezer and pop it in the microwave for a few minutes. Imagine making that lasagna from scratch!

We were recently throwing a scout food dinner party, a blend of informal fun and constructive criticism also designed to rid ourselves of the hundreds of pounds of "test" food that we were once again buried in. We had already hosted several such events in the past, but this would be the grand finale, during the frantic press to finish the cookbook. On hand were more than one dozen entrees in huge aluminum trays and an entire table covered in Dutch oven desserts. So much food that we had to ask neighbors to help us by storing much of it in their freezers before the event. Enough for over two hundred people.

Bags under our eyes, we mingled with the guests when one remarked, "You must have been up late last night making all of this food!" Recovering from the initial shock, we received it as the compliment it was intended to be. But our guest actually thought we were able to assemble two dozen massive dishes in one evening, a process that actually took nearly two weeks!

Preparing real food, especially outdoors, isn't always easy, nor should it be. Our recommendations and tips—in fact, this book—aren't about hastening the process. They've been written to help your mealtimes become more enjoyable. So roll up your shirtsleeves and, rather than saving time, get ready to make memories instead.

Getting Started in Outdoor Cooking

- If you are new to camp cooking, often the best advice is to keep it simple initially. As you become more skilled and confident in your abilities, increase the number of recipes prepared from scratch and raise the challenge level.

- Wind, rain, snow, bugs, and wild animals. Keep these in mind as you plan your outdoor meals. Be realistic about what you can handle under the expected circumstances, and don't overwhelm yourself with many complicated meals.

- Don't hesitate to ask other leaders and older, more mature scouts for assistance. But avoid accepting the offer from too many of the younger helpers until you become proficient and are better able to multitask.

- In the event you need a backup plan, it doesn't hurt to have a little extra food on the side or an escape route mapped to the nearest grocer!

Safe Cooking Habits

- An adult leader or experienced senior scout should always direct and supervise the cooking activities of younger scouts, especially when heat and sharp utensils are involved.

- Ensure that any water used for cooking has been properly treated or purified before using.

- To help prevent food-related illness, care should be taken when handling raw meat to prevent cross-contamination of other foods such as raw vegetables. Cutting surfaces and utensils should either be dedicated to preparing raw meats or thoroughly washed prior to use for other purposes. In addition, use a food thermometer to check meat and egg dishes for doneness prior to serving. This is especially important when preparing recipes that are new to you.

- Something mysterious often occurs when normally well-behaved kids are handed sticks and other sharp objects in the vicinity of campfires. Self-control rapidly regresses into behavior that may bring to mind the image of cavorting Neanderthals. It is imperative that cooking activities involving skewers be carefully monitored and controlled by a mature leader to prevent puncture wounds and burns.

- Pie irons remain hot for a long time after being removed from the fire. Their small size can be deceiving. To prevent burns, reload heated pie irons with care. While they are cooling, don't place them in an unsafe area where they can be accidentally forgotten, handled, or sat upon.

- Caution is required when pouring hot water into ziplock bags to reconstitute foods. To help protect against rupture, use thick-walled freezer-type bags. Brace the bag inside a cook pot to help keep the bag upright while pouring and to contain any spills.

Dutch Oven Cooking

- Avoid raising the lid on your Dutch oven while baking as heat is quickly lost in doing so. And when removing the lid, do so slowly and carefully to prevent coal ash from falling into the oven onto your food. This is especially true when cooking under windy conditions.

- Intense heat is transferred through the walls of the oven in those areas where coals are in direct contact with the metal. To prevent your food from charring, keep coals from touching the sides or bottom of the oven. And avoid stacking food so high that it touches the inside surface of the lid if coals are to be placed on top of the oven.

- To help prevent hot spots from burning your food while baking, rotate the oven one-quarter of a turn over the coals every 15 minutes of cooking time. At the same time, use a lid-lifter to carefully rotate the lid one-quarter turn relative to the base. When doing this, avoid lifting the lid completely from the oven to prevent excessive heat from escaping.

- Don't put hot briquettes directly on moist soil. Doing so will almost surely cause the coals to quickly fail. Instead, place your coals on a metal tray or other hard, fireproof surface to avoid this problem. Setting the legs of the oven on a tray or brick surface also prevents settling and direct contact with the coals under the oven.

- When camping in snow with no exposed soil surface available, it may be necessary to cook above the ground using a small sturdy metal table designed specifically for Dutch oven cooking. This type of device is also useful for reducing the amount of squatting and stooping otherwise required when cooking with Dutch ovens.

- A screen made from heavy-duty aluminum foil or sheet metal is a requirement in rainy weather or windy conditions. You might be surprised at how quickly a hot coal can erode in high wind.

- Always bring plenty of extra charcoal briquettes to cover contingencies. Many are the times we've started a batch of coals only to have the food preparation process take longer than expected. With the original batch of coals mostly eroded, more were required. Less than ideal weather conditions can also greatly increase the number of coals you may need.

- Use a wooden spoon for mixing and stirring. Metal can remove some of your Dutch oven's hard-won seasoned coating, and plastic can easily melt.

- A trivet is a three-point base used to provide an insulating air gap between a hot cooking surface and a tray, pie pan, or cake pan placed on the trivet. It is used to prevent particularly sensitive foods from burning. A trivet is easily fashioned from a trio of marble-size balls of foil or small pebbles placed directly on the inside bottom of the Dutch oven. When creating your own trivet, don't use large metal objects. These will transmit a lot of heat and create their own hot spots. Avoid using excessively large rocks that can block heat or explode when wet.

- It is a common belief that aluminum foil is often necessary to prevent foods from gluing to the interior of a Dutch oven. The reality is that virtually no food will strongly adhere to a well-seasoned oven. So aluminum foil isn't typically required for this purpose. However, for some goopy recipes, foil lining can make cleanup much easier, as once the foil is removed following the meal, most of the glop goes with it. Foil is not suitable for recipes that require a lot of stirring, such as stews, as the foil can snag and tear.

- The seasoned walls of a well-used Dutch oven carry a pleasant flavor that's an amalgam of everything cooked prior but which can transfer to subsequently prepared food. It's a wonderfully complementary flavor addition for many dishes. For others, such as some desserts or recipes with a delicate taste, it is definitely not. Use aluminum foil lining for these types of recipes to minimize flavor transfer.

- A single sheet of heavy-duty aluminum foil used as a liner can be gripped following cooking to lift and transport stiff foods, such as breads, cakes, and quiches, in their entirety from oven to the serving table.

- Many recipes can be prepared using more than one cooking method. A Dutch oven can often take the place of a pot or skillet and vice versa.

- Boiling water in a Dutch oven will remove some of the oily coating from the inside walls and can produce a greasy, brownish-colored liquid. Certainly not the best way to a good cup of tea!

Cooking with Younger Scouts

- Have a meeting with your scouts to plan your menu before leaving on your outing. By including them in the process and giving them a vote, you will help build the scouts' anticipation.

- When first teaching young scouts how to cook, keep it simple. Remember that some kids have never cracked an egg or used a can opener.

- For younger scouts, include a fair amount of previously prepared items that don't require heating or extensive preparation once in camp. From their perspective, this can make the process of outdoor cooking seem less daunting and help prevent them and you from becoming overwhelmed in your camp kitchen.

- It can be quite challenging for little hands to hold all four layers of s'mores. To make the stack easier to handle, remove the chocolate piece and substitute fudge-striped cookies, chocolate-covered graham crackers, or chocolate mint cookies for the standard graham crackers.

- To help prevent marshmallows from burning over a campfire, give them a quick dip in water first. When cooking on a stick or other skewer, use hot coals instead of open flame to allow your food to cook more evenly without burning.

Nutrition and Moderation

We've been avid students of food and nutrition for nearly two decades, and we're convinced that one of the secrets of a long and happy life is finding the middle ground between eating to live and living to eat. Establishing a habit of eating exceptionally healthy foods during day-to-day living allows the body to more easily shrug off the occasional dietary indulgence.

It's been said that nobody has ever starved on a scout campout. After testing all the recipes in this cookbook, we are certain that statement is true! While large quantities of whole foods are often used, this is not a diet book.

Many of the recipes in our cookbook taste amazing because they are rich. Use dietary discretion when cooking for your scouts, and reserve the more full-bodied dishes for particularly special occasions, when a bountiful meal would serve as a capstone for good times and wonderful memories.

Sunrise Surprise Coffee Cake

Servings: 6–8 | Challenge Level: Easy

"Three of us were camping one fall morning in a state park in the Adirondacks. I was up early preparing this coffee cake. Several people in the campground dropped by 'to see where that wonderful aroma was coming from'!"

Preparation at Camp:

1. Line sides and bottom of a Dutch oven with greased heavy-duty aluminum foil.

2. Preheat oven using 8 coals underneath and 17 briquettes on the lid.

3. In a medium-size bowl, mix all ingredients except the nuts.

4. Remove oven from heat and pour coffee cake batter into the oven, spreading evenly over the foil on bottom.

5. Sprinkle nuts over top of batter.

6. Return oven to the original set of coals and bake for 30 minutes or until the aroma fills the air and people come begging!

Required Equipment:

12-inch Dutch oven
Heavy-duty aluminum foil
Medium-size mixing bowl

2¼ cups all-purpose flour

½ teaspoon salt

1 tablespoon ground cinnamon

1 cup brown sugar

¾ cup granulated sugar

¾ cup vegetable oil

1 teaspoon baking soda

1 teaspoon baking powder

1 egg, beaten

1 cup buttermilk

1 cup chopped nuts (your choice)

Sherry Bennett, Rochester, New York

Former Den Leader and Merit Badge Counselor, Otetiana Council, Boy Scouts of America

Fiesta Omelet

Servings: 6–8 | Challenge Level: Easy

5 slices of bread, slightly dried

1 (8-ounce) package precooked sausage links

1 dozen eggs

1 (16-ounce) jar Newman's Own peach or mango salsa

1 (16-ounce) package shredded taco–or Mexican-flavored cheese blend

¼ cup (½ standard stick) butter

Hot sauce to taste

Preparation at Camp:

1. Tear dried bread slices into pieces, using them to line the bottom of greased Dutch oven.

2. Break sausage links into small chunks and sprinkle over bread pieces.

3. Whisk eggs in a medium-size bowl then spread evenly over the sausage.

4. Pour salsa evenly over the eggs.

5. Top the mixture with shredded cheese.

6. Slice butter into thin pats, laying the slices evenly across the cheese.

7. Using 12 coals under the oven and 12 briquettes on the lid, bake for about 20 minutes or until eggs congeal and cheese melts.

8. Serve, adding hot sauce to taste.

Required Equipment:

12-inch Dutch oven

Medium-size mixing bowl

Ed Newell, Ballston Lake, New York
Scoutmaster, Troop 65, Twin River Council, Boy Scouts of America

Flaming Eagle Chimichangas

Servings: 12 | Challenge Level: Easy

Preparation at Camp:

1. Line Dutch oven with heavy-duty aluminum foil.

2. Preheat covered oven using 10 briquettes under the oven and 20 coals on the lid.

3. Thoroughly blend cream cheese, ricotta cheese, sugar, preserves, and strawberries in a medium-size mixing bowl.

4. Spoon roughly ½ cup of strawberry-cheese mixture onto each tortilla.

5. Roll and seal tortilla like you would a burrito, folding one end of the tortilla over the mixture before rolling.

6. Brush each chimichanga with melted butter then sprinkle with sugar to taste.

7. Cross-layer all the chimichangas in the preheated oven.

8. Replace briquette-covered lid. Bake for 10 minutes or until the chimichangas are thoroughly warmed and cheese is melting.

Required Equipment:

14-inch Dutch oven
Heavy-duty aluminum foil
Medium-size mixing bowl

2 (8-ounce) packages cream cheese, softened

1 cup ricotta cheese

½ cup granulated sugar, plus enough additional sugar for sprinkling over each chimichanga

1 (18-ounce) jar strawberry preserves

1 pound fresh or frozen strawberries, chopped (if using frozen strawberries, thaw them first)

12 flour tortillas

4 tablespoons butter, melted

Options: Try other types of fruit and preserves, such as apricots. And if you really want to serve these flaming, you can soak a sugar cube in lemon extract, put it on top of the chimichanga, and carefully light it on fire!

Ed Bedford, Chapel Hill, North Carolina
Scoutmaster, Troop 820, Occoneechee Council, Boy Scouts of America

Breakfast Bread

Servings: 12–14 | Challenge Level: Easy

2 pounds uncooked breakfast sausage

2 dozen eggs

1 loaf bread (your choice)

2 cups shredded cheese

Maple syrup to taste

Preparation at Camp:

1. Brown sausage in Dutch oven, then drain grease. Crumble sausage and set aside.

2. Whisk eggs in a large mixing bowl.

3. Pour a thin layer of egg mixture into the bottom of the oven.

4. Layer half of the loaf of bread on top of the eggs, evenly stacking the pieces in an overlapping fashion.

5. Spread the browned sausage across the top of the bread.

6. Sprinkle the cheese over the sausage.

7. Pour half of the remaining eggs over the cheese.

8. Layer the remaining slices of bread over the top of the mixture.

9. Pour the remaining eggs into the oven.

10. Heat using 12 briquettes under the oven and 16 coals on the lid. Cook for 45 to 60 minutes or until eggs set, replenishing coals as required.

11. Serve with maple syrup to taste.

Required Equipment:

14-inch Dutch oven
Large-size mixing bowl

Freddie Tuten, Guyton, Georgia
Committee Member, Troop 295, Coastal Empire Council, Boy Scouts of America

Michelle Tuten, Guyton, Georgia
Volunteer, Troop 295, Coastal Empire Council, Boy Scouts of America

Feed-'em-and-Go Dutch Oven Breakfast

Servings: 8–10 | Challenge Level: Easy

"This is a favorite of our troop. We usually prepare this recipe on the last morning of our outings, when we are in a hurry to break camp. While the food is cooking, we have time to pack our equipment and take down our tents. After eating, cleanup is easy, and we are on our way."

Preparation at Camp:

1. Brown sausage in Dutch oven, then drain grease. Crumble sausage and set aside.

2. Line bottom of oven with hash browns, lightly pressing them down.

3. Place optional vegetables on top of hash browns.

4. Spread sausage over hash browns.

5. Sprinkle cheese evenly over the sausage.

6. Whisk eggs and milk together in a medium-size bowl then gently pour the liquid over the cheese. Ensure that the mixture thoroughly saturates the hash browns.

7. Cook using 10 briquettes under the oven and 17 coals on the lid, heating for 1 hour or until the eggs set. Replenish coals as required to maintain heat.

8. Remove oven from coals and let stand for 15 minutes. Serve and season to taste.

Required Equipment:

12-inch Dutch oven
Medium-size mixing bowl

1 pound uncooked spicy breakfast sausage

1 (30-ounce) package frozen hash browns, thawed

1 small bunch green onions, diced (optional)

1 bell pepper, chopped (optional)

2 cups shredded sharp cheddar cheese

12 large eggs

½ cup milk

Salt, ground black pepper, and hot sauce to taste

Daniel Czarnecki, Grand Haven, Michigan
Advancement Chairperson, Troop 165, Gerald R. Ford Council, Boy Scouts of America

Linda Czarnecki, Grand Haven, Michigan
Committee Member, Troop 165, Gerald R. Ford Council, Boy Scouts of America

Uwharrie Hash Brown Casserole

Servings: 6–8 | Challenge Level: Easy

"This recipe is named for North Carolina's Uwharrie National Forest, an area rich in history. The mountains in this area may be the oldest in North America. Some geologists believe the Uwharrie Mountains are descended from an ancient chain of volcanoes, with the 1,000-foot high hills of today once being mighty peaks 20,000 feet tall. The region is at the crossroads of both prehistoric and historic settlements, providing one of the greatest concentrations of archaeological sites in the Southeast. The first large gold discovery in the United States occurred in the late 1700s at the nearby Reed Gold Mine. Old mining sites remain, and part-time prospectors can still be found panning in the streams to find traces of gold dust."

2 (10-ounce) cans condensed cream of potato soup

2 cups sour cream

1 cup grated cheddar cheese

1 small onion, diced

1 (30-ounce) package frozen hash browns, thawed

Grated Parmesan cheese to taste

Preparation at Camp:

1. In greased Dutch oven, combine soup, sour cream, cheddar cheese, and onion.

2. Stir in hash browns then top with grated Parmesan cheese.

3. Bake using 8 briquettes under the oven and 17 coals on the lid for about 30 minutes or until top is lightly browned.

Required Equipment:

12-inch Dutch oven

Ed Bedford, Chapel Hill, North Carolina
Scoutmaster, Troop 820, Occoneechee Council, Boy Scouts of America

Emma Woods Easy Beach Quiche

Servings: 6–8 | Challenge Level: Easy

"I call this recipe 'easy' because all the ingredients are just dumped in the Dutch oven. No need to actually make a crust like a real quiche. I remember cooking this dish for the first time while camping at Emma Woods State Beach, just outside Ventura."

Preparation at Camp:

1. In a greased Dutch oven, combine cheese, onion, and turkey, spreading evenly on the bottom.

2. In a medium-size bowl, combine milk, eggs, baking mix, and seasoning blend. Pour over the turkey mix in Dutch oven.

3. Using 7 briquettes under the oven and 16 coals on the lid, bake for approximately 30 minutes or until eggs have congealed.

Required Equipment:

12-inch Dutch oven
Medium-size mixing bowl

1½ cups shredded cheese (your choice)

1 onion, chopped

1 pound cooked turkey, diced

2 cups milk

4 eggs

½ cup baking mix (Bisquick preferred)

Seasoning blend (such as Morton Nature's Seasons Seasoning Blend), to taste

Katie Salyer Cox, Tucson, Arizona
Leader and Trainer, USA Girl Scouts Overseas and Sahuaro Council, Girl Scouts of the USA

The Egg Has Landed Casserole

Servings: 12–14 | Challenge Level: Easy

"Wapakoneta is the birthplace of Astronaut and Eagle Scout Neil Armstrong, thus the tongue-in-cheek title for this recipe!"

18 eggs, whisked

1 quart half-and-half

1 cup milk

2 teaspoons salt

¼ teaspoon ground black pepper

2 teaspoons dry ground mustard

1 teaspoon Worcestershire sauce

2 pounds cooked ham, finely diced

2 cups (8-ounce package) shredded cheddar cheese

1 (15-ounce) container seasoned bread crumbs

Preparation at Camp:

1. Combine all ingredients in a large-size bowl. Mix well.

2. Preheat greased Dutch oven over coals and pour in egg mixture.

3. Using 11 coals under the oven and 21 briquettes on the lid, bake for 45 minutes to 1 hour, refreshing coals as required.

4. When ready to serve, the casserole will have risen slightly and have a golden brown top.

Required Equipment:

14-inch Dutch oven

Large-size mixing bowl

Tip: Before leaving home for camp, all ingredients, except bread crumbs, can be placed in a 1-gallon plastic, screw-top milk jug and stored in a cooler. A wide-mouth food funnel can be used to pour the ingredients into the jug. The egg mixture and bread crumbs are combined at camp.

Marty Borchers, Wapakoneta, Ohio
Assistant Scoutmaster, Troop 4, Black Swamp Area Council, Boy Scouts of America

Camp Guyasuta Breakfast Pizza

Servings: 6–8 | Challenge Level: Moderate

"You can't go wrong with this great recipe. I've prepared it for scouts on campouts, family at Christmas, and even during a cooking demonstration for the National Wild Turkey Federation's 'Women in the Outdoors' training series. There are never any leftovers and always plenty of compliments."

Preparation at Camp:

1. Brown sausage in Dutch oven then drain grease. Crumble sausage and set aside.

2. Line bottom of oven with heavy-duty aluminum foil.

3. Unroll crescent roll dough and flatten evenly across top of foil.

4. Spread sausage, bell pepper, cheddar cheese, green onion, and hash browns over dough.

5. Whisk eggs, milk, salt, and black pepper in a medium-size bowl.

6. Pour egg blend over the ingredient mix in the bottom of the oven.

7. Sprinkle Parmesan cheese over the top of the egg blend.

8. Using 10 coals under the oven and 12 briquettes on the lid, bake for approximately 25 minutes or until eggs are firm.

9. Holding the foil, lift pizza from oven, and slice into wedges with a knife or pizza cutter.

Required Equipment:

12-inch Dutch oven
Heavy-duty aluminum foil
Medium-size mixing bowl

1 pound uncooked breakfast sausage

1 (8-ounce) container refrigerated crescent roll dough

1 medium bell pepper, diced

1 cup shredded sharp cheddar cheese

1 green onion, chopped

1 cup plain shredded frozen hash brown potatoes, thawed

3 eggs

3 tablespoons milk

½ teaspoon salt

1 teaspoon ground black pepper

3 tablespoons grated Parmesan cheese

Option: Use a mix of chopped red, yellow, and green bell peppers for a festive touch.

Page Davies, Glenshaw, Pennsylvania
Japeechen District Commissioner, Greater Pittsburgh Council, Boy Scouts of America

Beaver Patrol Saturday Breakfast

Servings: 8–10 | Challenge Level: Moderate

"This is a great breakfast to prepare ahead of an active day. We even make this during winter at our Klondike Derby. I often gather some of the ingredients ahead of time and store them in the freezer in ziplock bags."

1 pound uncooked pork sausage

1 cup chopped green onions

1 (4-ounce) can mushrooms with stems and pieces, drained and chopped

2 medium tomatoes, diced

2 cups shredded Colby or mozzarella cheese

1 cup original-type pancake mix

1 dozen large eggs

1 cup milk

1 teaspoon ground oregano

½ teaspoon salt

½ teaspoon ground black pepper

Option: Use spicy sausage if your scouts like a little zing.

Preparation at Camp:

1. Brown sausage in Dutch oven, then drain grease. Crumble sausage.

2. Mix sausage, onions, mushrooms, and tomatoes in greased oven.

3. Gently blend cheese throughout the mixture.

4. In a large-size bowl, whisk together the pancake mix, eggs, milk, oregano, salt, and black pepper, then pour the batter over the sausage mixture in the oven.

5. Heat using 8 briquettes under the oven and 17 coals on the lid. Bake for 35 minutes or until the top of the breakfast mix is firm and lightly browned

Required Equipment:

12-inch Dutch oven
Large-size mixing bowl

Todd Campbell, Idaho Falls, Idaho
Cubmaster, Troop 327, Grand Teton Council, Boy Scouts of America

HT Ranch Hash

Servings: 10–12 | Challenge Level: Moderate

"The HT Ranch is located near the town of Amidon in the southwest corner of North Dakota. It is one of our troop's favorite places to camp. The land is owned by the family of a former Scoutmaster of our troop. Still standing on the property, The Shackford is the original log ranch house. It is over one hundred years old.

The ranch is in the badlands on what was once part of a 23,000-acre parcel acquired in 1882 by A.C. Huidekoper. Using purebred Percheron horses from France, stallions from Illinois, mares from Oregon, and ponies acquired from Sitting Bull, the Lakota Indian Chief, Huidekoper increased his herd to 4,000 head in 10 years.

This recipe was born on one of our many campouts at the ranch."

Preparation at Camp:

1. Spread diced potatoes in greased Dutch oven.

2. Whisk eggs in a medium-size bowl along with black pepper and garlic, thyme, and sage powders to taste.

3. Pour egg mixture over potatoes.

4. Place links over potato-egg mix.

5. Lay ham pieces over links, covering entirely, then distribute bacon pieces over ham.

6. Using 10 coals under the oven and 19 briquettes on the lid, bake for approximately 1 hour or until egg mix is firm throughout and bacon is fully cooked. Refresh coals as required.

7. Remove oven from heat, uncover, and add cheese slices to top of hash.

8. Replace lid and allow cheese to melt before serving.

Required Equipment:

12-inch Dutch oven
Medium-size mixing bowl

5 pounds potatoes, peeled and diced

1 dozen eggs

Ground black pepper to taste

Garlic powder to taste

Thyme powder to taste

Sage powder to taste

1 (16-ounce) package smoked sausage cocktail links (such as Lit'l Smokies)

6 ounces precooked sliced ham, each slice cut into quarters

4 slices uncooked bacon, each strip cut into quarters

8 slices cheese (your choice)

Darryl Wehner, Dickinson, North Dakota
Assistant Scoutmaster / Treasurer, Troop 32, Northern Lights Council, Boy Scouts of America

WHOMP! Donuts

Servings: 8 Donuts | Challenge Level: Moderate

"A real scout favorite, this recipe is fun to prepare and tastes great. The donuts are made from refrigerated biscuit dough. (Remember the ones your mom used to make by whomping the dough container open on the side of the counter?)

1 (8-count) large tube refrigerated biscuit dough (do not use flakey type)

4 cups canola oil

1 cup powdered sugar

1 cup granulated sugar

8 teaspoons ground cinnamon

Options: Honey, honey butter, or melted chocolate are other great toppings to try.

Preparation at Camp:

1. Place canola oil in Dutch oven or large pot and heat over coals until oil reaches 350 degrees F. If oil becomes too hot, carefully remove some of the briquettes from under the oven. The oil should not be so hot that the donuts turn dark brown before cooking through.

2. While oil is heating, WHOMP! open the biscuit dough container, separate the biscuits, and place on a clean surface.

3. Grease the top of an empty, clean soda bottle with a little unheated canola oil. Use the bottle to punch holes in the center of each biscuit by pressing the opening into the dough. The residual dough should slide from the opening.

4. Place the donuts into hot oil, being careful to avoid splattering. Do not overload your oven or cook pot; you'll have better results by cooking a few at a time rather than all of them at once. Don't forget to cook the donut "holes" also!

5. Once the donuts are a golden brown, remove from oil and place on paper towels to draw off excess grease.

6. Fill a paper lunch bag with the powdered sugar and another with a combination of the granulated sugar and cinnamon. Carefully place a drained donut into one of the paper bags and shake to coat. Repeat for each of the remaining donuts.

Required Equipment:

12-inch Dutch oven or large pot
Cooking thermometer
Empty and clean plastic soda bottle
Paper lunch bags

Bill Britt, Hurlburt Field, Florida
Scoutmaster, Troop 509, Gulf Coast Council, Boy Scouts of America

Buckeye Biscuits and Gravy

Servings: 8–10 | Challenge Level: Moderate

"This recipe is dedicated to the Ohio State Buckeyes!"

Preparation at Camp:

1. Pour Bisquick and 1⅓ cups milk into gallon-size ziplock freezer bag. Knead.

2. Place a small amount of flour in your hands and rub together. From the ziplock bag, remove a dough piece about the size of a pool ball, and form a patty about 3/4-inch thick and 2 inches in diameter. Using same process, make a total of 12 biscuits and arrange them in greased Dutch oven.

3. Bake biscuits using 8 briquettes under the oven and 17 coals on the lid. Cook until biscuits have risen to a light golden brown, about 20 to 25 minutes.

4. While biscuits bake, begin to prepare the gravy by pouring oil in heated skillet and browning the sausage.

5. Add flour to the skillet and stir well. Blend in milk, stirring as the gravy comes to a slow boil.

6. Gravy is ready to serve once it thickens. If the gravy becomes too thick, mix in a little more milk or water. Add salt and black pepper to taste.

7. Crumble each biscuit or slice each in half, then cover with gravy.

Required Equipment:

12-inch Dutch oven
Large-size frying pan
Gallon-size ziplock freezer bag

4½ cups Bisquick

1⅓ cups milk

½ cup unbleached all-purpose flour (to work dough)

2 pounds breakfast sausage

2 tablespoons vegetable oil

⅔ cup all-purpose flour

5 cups milk

Salt and ground black pepper to taste

Dennis L. Elliott, Dublin, Ohio
Church Committee Representative, Troop 200, Simon Kenton Council, Boy Scouts of America

Brat Bake

Servings: 8–10 | Challenge Level: Moderate

"Brat Bake received two outdoor cooking awards in 2004, the first during a cooking competition at Wood Badge and the other at the Arapaho District Scout Show."

2 pounds fresh bratwurst, chopped into bite-size pieces

2 pounds potatoes, peeled and thinly sliced

2 pounds unpeeled baking apples, cored and sliced into thin wedges

2 medium onions, peeled and thickly sliced into quarters

2 teaspoons salt

½ teaspoon ground black pepper

1 teaspoon thyme

Options: Baking apples that work well with this recipe include Granny Smith, Golden Delicious, McIntosh, Rome, and Cortland.

Preparation at Camp:

1. Brown bratwurst in Dutch oven over 25 coals. Stir occasionally.

2. Add remainder of ingredients and stir.

3. Relocate 17 coals to the lid of the oven, keeping 8 briquettes underneath. Bake for 45 to 60 minutes or until the potatoes become tender. Refresh coals as required.

Required Equipment:

12-inch Dutch oven

June Eakin, Silver Spring, Maryland
Advisor, Crew 1444, National Capital Area Council, Boy Scouts of America

Peachy Dutch Oven French Toast

Servings: 10–12 | Challenge Level: Moderate

"This recipe took second place in the 'entrees' category of *Scouting* magazine's 2001 'Great Tastes in Camp Cooking' recipe contest. With the caramelized topping, you won't need syrup on this French toast!"

Preparation at Camp:

1. Preheat oven for 15 minutes using 21 coals on top and 11 briquettes under the oven.

2. While oven is warming, beat eggs, milk, vanilla, and cinnamon in a medium-size bowl.

3. Place bread slices into egg mixture to soak.

4. Move oven away from bottom coals and remove lid.

5. Melt butter in heated oven. Blend brown sugar into the melted butter.

6. Once sugar-butter turns light brown, place drained peaches into the caramel.

7. Spread egg-soaked bread on top of peaches.

8. Return lid to oven and place oven back over coals.

9. Bake for 35–45 minutes, refreshing coals if required. Occasionally check the bread mixture to ensure that the edges don't burn.

1 dozen eggs

2 cups milk

½ teaspoon vanilla extract

1 tablespoon ground cinnamon

1 loaf French or Italian bread, sliced

½ pound (2 standard sticks) butter

2½ cups brown sugar, tightly packed

3 (16-ounce) cans peaches, drained and quartered

Required Equipment:

14-inch Dutch oven
Medium-size mixing bowl

Ken Vetrovec, Racine, Wisconsin
Unit Commissioner, Troop 400, Southeast Wisconsin Council, Boy Scouts of America

Fisherman's Hearty Cajun Breakfast

Servings: 4 | Challenge Level: Difficult

1½ pounds fresh fish (such as northern pike or largemouth bass)

Salt and ground black pepper to taste

1 cup all-purpose flour

1 tablespoon cayenne pepper or Cajun seasoning

1 pound bacon

1 large onion, chopped

Vegetable oil as required to fry fish (about ¼ to ½ cup)

Preparation at Camp:

1. Clean and rinse fish, remove bones, and cut into pieces. Add salt and black pepper to taste.

2. Combine flour and cayenne pepper or Cajun seasoning in a gallon-size ziplock freezer bag.

3. Place fish pieces in ziplock bag and coat with flour mix by shaking. Set bag aside in a cool place until ready to cook.

4. In an uncovered Dutch oven, fry bacon over medium heat from wood fire or coals. When bacon is crispy, set aside on a paper towel to remove excess grease.

5. Drop chopped onion into hot bacon grease.

6. If quantity of remaining bacon grease is insufficient to fry fish, add vegetable oil as needed. Allow vegetable oil to warm. Carefully pour coated fish into hot oil.

7. Occasionally turn fish and onions. Onions are ready when they begin to turn crispy; the fish once the outside is crispy and the inside flakey.

8. While onions and fish are cooking, place Dutch oven lid upside down on coals or over medium heat from a wood fire and begin preparing the "bird nests," next step.

9. Remove center portion of wheat bread slices to form a hole (the nest). Set center bread portions aside.

10. Melt butter on frying surface of Dutch oven lid to prevent sticking.

11. Place four wheat bread slices on hot lid, cracking one egg into each hole. While they are frying, flip eggs with bread once. Add salt, black pepper, and hot sauce to taste.

12. Spread jam or preserves on saved centers.

13. Divide bacon, fish, and bird nests among your four hungry scouts. This is a spicy dish, so have plenty of cold water or milk handy!

Required Equipment:

12-inch Dutch oven

Gallon-size ziplock freezer bag

Bird Nests:

4 slices wheat bread

2 tablespoons butter

4 eggs

Salt and ground black pepper to taste

Hot sauce to taste

4 tablespoons fruit jam or preserves

Ronald G. Behrens, Hawthorn Woods, Illinois
Assistant Scoutmaster, Troop 92, Northwest Suburban Council, Boy Scouts of America

Brazos River Pecan Sticky Buns

Servings: 8–10 | Challenge Level: Difficult

"I taught each of our troop's patrols how to prepare this recipe for dessert at one of our camping cookouts. There weren't any leftovers! The name comes from the Brazos River region in central Texas, home to many pecan trees, and an area where I have camped many times."

Dough:

Ziplock bag 1:

1 tablespoon active dry yeast

1 teaspoon sugar

Ziplock bag 2:

¼ cup nonfat powdered milk

¼ teaspoon salt

1 cup sugar

Ziplock bag 3:

4 cups unbleached all-purpose flour

Ziplock bag 4:

1 cup unbleached all-purpose flour (to work dough)

Preparation at Home:

1. Use quart-size ziplock freezer bags for all bags except number 3, which should be gallon size. Label each of the six bags sequentially, 1 through 6.

2. Assemble each bag with dry ingredients according to the list.

Preparation at Camp:

1. To prepare dough, add about ½ cup warm water to the contents of bag 1.

2. After the yeast swells, add the contents of bag 2 to bag 1 along with the remaining ¾ cup water.

3. Add the water-yeast mixture from the preceding step to the flour in bag 3 along with ¼ cup butter. Knead the bag thoroughly.

4. Seal bag 3 and place in a warm place to rise until it doubles in bulk, about 1 to 2 hours. On a cold day, the bag can be placed inside your shirt for warmth.

5. Make a clean workspace by spreading out sheets of aluminum foil. Dust the aluminum foil surface using some of the flour from bag 4.

6. Roll the dough into a rectangle about 30x8 inches on the side. It will be soft. Spread ¼ cup softened butter over top of dough.

7. Sprinkle the contents of bag 5 evenly over the top of the dough. Roll up the long-side of the dough like a jellyroll, then cut into 24 slices.

8. Dot the bottoms of two 9-inch round cake pans with the remaining softened butter, using about 2 table-spoons per pan.

9. Sprinkle the contents of bag 6 in the cake pans and arrange the dough slices on top of the sugar mixture. Cover with aluminum foil and allow the dough to rise again in a warm place until almost doubled in size.

10. Set a pan on trivets in each of two 12-inch Dutch ov-ens. Using 8 briquettes under each oven and 17 coals on each lid, bake for 20–30 minutes or until the dough is golden brown.

11. Remove pans from ovens and run a knife around the edge of the sticky buns. Immediately flip contents onto plates so that the buns are upside down.

12. There will be some caramelized sauce in the bottom of each pan. Scrape it off and add to the top of the buns. Serve warm.

Required Equipment:

2 12-inch Dutch ovens (if cooking the two batches concurrently)
2 sets of trivets for Dutch ovens
2 9-inch round cake pans
Aluminum foil
Cooking thermometer

Tips: If the buns will be prepared for breakfast, the second rising can take place overnight if the dough is kept in a cool location such as an ice chest. The buns can then be baked in the morning as soon as the coals are ready. This recipe can also be pre-pared in a box oven.

Jim Russell, Houston, Texas
Scoutmaster, Troop 211, Sam Houston Area Council, Boy Scouts of America

Filling:

Ziplock bag 5:

½ cup brown sugar

3/8 teaspoon ground cinnamon

¼ cup raisins

Ziploc bag 6:

½ cup brown sugar

⅜ teaspoon ground cinnamon

¼ cup raisins

⅔ cup roughly chopped pecans

1¼ cups warm water (about 110 degrees F)

¾ cup (1½ standard sticks) butter, softened

Omelet-in-a-Bag

Servings: 1 / Multiply as Required | Challenge Level: Moderate

"We receive some strange looks from other Packs when we prepare this recipe. But do their mouths ever water once they see the end-product!"

2 eggs

Water sufficient for boiling eggs

Choose from your favorite ingredients in quantities ample for your group:

Green, yellow, or red peppers, chopped

Onions, finely chopped

Tomatoes, chopped

Mushrooms, sliced

Olives, sliced

Precooked sausage, ham, or bacon, sliced or cubed

Shredded cheese

Salt and ground black pepper

Barbeque sauce

Worcestershire sauce

Hot sauce

Milk

Preparation at Camp:

1. Fill a large pot ¾ full of water and bring to a boil.

2. Ask each scout to write their name on a quart-size ziplock freezer bag.

3. Have each scout hold their bag open while another scout cracks two eggs into it.

4. Ask each scout to add their favorite ingredients to their "omelet" bag. Have the scouts take care not to overload the bag with vegetables or liquids; otherwise too much water may be released during the cooking process and the eggs won't set properly.

5. Seal bag, ensuring it is tightly closed, then shake it.

6. Placing no more than four omelet bags at a time into the pot of hot water, boil for 4 minutes. Occasionally stir to prevent bags from adhering to sides of the pot.

7. Using tongs, remove the bags from the boiling water and shake each to remix the contents, carefully holding by the corners of the bag to do this.

8. Return bags to the boiling water for four additional minutes or until eggs appear to be set and scrambled.

9. Remove bags from hot water. Carefully open and pour each omelet onto a serving plate.

Required Equipment:

Large-size cook pot
Quart-size ziplock freezer bags (one per scout)
Cooking tongs

Kay Taylor, Eau Claire, Wisconsin
Assistant Cubmaster, Troop 128, Chippewa Valley Council, Boy Scouts of America

Great Southwest Council Hash

Servings: 4 | Challenge Level: Easy

Preparation at Camp:

1. Heat corned beef, hominy, and chilies in a large frying pan over medium heat. Stir occasionally.

2. Crack eggs over corned beef mixture.

3. Cover frying pan and continue cooking until eggs set.

4. Serve on tortillas and top with salsa.

Required Equipment:

Large-size frying pan
Aluminum foil (if frying pan has no lid)

1 (15-ounce) can corned beef

1 (16-ounce) can hominy, drained

1 (4-ounce) can chopped green chilies

4 eggs

4 flour tortillas

Salsa to taste

Vince Wahler, Albuquerque, New Mexico
Assistant Scoutmaster, Troop 395, Great Southwest Council, Boy Scouts of America

Vogelheu

Servings: 1 / Multiply as Required | Challenge Level: Easy

"Vogelheu originates from an old Swiss recipe. The German name means 'bird's hay.' This is a favorite winter campout breakfast among scout leaders. Vogelheu is very easy to prepare and has two other qualities that are valuable for winter camping: (1) it is high in fat calories, and (2) the fried bread acts as an insulator to help keep the eggs from becoming cold by the time you've finished eating them."

2 slices caraway rye bread

2 tablespoons butter

2 eggs

Option: Emmental cheese and spices can be added; but the basic recipe, using only butter and caraway rye, is delicious.

Preparation at Camp:

1. Cut each slice of caraway rye bread into long strips that are as wide as they are thick.

2. Fry strips in butter until bread is golden and crispy.

3. Break eggs over the fried strips, scramble, then serve.

Required Equipment:

Medium-size frying pan

G. John Marmet, Glenview, Illinois
Assistant Scoutmaster and Former Brownsea Junior Leader Training Cook, Troop 156, Northeast Illinois Council, Boy Scouts of America

Cattle Kate's Fancy Flapjacks

Servings: 4–6 | Challenge Level: Easy

Preparation at Camp:

1. In a medium-size bowl, mix together flour, salt, sugar, and baking powder.

2. Add eggs and milk. Stir well.

3. Grease skillet with butter to taste over medium heat.

4. Once butter melts, pour about 1/2 cup batter into skillet. When top of flapjack begins to bubble, flip and brown the other side.

5. Repeat step 4 until all batter is used. Serve with maple syrup or optional secret topping.

Required Equipment:

Medium-size frying pan
Medium-size mixing bowl

2 cups all-purpose flour

¼ teaspoon salt

¼ cup sugar

1 tablespoon baking powder

2 eggs

2 cups milk

Butter to taste

Maple syrup or optional Cattle Kate's secret topping (see below)

Option: To prepare Cattle Kate's secret flapjack topping, combine 1 pound of your favorite frozen fruit with a little water and sugar in a skillet. Get it good and hot, mix together, then pour over your flapjacks to taste.

Christine Conners, Statesboro, Georgia
Former Girl Scout, Hawaii Council, Girl Scouts of the USA

Laguna Beach Scrambled Eggs

Servings: 2 / Multiply as Required | Challenge Level: Easy

2 tablespoons butter

3 large eggs

2 tablespoons water

2/3 cup cottage cheese

1/3 cup grated cheese (your choice)

Salt and ground black pepper to taste

Preparation at Camp:

1. Melt butter in medium-size frying pan over low heat.

2. While butter is melting, whisk eggs and water in a medium-size bowl.

3. Spread cottage cheese in frying pan and bring to a simmer over low heat. Add grated cheese and stir.

4. Once cheese begins to simmer once more, add egg mixture to pan, stirring constantly.

5. Once eggs set, add salt or black pepper to taste and serve.

Required Equipment:

Medium-size frying pan
Medium-size mixing bowl

Charles E. Hirsch, Laguna Beach, California
Advisory Board Member, Orange County Council, Boy Scouts of America

Scout Breakfast Sandwich

Servings: 6 | Challenge Level: Easy

Preparation at Camp:

1. In medium-size bowl, whisk eggs, vanilla extract, and milk.

2. Make six traditional sandwiches using bread and peanut butter.

3. Dip each sandwich in the egg mixture.

4. Melt butter in large skillet and fry both sides of each sandwich until brown.

5. Serve with syrup.

Required Equipment:

Large-size frying pan
Medium-size mixing bowl

6 eggs

½ teaspoon vanilla extract

1 cup milk

12 slices bread

1 cup peanut butter

3 tablespoons butter

Syrup to taste

Eric Simonsen, Brooklyn, New York
Assistant Scoutmaster, Troop 76, Greater New York Councils, Boy Scouts of America

Crunchy French Toast

Servings: 6 | Challenge Level: Easy

1 (12-ounce) box cornflakes cereal

6 eggs

½ teaspoon vanilla extract

1 cup milk

3 tablespoons butter

12 slices bread

Syrup to taste

Preparation at Camp:

1. Crush cornflakes in a large bowl.

2. In a separate, medium-size bowl, whisk eggs, vanilla, and milk.

3. Melt butter in heated skillet.

4. Dip each slice of bread in the egg batter, then quickly place in the bowl of cornflakes, covering both sides with crushed flakes.

5. Fry both sides of each slice until brown.

6. Serve with syrup.

Required Equipment:

Large-size frying pan
Large-size mixing bowl
Medium-size mixing bowl

Eric Simonsen, Brooklyn, New York
Assistant Scoutmaster, Troop 76, Greater New York Councils, Boy Scouts of America

Santa Cruz Scrambled Eggs

Servings: 2 / Multiply as Required | Challenge Level: Easy

"This recipe had its beginnings at our family cabin on the San Lorenzo River in the coastal redwoods near Santa Cruz, California. The cabin was built by my grandfather in the late 1920s, and we love the area. My wife, Pat, developed the recipe, and it originally used English Cotswold cheese, which is quite tangy and a real treat in the winter around the wood stove or in the summer out on the porch. Unfortunately, Cotswold cheese can be hard to find, hence the substitute herein with cheddar. For the adults, enjoy this recipe with lots of scoutmaster juice (hot black coffee) and some crunchy toast (we recommend pain de campagne, a round loaf of French sourdough bread)."

Preparation at Camp:

1. Combine sour cream and dried onion in a medium-size bowl. Stir well and let sit for a few minutes to allow onion to rehydrate.

2. Add eggs, Fines Herbes blend, and tarragon to the sour cream mix and beat with a fork to combine.

3. Stir precooked potatoes into the egg mixture.

4. Melt butter in a hot frying pan.

5. Add the egg mixture and cook to taste.

6. Sprinkle cheese over the eggs, then add salt and black pepper to taste. Serve once cheese has melted.

Required Equipment:

Medium-size frying pan
Medium-size mixing bowl

George Brown, Los Osos, California
Former Scoutmaster, Troop 216, Los Padres Council, Boy Scouts of America

¼ **cup sour cream**

2 **tablespoons dried onion**

4 **eggs**

½ **teaspoon Spice Islands Fines Herbes spice blend**

½ **teaspoon tarragon**

½ **cup finely diced red potato, precooked at home**

2 **tablespoons butter**

¼ **cup shredded sharp cheddar cheese (or any hard, aromatic cheese, such as feta)**

Salt and ground black pepper to taste

Option: One of my personal additions is a squirt of Tabasco sauce, considered essential by many Scouters here in the Western United States. The eggs in this recipe can be cooked to your liking: My wife prefers eggs like vulcanized rubber; I go for the soft type.

Bird Nests

Servings: 1 / Multiply as Required | Challenge Level: Easy

1 slice bread (your choice)

1 tablespoon butter

1 egg

Salt and ground black pepper to taste

Options: Substitute a slice of Spam for the bread. Center cuts of bread can be eaten with jelly.

Preparation at Camp:

1. Cut a circle from the center of a slice of bread using the rim of a small drinking cup as a cutter.

2. Melt butter in frying pan, and place bread slice in frying pan.

3. Crack an egg into the hole in the bread.

4. Fry egg and bread together on both sides until cooked.

5. Add salt and black pepper to taste.

Required Equipment:

Small-size frying pan

Ronald G. Behrens, Hawthorn Woods, Illinois
Assistant Scoutmaster, Troop 92, Northwest Suburban Council, Boy Scouts of America

Sahuaro Breakfast Burritos

Servings: 8 | Challenge Level: Easy

"This recipe was adapted from an outdoor cooking class I attended at North Atlantic Girl Scouts' Annual Training Conference in 2002."

Preparation at Camp:

1. Scramble eggs in a medium-size bowl.

2. Melt butter in a large skillet. Add optional chorizo sausage, if desired.

3. To the frying pan, add both the eggs and hash browns and scramble until eggs are cooked.

4. Add cheese and stir until melted. Season with salt and ground black pepper to taste.

5. On each tortilla, place approximately ¾ cup egg mixture. Add hot sauce or salsa if desired. Roll up like a burrito and serve.

Required Equipment:

Large-size frying pan
Medium-size mixing bowl

1 dozen eggs

1 tablespoon butter

precooked chorizo sausage (optional)

1 (20-ounce) bag frozen hash browns with onions and peppers (such as Ore-Ida Potatoes O'Brien)

2 cups (8-ounce package) shredded cheese (your choice)

Salt and ground black pepper to taste

8 flour tortillas, burrito style

Hot sauce and salsa to taste

Katie Salyer Cox, Tucson, Arizona
Leader and Trainer, USA Girl Scouts Overseas and Sahuaro Council, Girl Scouts of the USA

Wagon Wheels

Servings: 4 | Challenge Level: Moderate

"We were running low on groceries during an extended campout. Only a few items remained in the trailer to prepare one last breakfast. After observing a neighboring troop making egg-muffin sandwiches, I came up with the idea of Wagon Wheels. We had to disguise the hash because most boys won't try corned beef just because of its name. The ruse worked: They ate it all!"

2 teaspoons prepared mustard

1 teaspoon garlic powder

¼ teaspoon Tabasco sauce

1 tablespoon vegetable oil

1 (15-ounce) can corned beef hash

½ onion, diced

½ bell pepper, diced

1 cup shredded cheddar cheese

2 English muffins, each sliced in half and toasted

Butter to taste

Options: Use ketchup instead of mustard, or top with scrambled eggs instead of onions and peppers.

Preparation at Camp:

1. In a small cup or bowl, mix mustard, garlic powder, and Tabasco sauce. Set aside.
2. Heat oil in a large-size skillet over medium heat.
3. Remove hash whole by opening both ends of can and running a knife around the sides if necessary. Slice hash into four rounds and place in hot oil.
4. Cook hash on one side for 5 minutes. Carefully flip rounds. Spread mustard mixture equally over each.
5. Top each hash round with onions and peppers. Place lid over skillet and cook for 3–5 more minutes. Add cheese to top of pepper-onion mix on each round.
6. Remove rounds from heat and place each on a buttered English muffin half.

Required Equipment:

Large-size frying pan
Aluminum foil (if frying pan has no lid)

Tip: English muffins can be toasted over the lid of the skillet during cooking or in the pan prior to cooking the rounds.

Michael A. Shively, Anderson, Indiana
Assistant Scoutmaster, Troop 249, Crossroads of America Council, Boy Scouts of America

National Trails Scramble

Servings: 8–10 | Challenge Level: Moderate

"If you use frozen hash browns in this recipe, thaw them overnight in an animal-proof container, not in your tent. Be sure the bears can't get at your food during the night, or breakfast will be pretty lame. Experience talking here!"

Preparation at Camp:

1. Pull the sausage into small pieces and brown in a large-size frying pan over medium heat.

2. While the sausage is browning, peel potatoes and then shred with a cheese grater.

3. Slowly add vegetable oil, shredded potatoes, and green onions to the browned sausage. Stir frequently, but gently, to avoid turning the potatoes into mush.

4. While the potatoes are browning, crack the eggs in a medium-size bowl and beat them as you would for scrambled eggs.

5. Once the potatoes are golden brown, stir in the beaten eggs, bell pepper, and shredded cheese.

6. Cook until eggs are firm. Serve hot and add salt and pepper to taste.

Required Equipment:

Large-size frying pan
Cheese grater
Medium-size mixing bowl

1 pound uncooked pork sausage

4 potatoes

⅛ cup vegetable oil

4 green onions, finely sliced

12 large eggs

1 green or red bell pepper, chopped

2 cups shredded cheddar cheese

Salt and ground black pepper to taste

Options: If you prefer, you can substitute regular frozen hash browns for the kind with peppers and onions already in the mixture. This spares you the slicing and dicing of the potatoes, peppers, and onions while in the field. The mix can also be rolled into tortillas for breakfast burritos.

Bob Ballou, Minden, Nevada
Eagle Scout–1958 / Former Professional Staff Member, Boy Scouts of America

Misty Morning Stuffed Toast

Servings: 10–12 | Challenge Level: Moderate

"Tim and I had this wonderful stuffed toast for breakfast in a little restaurant by the Pacific Ocean on the misty morning he proposed to me on the beach."

1 dozen eggs

1 teaspoon vanilla extract

½ cup milk

2 (8-ounce) packages cream cheese, softened

1 (21-ounce) can fruit filling (such as Comstock) (your choice of flavor)

2 (1-pound) loaves French bread, sliced ½-inch thick

Butter to taste for frying the stuffed toast

Maple syrup to taste

Preparation at Camp:

1. In a medium-size bowl, whisk eggs, vanilla extract, and milk.

2. In a second medium-size bowl, combine cream cheese and fruit filling.

3. With slices arranged in pairs as if making sandwiches, smear fruit filling–cream cheese mixture on one side of bread slice. Cover with a plain slice of bread. Repeat until all bread slices have been used to make stuffed sandwiches.

4. Dip each sandwich into the egg batter, coating both sides.

5. In melted butter to taste, cook each side over low heat. Cover pan while frying.

6. Toast is ready once filling is hot. Serve with maple syrup.

Required Equipment:

Large-size frying pan
2 medium-size mixing bowls
Aluminum foil (if frying pan has no lid)

Christine Conners, Statesboro, Georgia
Former Girl Scout, Hawaii Council, Girl Scouts of the USA

Cheesy Eggs Frederick

Servings: 12–14 | Challenge Level: Moderate

Preparation at Camp:

1. Melt one stick of butter in a large skillet. Reduce heat. Add flour and stir.

2. Peel and cut eggs into small pieces and add to butter-flour mixture.

3. Stir in half-and-half until mixture has a creamy consistency.

4. Add dried beef and cheese, heating on low and stirring constantly until mixture is warm.

5. Pour egg mixture into a medium-size bowl and set aside.

6. Toast English muffins in skillet with butter to taste.

7. Place approximately 2 tablespoons egg mixture onto each of the 36 English muffin halves, serving two or three per scout.

Required Equipment:

Large-size frying pan
Medium-size mixing bowl

Tip: For cooking on the trail, eggs can be boiled and refrigerated the night before your trip. Chop dried beef into small pieces and place in a quart-size ziplock freezer bag. Shredded cheese can be carried in its own packaging. Carry cold items in an insulated bag chilled with small ziplock bags filled with ice cubes. With proper care, food items should stay cool for as long as 36 hours.

½ cup (1 standard stick) butter

¼ cup all-purpose flour

18 eggs, hard-boiled

1 cup half-and-half

1 (2½-ounce) jar dried beef, cut into small pieces

2 cups (8-ounce package) shredded cheddar cheese

18 English muffins

Butter to taste for toasting English muffins

Frederick Smith, Lynchburg, Virginia
Assistant Scoutmaster, Troop 10, Blue Ridge Mountain Council, Boy Scouts of America

Paper Bag Bacon and Eggs

Servings: 1 / Multiply as Required | Challenge Level: Easy

2 thick strips of bacon

2 eggs

Preparation at Camp:

1. Cut the bacon strips in half and lay the pieces side by side in a paper lunch bag. If the bag is not sturdy, double up using a bag within a bag.

2. Crack two eggs within the bag over the bacon.

3. Roll the top of the bag in flattened sections as you would the end of a tube of toothpaste and skewer it closed with a toasting fork so that the bag hangs at the end of the fork.

4. Toast the food in the bag by holding it with the fork above hot coals, being careful not to set the bag on fire. The bacon fat will be absorbed by the paper and protect the bag from burning. The bag shouldn't drip unless it is torn.

5. Once the egg becomes firm, carefully tear the bag open to make a bowl. Eat your breakfast right from the bag!

Required Equipment:

Paper lunch bags
Toasting forks

Tip: If you burn your paper trash after breakfast, reduce the risk of wildfire by first tearing the used lunch bags into small pieces or by weighing the bags down once they are in the fire. This will decrease the tendency of the burning ash to float away.

Georgia Bosse, Portland, Oregon
Leave No Trace Master Educator, Columbia River Council, Girl Scouts of the USA

Corn Bread in an Orange

Servings: 4 | Challenge Level: Easy

4 medium oranges

1 (8½-ounce) box Jiffy corn muffin mix

1 egg

1 teaspoon sugar

⅓ cup milk

Options: Hollowed orange halves can be used in this manner to cook any of your favorite cake, muffin, or bread mixes.

Preparation at Camp:

1. Cut oranges in half and remove pulp, being careful not to tear the skin. The pulp isn't required for this recipe, so pass the orange pieces around to your scouts.

2. In a medium-size bowl, combine corn muffin mix with the egg, sugar, and milk.

3. Fill each of the orange halves with the corn muffin mixture, dividing it equally among the eight pieces.

4. Realign orange halves into four spheres, then wrap each sphere in heavy-duty aluminum foil.

5. Place foil spheres directly on hot coals. Heat for 8–10 minutes or until corn muffin mix has fully cooked.

6. Serve. The skins provide natural bowls for the baked muffins and impart an orange flavor to the corn cake!

Required Equipment:

Medium-size mixing bowl
Heavy-duty aluminum foil

Beth Ann Ast, Michigan City, Indiana
Advancement Chair / Cooking Merit Badge Counselor, Troop 871, La Salle Council, Boy Scouts of America

Jacob's Tastee Egg and Bacon Breakfast

Servings: 1 / Multiply as Required | Challenge Level: Easy

"Jacob is one of the scouts who helped prepare meals for Central New Jersey Council's Camporee in 2004. Jacob has since gone on to become the cooking instructor for Troop 33."

1 teaspoon butter

1 slice Canadian bacon

1 egg

1 slice cheese (your choice)

1 Pillsbury Grands! Homestyle refrigerated biscuit dough round

Option: A precooked sausage patty can be substituted for the Canadian bacon.

Preparation at Camp:

1. Place butter in the bottom of a small, clean tin can. Lay bacon on top of butter.

2. Crack egg over top of bacon. Cover with slice of cheese. Place biscuit dough on cheese slice.

3. Wrap can with heavy-duty aluminum foil, leaving room for the biscuit to puff up while heating.

4. Cook over hot coals for about 20 minutes or until the biscuit has browned. Serve straight from the can.

Required Equipment:

Empty tin can, approximately 8 ounces in size, label removed

Heavy-duty aluminum foil

Kathleen Kirby, Milltown, New Jersey
Cooking Merit Badge Counselor, Troop 33, Central New Jersey Council, Boy Scouts of America
Former Leader, Troop 12, Delaware-Raritan Council, Girl Scouts of the USA

Orange Shell Breakfast

Servings: 1 / Multiply as Required | Challenge Level: Easy

"The shell of an orange can be used as a unique cooking tool for eggs, vegetables, or cakes. Our troop in Kuwait loved this on campouts. Using turkey bacon was a great addition because it isn't pork-based so the Muslim girls in our troop could eat it."

Preparation at Camp:

1. Have scout carefully eat the pulp from orange half, leaving behind the peel with any remaining membrane removed. If preparing more than one, label peel of each orange with marker to keep track of whom it belongs to.

2. Lay 2 bacon slices in the orange shell, making a criss-cross in the bottom.

3. Break egg into orange shell. Season with salt and black pepper to taste.

4. Take the 4 corners of a sheet of heavy-duty aluminum foil and pull them together above the orange.

5. Squeeze the foil together around the bottom and sides of the orange shell while keeping the rest of the foil standing up straight above the orange.

6. Squish in the top of foil to retain heat, but leave it loosely packed to make it easier to check on the egg while it is cooking.

7. Set the foil-covered orange shell in the coals or on a very hot grill and bake for 3–5 minutes until egg is cooked to your liking.

8. Serve right out of the orange!

Required Equipment:

Heavy-duty aluminum foil

Half-shell from a large orange

2 slices turkey bacon

1 egg

Salt and ground black pepper to taste

Option: Try cooking pumpkin muffins in orange shells. They taste great with the slight orange flavor imparted by the shells.

Katie Salyer Cox, Tucson, Arizona
Leader and Trainer, USA Girl Scouts Overseas and Sahuaro Council, Girl Scouts of the USA

Egg on a Stick

Servings: 1 / Multiply as Required | Challenge Level: Moderate

"My husband and I have cooked this recipe many times. It works!"

1 egg

Salt and ground black pepper to taste

Option: Bore hole in top of egg, then stand the egg, large-end down, on a bed of ashes or hot rocks near your campfire. Bake for about 5 minutes before serving.

Preparation at Camp:

1. Using the tip of a knife, bore a small hole through the shell in one end of the egg.

2. Insert stick through the hole and into the egg, being careful not to crack the shell. Do not drive the stick all the way through the egg.

3. Carefully bore a second very small hole through the shell on the other end of the egg. This will prevent the egg from exploding by allowing steam to escape while cooking.

4. Using the stick, suspend the egg above the flame of a campfire for about 6 minutes. Note that the shell will char and the egg white may protrude from the holes.

5. Remove egg shell and sprinkle on salt and black pepper to taste.

Required Equipment:

Green stick, 2–3 feet long and no more than ¼ inch diameter at the end

Caution: Do not use a limb from a poisonous plant!

Tina Welch, Harper, Kansas
Assistant Scout Leader, Pack 853, Quivera Council, Boy Scouts of America

Bags of Gold

Servings: 2 / Multiply as Required | Challenge Level: Easy

"I learned of this recipe at a gourmet outdoor cooking class with USA Girl Scouts Overseas North Atlantic. It makes a great rainy day lunch!"

Preparation at Camp:

1. In a medium-size cook pot, stir milk and water into the tomato soup and heat to a gentle boil.

2. Tightly wrap each cube of cheese with the dough from one biscuit and drop into the hot tomato soup.

3. Reduce heat, cover pot, and simmer for 15 minutes.

Required Equipment:

Medium-size cook pot

1 (10¾-ounce) can condensed tomato soup

½ can milk (use empty tomato soup can to measure)

½ can water (use empty tomato soup can to measure)

4 ounces cheddar cheese, cut into four cubes

4 regular-size refrigerated biscuits (such as Pillsbury)

Katie Salyer Cox, Tucson, Arizona
Leader and Trainer, USA Girl Scouts Overseas and Sahuaro Council, Girl Scouts of the USA

Scoutmaster Steve's Revenge

Servings: 6–8 | Challenge Level: Easy

"Warning: Don't serve this just before a long drive home… unless you have control of the car windows!"

2 (28-ounce) cans pork and beans

1 cup brown sugar

½ cup ketchup

1 (8- or 10-count) package hot dogs

Preparation at Camp:

1. Open pork and beans and drain the thick juice. Pour into large cook pot.

2. Add brown sugar and ketchup to the pork and beans.

3. Cut hot dogs into ¼-inch round slices and stir into mixture.

4. Heat and serve.

Required Equipment:

Large-size cook pot

Steven Boyack, Poway, California
Assistant District Commissioner / Former Scoutmaster, Imperial Council, Boy Scouts of America

Southern New Jersey Clam Chowder

Servings: 6–8 | Challenge Level: Easy

"This recipe is also great for short backpacking trips and can be multiplied indefinitely to serve larger groups."

Preparation at Camp:

1. In a pot, bring water to a boil. Add potato soup mix and stir. Reduce heat and simmer, uncovered, about 15 minutes, stirring occasionally.

2. Once the potatoes from the soup mix become soft, add clams and corn. Stir.

3. Garnish with dried parsley and black pepper. Serve with oyster crackers or saltines.

Required Equipment:

Medium-size cook pot

6 cups water

1 (11-ounce) bag Bear Creek creamy potato soup mix

1 (10-ounce) can clams (do not drain)

1 (15¼-ounce) can corn (do not drain)

Dried parsley to taste

Ground black pepper to taste

Handful of oyster crackers or saltines per serving

William Sheehan, Pitman, New Jersey
Assistant Scoutmaster, Troop 55, Southern New Jersey Council, Boy Scouts of America

2 X 4 Soup

Servings: 8–10 | Challenge Level: Moderate

"When I was given this recipe at a campout one weekend, I was told it was a Boy Scout favorite. Sure enough, every time I've cooked it, there haven't been any leftovers. In fact, when we go camping, all I have to say is 'We're having 2 X 4 tonight,' and the boys automatically pitch in to help."

2 pounds ground beef

2 (10-ounce) cans diced tomatoes and green chilies (such as original-style Ro-Tel) [do not drain]

2 (15-ounce) cans pinto beans, drained

2 (10½-ounce) cans condensed vegetable soup

Crackers (optional)

Preparation at Camp:

1. Brown ground beef in a large-size skillet. Drain grease.

2. In a large-size pot, combine browned meat, tomatoes, pinto beans, and vegetable soup. Stir.

3. Heat thoroughly and serve.

Required Equipment:

Large-size frying pan
Large-size cook pot

Tip: This recipe can be easily adapted for cooking in a Dutch oven.

Roberta Kleinik, Jacksonville, Florida
Troop Advancement Chair, Troop 131, North Florida Council, Boy Scouts of America

Travelin' Tacos

Servings: 4 | Challenge Level: Easy

Preparation at Camp:

1. Cook the ground beef in a frying pan. Remove from heat and drain off excess grease.

2. Stir the taco seasoning and water into the ground beef.

3. With the chip bags still sealed, carefully crush corn chips in the bag.

4. Cut each bag open along one side.

5. Add beef mix, lettuce, tomato, cheese, salsa, and sour cream to the chip bag.

6. Eat right out of the bag with a fork!

Required Equipment:

Medium-size frying pan

1 pound lean ground beef

1 (1¼-ounce) package taco seasoning mix

¾ cup water

4 (2-ounce) single-serving bags corn chips

1 cup shredded lettuce (about ¼ of an average-size head)

1 tomato, chopped

1 cup shredded cheddar cheese

¼ cup salsa

¼ cup sour cream

Millie Hutchison, Pittsburgh, Pennsylvania
Girl Scout Trainer, Trillium Council, Girl Scouts of the USA

Croque Monsieur a la Scout

Servings: 1 / Multiply as Required | Challenge Level: Easy

"Croque Monsieur is a classic French lunch that brings a little gourmet to the traditional scout lunch fare."

1 tablespoon butter

2 slices bread (your choice)

3 ounces sliced or shredded Swiss Gruyere, Emmentaler, or Jarlsberg cheese

3 ounces sliced ham

Option: For Croque Madame a la Scout, prepare Croque Monsieur as above. Fry an egg in butter, turning over after the white has set. Place cooked egg on the sandwich and serve immediately.

Preparation at Camp:

1. Spread half of the butter over one side of a slice of bread. Repeat for the other slice.

2. Put half of the cheese on the unbuttered side of one slice of bread. Add the ham then the remainder of the cheese.

3. Top with the other slice of bread, buttered side up.

4. Fry in a skillet until the bottom is golden brown, then turn and cook the other side. Or, alternatively, cook sandwich in a pie iron until bread browns and the cheese melts.

Required Equipment:

Medium-size frying pan or pie iron

Ken Harbison, Rochester, New York
Former Boy Scout, Washington Trail Council, Boy Scouts of America

Judy Harbison, Rochester, New York
Lifetime Member, Genesee Valley Council, Girl Scouts of the USA

Turkey Joes

Servings: 8 | Challenge Level: Easy

Preparation at Camp:

1. Fry diced onion and turkey in lightly oiled skillet, stirring well to break up any clumps of meat. Cook until turkey is no longer pink.

2. Blend chili sauce, applesauce, mustard, and Worcestershire sauce into the ground turkey.

3. Simmer until liquid thickens, about 15 minutes.

4. Serve on buns.

Required Equipment:

Medium-size frying pan

½ **tablespoon vegetable oil**

1 medium onion, finely diced

1 pound ground turkey

1 cup chili sauce

1 cup applesauce

2 teaspoons prepared mustard

1 teaspoon Worcestershire sauce

8 hamburger buns

Ken Harbison, Rochester, New York
Former Boy Scout, Washington Trail Council, Boy Scouts of America

Judy Harbison, Rochester, New York
Lifetime Member, Genesee Valley Council, Girl Scouts of the USA

Jenny Jump Sandwiches

Servings: 4 | Challenge Level: Easy

"The story behind these sandwiches was simple necessity. My three grandchildren and I were staying in a shelter at Jenny Jump State Park in Hope, New Jersey. The cheese slices for grilled cheese had become soggy in the cooler—yuck! The local convenience store had only cream cheese in stock. So, I thought, 'Why not? Cream cheese is not just for bagels anymore!'"

8 slices bread (your choice)

1 (8-ounce) package cream cheese

4 tablespoons butter

Option: Goes great with a cup of soup!

Preparation at Camp:

1. Using the eight slices of bread, make four sandwiches with the cream cheese.

2. Butter outside of each slice of bread.

3. Fry each cream cheese sandwich until golden brown on both sides.

Required Equipment:

Medium-size frying pan

Brigitta M. Pereillo, Landing, New Jersey
Webelos Leader, Pack 188, Patriots' Path Council, Boy Scouts of America

Daisy Dog Delight

Servings: 10–12 | Challenge Level: Easy

" 'Daisy' was the nickname of Girl Scout founder Juliette Gordon Low."

Preparation at Camp:

1. Combine all ingredients in a large skillet.

2. Simmer for about 15 minutes then serve.

Required Equipment:

Large-size frying pan

1 (12-ounce) jar chili sauce

1 (12-ounce) jar currant jelly

3 tablespoons lemon juice

1 tablespoon prepared mustard

3 pounds cocktail franks, or frankfurters cut into 1-inch thick slices

2 (20-ounce) cans pineapple chunks, drained

Options: Can be eaten as is or served over rice or on hamburger buns, like a sloppy Joe.

Julie Terranera, Port Orange, Florida
National Operational Volunteer / Instructor of Trainers / Lifetime Member, Citrus Council, Girl Scouts of the USA

River Run Reubens

Servings: 6 | Challenge Level: Easy

12 slices rye or pumpernickel bread

6 slices Swiss cheese

1 (12-ounce) can corned beef

1 (15-ounce) can sauerkraut, drained

¾ cup Thousand Island dressing

4 tablespoons butter

Preparation at Camp:

1. Lay out 6 slices of bread.

2. On each, place one slice of Swiss cheese.

3. Divide the corned beef among the six slices.

4. Place 2 or 3 tablespoons of sauerkraut on top of beef on each slice.

5. Add 2 tablespoons dressing to top of the sauerkraut on each of the slices.

6. Cover each with another slice of bread.

7. Melt butter in a large skillet over a medium-low heat source. Cook each side of bread in skillet until the insides become warm.

Required Equipment:

Large-size frying pan

Tip: River Run Reubens also make for a great pie iron recipe.

Millie Hutchison, Pittsburgh, Pennsylvania
Girl Scout Trainer, Trillium Council, Girl Scouts of the USA

Mexican Grilled Cheese Sandwiches

Servings: 8 | Challenge Level: Easy

"When teaching leaders and girls how to prepare food outdoors, I try to choose recipes that help them become relaxed and confident when cooking. This is one of those recipes."

Preparation at Camp:

1. For each sandwich, sprinkle a little taco seasoning mix on one slice of bread.

2. Spread one-eighth of Velveeta cheese block on top of seasoning mix.

3. Close the sandwich with another slice of bread. Melt ½ tablespoon butter in frying pan. Cook on medium-low heat until side is lightly browned. Flip and repeat on the other side.

4. With cheese slightly melted, remove sandwich from pan, open, and add 2 tablespoons of black bean and corn salsa.

5. Cut and serve, repeating the process for the remainder of the sandwiches.

16 slices bread

1 (1 ¼-ounce) packet taco seasoning mix

1 (16-ounce) package Velveeta Mexican cheese product

4 tablespoons (½ standard stick) butter

1 (16-ounce) jar black bean and corn salsa

Option: Hot jalapeño cheese slices work well as a substitute for Velveeta.

Required Equipment:

Large-size frying pan

Tip: This recipe can also be prepared using a pie iron or in foil instead of in a frying pan. Simply butter the outside of the bread first.

Millie Hutchison, Pittsburgh, Pennsylvania
Girl Scout Trainer, Trillium Council, Girl Scouts of the USA

Pie Iron Pizza

Servings: 1 / Multiply as Required | Challenge Level: Easy

"This recipe was adapted from a collection of recipes compiled in 1988 from the Girl Scouts of Genesee Valley."

2 slices bread, or one English muffin, sliced in half

1 tablespoon butter

1 tablespoon pizza sauce

4 slices pepperoni

1 slice mozzarella cheese

Preparation at Camp:

1. Spread butter on one side of each slice of bread.

2. Place bread in the pie iron with the buttered sides against the iron surface.

3. Spread pizza sauce on one slice of bread. Add pepperoni and cheese. Close the pie iron.

4. Cook over campfire for several minutes, turning once, until the bread is golden brown.

Required Equipment:

Pie iron

Tip: If your bread is too large for the pie iron, trim it to fit before buttering.

Ken Harbison, Rochester, New York
Former Boy Scout, Washington Trail Council, Boy Scouts of America

Judy Harbison, Rochester, New York
Lifetime Member, Genesee Valley Council, Girl Scouts of the USA

Gold Rush Grilled Cheese

Servings: 1 / Multiply as Required | Challenge Level: Easy

"This recipe was adapted from a collection of recipes compiled in 1988 from the Girl Scouts of Genesee Valley."

2 slices bread, or one English muffin, sliced in half

1 tablespoon butter

1 slice American cheese

Preparation at Camp:

1. Spread butter on one side of each slice of bread.

2. Place bread in the pie iron with the buttered sides against the iron surface.

3. Place cheese between the slices of bread and close the pie iron.

4. Cook over the fire for several minutes, turning once, until bread is golden brown.

Required Equipment:

Pie iron

Tip: If your bread is too large for the pie iron, trim it to fit before buttering.

Ken Harbison, Rochester, New York
Former Boy Scout, Washington Trail Council, Boy Scouts of America

Judy Harbison, Rochester, New York
Lifetime Member, Genesee Valley Council, Girl Scouts of the USA

Fencepost Hobo Burgers

Servings: 4 | Challenge Level: Easy

"Mawmaw, my grandmother, taught me this recipe. She explained that, during the Great Depression, hobos would prepare a similar dish by finding a little meat and a few vegetables and tossing them together to make a meal fit for kings. During this difficult time in our country's history, my grandparents placed a cat symbol on their fencepost. This was a sign to passing hobos that they could count on a meal from the friendly folks inside."

1 pound ground beef

1 medium potato

1 medium onion

Celery, carrots, bell peppers, cabbage (optional vegetables)

Garlic salt to taste

Mrs. Dash seasoning to taste

4 hamburger buns

Cheese, lettuce, tomato slices, and ketchup (optional burger toppings)

Preparation at Camp:

1. Form four hamburger patties from the ground beef. Place each patty on its own piece of heavy-duty aluminum foil.

2. Slice the potato, onion, and other optional vegetables and place on top of the hamburger patties. Season with garlic salt and Mrs. Dash to taste.

3. Wrap the hamburger and vegetables tightly in the foil. One method is to fold a sheet of foil over the vegetables and burger, forming a foil triangle. Seal the edges.

4. Place packets over coals or on a grill, and allow all to thoroughly cook, approximately 15–30 minutes. Packets are ready to serve once internal temperature of patty exceeds 160 degrees F.

5. Remove packets with tongs, and carefully open the foil. Place patty on hamburger bun with cheese and optional toppings. Enjoy the vegetables as a side or on the burger.

Required Equipment:

Heavy-duty aluminum foil

Tip: Hobo Burgers can be prepared ahead of time and packed in a cooler until ready to cook.

Tina Welch, Harper, Kansas
Assistant Scout Leader, Pack 853, Quivera Council, Boy Scouts of America

Kipawa Campfire Onion

Servings: 2 / Multiply as Required | Challenge Level: Easy

"For the last 40 years, Troop 405 has made the pilgrimage to the Kipawa Lake Region of Quebec for its biennial week-long canoe trip. As far as I'm concerned, that place is heaven on earth. This will be my tenth trip. Maintaining this special troop tradition, for the benefit of my son and other young men, has been my way of thanking the scout leaders who took the time and trouble to bring me to beautiful Kipawa Lake when I was young."

1 large sweet onion

1 beef bouillon cube (2 cubes if the onion is unusually large)

1 tablespoon butter

Preparation at Camp:

1. Peel onion and slice the ends off.

2. Cut the onion in half, across the ring grain.

3. Score the flat side of each half so that the notches define eight segments. In each score, cut the onion deeply enough so it begins to open up, but not so deep that the onion comes apart.

4. Scoop the center from each half to make a void for the bouillon cube. Place the bouillon cube in the void and cover each cut side of the onion with butter.

5. Close the onion back up by realigning the cut halves. Double wrap the onion in heavy-duty aluminum foil and place over coals or on the grill. Cook for 20–30 minutes or until tender enough to easily pierce with fork.

6. Serve from the foil. The onion will open up some once the foil is removed, and there will be broth in the bottom of the packet that can be used to marinate the onion prior to eating.

Required Equipment:

Heavy-duty aluminum foil

Kurt Larson, Harmony, Pennsylvania
Committee Member, Troop 405, Greater Pittsburgh Council, Boy Scouts of America

Lincoln Forest Cannon Balls

Servings: 8 | Challenge Level: Easy

"Warning: Coyotes will call each other by cell phone to make sure that they all get leftovers from this scout supper!"

4 very large onions

1 pound lean ground beef

½ cup oatmeal

¼ teaspoon garlic powder

Salt, ground black pepper, and cayenne pepper to taste

1 tablespoon Worcestershire sauce

1 egg

Options: Your favorite ingredients can be combined to create a tailored meat mixture. Consider substituting bread crumbs, crackers, diced bell peppers, minced garlic, or your other favorite fillers.

Preparation at Camp:

1. Cut each onion in half, against the ring grain. Trim outer skin. Remove center of onion from each half, leaving two or three thick outer layers, creating half-shell "bowls." Set aside.

2. In medium-size mixing bowl, combine ground beef, oatmeal, spices, Worcestershire, and egg. If desired, a portion of the onion pieces previously removed from the onion center can be diced and added to the meat mixture at this time. Knead.

3. Fill each onion shell with the meat mixture.

4. Reassemble each onion by aligning the cut layers from two halves. Wrap each of the four onion balls with a sheet of heavy-duty aluminum foil.

5. Bake on hot coals for about 30 minutes or until meat is thoroughly cooked. Hot fires work best, as the outer layers of the onion will caramelize and sweeten the meat mixture.

Required Equipment:

Medium-size mixing bowl
Heavy-duty aluminum foil

Cal Beard, Cedar Hills, Texas
Assistant Scoutmaster, Troop 783, Circle 10 Council, Boy Scouts of America

Dustin Beard, Cedar Hills, Texas
Eagle Scout, Troop 783, Circle 10 Council, Boy Scouts of America

Brandon Beard, Cedar Hills, Texas
Boy Scout, Troop 783, Circle 10 Council, Boy Scouts of America

Flying Pigs in Sleeping Bags

Servings: 8 | Challenge Level: Easy

Preparation at Camp:

1. Press pairs of triangular crescent rolls together to make four rectangular dough shapes.

2. Cut each rectangle in half to make 8 squares.

3. Place a hot dog on top of each square. Sprinkle with cheese, if desired.

4. Roll dough around hot dog, allowing one end to peek out, like a head from a sleeping bag. Pinch the bottom closed.

5. Stick with a camp fork, and heat over coals until dough becomes golden brown.

6. Serve, dipping in ketchup, if desired.

Required Equipment:

Camp forks

1 (8-ounce, 8 count) container refrigerated crescent rolls

8 hot dogs

Shredded cheese (optional)

Ketchup (optional)

Donna Pettigrew, Anderson, Indiana
Tanglewood Day Camp Director and Master Trainer, Central Indiana Girl Scout Council, Girl Scouts of the USA

Lazy Dogs in Canoes

Servings: 8 | Challenge Level: Easy

2 (8-ounce, 8 count) containers refrigerated crescent rolls

8 hot dogs

Southwest-style chili and shredded cheese (optional)

Option: Hot dog buns can be used instead of crescent rolls.

Preparation at Camp:

1. Press pairs of triangular crescent rolls together to make eight rectangular dough shapes.

2. Place 1 hot dog in the center of each rectangle. Pinch up the edges of dough around the hot dog to form a canoe shape. Repeat for each.

3. Top with chili and cheese, if desired.

4. Wrap each dog in heavy-duty aluminum foil, and lay on a grate over campfire or grill for a few minutes or until hot dog is heated throughout.

5. Unwrap and add toothpicks, one on each side, for oars.

Required Equipment:

Heavy-duty aluminum foil
Toothpicks

Donna Pettigrew, Anderson, Indiana
Tanglewood Day Camp Director and Master Trainer, Central Indiana Girl Scout Council, Girl Scouts of the USA

Angels on Horseback

Servings: 1 / Multiply as Required | Challenge Level: Easy

"This fun camp recipe has been around for a long time."

Preparation at Camp:

1. Slice hot dog halfway through along its length.

2. Tear cheese into strips and place into notch in the hot dog.

3. Wrap hot dog with bacon, like a stripe on a candy cane, beginning on one end and finishing on the other. Fasten bacon into hot dog with toothpicks.

4. Cook hot dog on a camping fork over a campfire or in foil on coals. Hot dog is ready once bacon begins to turn crispy.

5. Serve alone or on a hot dog bun.

Required Equipment:

Camping forks
Toothpicks

Tip: Be sure to cover as much cheese as possible with the bacon strip. This will help prevent the cheese from dripping once it melts.

1 hot dog

1 slice bacon

½ slice cheese, your choice

Hot dog bun (optional)

Donna Pettigrew, Anderson, Indiana
Tanglewood Day Camp Director and Master Trainer, Central Indiana Girl Scout Council, Girl Scouts of the USA

Potatoes Walz

Servings: 1 / Multiply as Required | Challenge Level: Easy

"This recipe took second place in the 'side dish' category of *Scouting* magazine's 2001 'Great Tastes in Camp Cooking' recipe contest. It is named for its creator, Eagle Scout Gary Walz."

Nonstick cooking spray

1 large potato per person

Toppings to taste:

Grated Parmesan cheese (or your choice)

Seasoning salt

Garlic powder

Dried minced onion, fresh minced onion, or onion powder

Dried parsley flakes

Italian seasoning

Mesquite seasoning

Butter

Preparation at Camp:

1. Lay out a large sheet of heavy-duty aluminum foil. Grease foil with cooking spray.

2. Cut potato into ⅛-inch slices, like potato chips.

3. Place potato slices on foil. Fan them like cards so they overlap but still spread out.

4. Sprinkle seasonings and cheese over the top of potato slices. Dot with pats of butter.

5. Carefully wrap foil over top of potatoes, being careful to keep the slices arranged in a flat row.

6. Seal edges of foil and cook directly on coals for about 25 minutes or until potatoes are tender.

Required Equipment:

Heavy-duty aluminum foil

Jeff Osorio, Cupertino, California
Former Assistant Cubmaster, Pack 103, Pacific Skyline Council, Boy Scouts of America

Flaming Gorge Hot Dog

Servings: 1 / Multiply as Required | Challenge Level: Easy

"This visually exciting cooking technique transforms a plain old hot dog into something spectacular! The first time I tried this method with my girls, they were pretty worried. There was concern that the hot dog might catch fire, that the carton could become a mini inferno, that they might set the forest afire. None of their worries came to pass. Instead, the girls sat mesmerized as their cartons burned at a slow, almost Zen-like, speed. Once the cartons turned to ash, the girls were amazed to discover their hot dogs and buns had been cooked to perfection."

1 hot dog

1 hot dog bun

Standard condiments: ketchup, mustard, and pickle relish to taste

Preparation at Camp:

1. Place hot dog in the bun. Wrap in heavy-duty aluminum foil, then roll foil in a sheet of newspaper.

2. Open the top of a half gallon–size milk carton, removing any plastic spout.

3. Insert wrapped hot dog into the carton and place carton upright in a fire pit.

4. Set top of carton on fire. The wax on the carton will control the burn rate, and the carton will be slowly consumed downward.

5. Once the carton has turned to ash, the hot dog is ready to unwrap and serve.

Required Equipment:

Heavy-duty aluminum foil

Sheets of newspaper

Wax-coated, cardboard, half gallon–size milk carton, plastic spout removed

Katie Salyer Cox, Tucson, Arizona
Leader and Trainer, USA Girl Scouts Overseas and Sahuaro Council, Girl Scouts of the USA

Cat Can Pizza

Servings: 1 / Multiply as Required | Challenge Level: Easy

"Makes a purrrrrfect pizza every time!"

1 teaspoon cooking oil

1 regular-size refrigerated biscuit dough or half an English muffin

2 teaspoons pizza sauce (Boboli works well)

1 teaspoon shredded cheese

Your favorite pizza toppings (optional)

Preparation at Camp:

1. Rub inside of empty tuna can with cooking oil.

2. Place biscuit dough or English muffin in the bottom of the can. Flatten out dough.

3. Add pizza sauce, cheese, and optional toppings.

4. Cover can with heavy-duty aluminum foil and place on grate over coals. Heat just long enough for the dough to cook.

Required Equipment:

Clean, empty 6-ounce tuna can, label removed

Heavy-duty aluminum foil

Donna Pettigrew, Anderson, Indiana
Tanglewood Day Camp Director and Master Trainer, Central Indiana Girl Scout Council, Girl Scouts of the USA

Bear Valley Tortillas

Servings: 8 | Challenge Level: Easy

Preparation at Camp:

1. Tear off two sheets of heavy-duty aluminum foil, each about 1 foot long.

2. Combine rice, salsa, and beans in a large-size bowl, mixing to ensure that rice is adequately coated.

3. Add chicken tenders to bowl and stir to distribute meat throughout rice and bean mix.

4. Spread chicken, rice, and bean mix evenly over one of the sheets of aluminum foil. Avoid mounding the food; otherwise it will not cook evenly.

5. Place second sheet of foil over the food. Thoroughly seal together all four edges.

6. Poke a few small holes on the top piece of foil to allow steam to escape.

7. Place foil-wrapped food directly on hot briquettes in a camp fire or grill. Coals should be at roughly medium heat, ashed over, and not flaming hot.

8. Heat for approximately 30 minutes or until chicken is warmed through.

9. Remove from coals, and carefully open foil. Scoop chicken, beans, and rice onto tortillas, adding any optional toppings.

10. Fold tortillas either taco- or burrito-style and serve.

Required Equipment:

Large-size mixing bowl
Heavy-duty aluminum foil

2 cups instant brown rice (Uncle Ben's preferred)

1 (16-ounce) jar salsa

1 (15-ounce) can black beans, drained

2½ pounds pre-cooked frozen chicken tenders, thawed

8 large tortillas

Toppings (optional): shredded cheese, sour cream, chopped chives

Christine Conners, Statesboro, Georgia
Former Girl Scout, Hawaii Council, Girl Scouts of the USA

Tim Conners, Statesboro, Georgia
Former Leader, Coastal Empire Council, Boy Scouts of America

Brownsea Chicken

Servings: 2 / Multiply as Required | Challenge Level: Easy

"I learned this fun recipe from another Scouter while training at Philmont Scout Ranch."

4 precooked frozen chicken tenderloin strips, thawed

1 (8½-ounce) can baby green peas

1 cup instant rice

½ (10½-ounce) can condensed cream of mushroom soup

Salt and ground black pepper to taste

Preparation at Camp:

1. Using a large sheet of heavy-duty aluminum foil, bring opposite ends together, creating a bowl or pot shape, with the open end facing up.

2. Place chicken strips, green peas with their juice, and rice in foil pouch. Pour in mushroom soup. Gently stir.

3. Firmly seal open end of pouch by folding edges over each other.

4. Place pouch on hot coals, folded end facing upwards and positioned so that it sits like a pot. At top of pouch, make two small slits for steam to escape.

5. Cook for 15–20 minutes. Using tongs, remove pouch from coals and carefully open top, being careful to avoid escaping steam.

6. Season to taste with salt and black pepper. Can be eaten from pouch or poured onto plates.

Required Equipment:

Heavy-duty aluminum foil

Corbin Sarchet, Gotha, Florida
Scoutmaster, Troop 48, Central Florida Council, Boy Scouts of America

Cabin Packets

Servings: 4 | Challenge Level: Moderate

Preparation at Camp:

1. Crush the Chex cereal in a gallon-size ziplock freezer bag.

2. Add ground beef, minced onion, basil, parsley, and egg. Seal bag, and knead mixture.

3. Form four patties from the meat mixture.

4. To make foil packets, tear off four large sheets of heavy-duty aluminum foil. Grease the center of one side of each sheet with a small amount of butter.

5. On each sheet, distribute potato and onion slices and cover with thinly sliced butter. Add salt and black pepper to taste.

6. Place a patty on the potato and onion slices, one for each sheet of foil.

7. Close the packets and fold edges several times over to form a tight seal.

8. Place packets on a rack over fire or hot coals and cook for approximately 10–12 minutes.

9. Using tongs, flip packets and continue cooking for an additional 10–12 minutes. Packets are ready to serve once internal temperature of patty exceeds 160 degrees F.

10. Serve directly from the packets.

Required Equipment:

Gallon-size ziplock freezer bag
Heavy-duty aluminum foil

1 cup Rice Chex cereal

1 pound lean ground beef

1 large onion, minced

1 tablespoon dried basil

2 teaspoons dried parsley

1 egg

½ cup (1 standard stick) butter

4 medium potatoes, thinly sliced

1 large onion, halved and thinly sliced

Salt and ground black pepper to taste

Nancy Gilbert, Cut Bank, Montana
Troop Assistant, Troop 559, Montana Council, Boy Scouts of America

Worm Burgers

Servings: 4 | Challenge Level: Easy

"This recipe is sure to make your scouts wiggle, giggle, and squirm! The juice from the meat swells the noodles, causing them to hang out of the burgers like juicy worms. Eeew!"

1 pound ground beef

½ cup dried chow mein noodles

Salt and ground black pepper to taste

4 hamburger buns

Toppings: cheese, tomatoes, lettuce, onions, ketchup, mayonnaise, or mustard (your choice)

Preparation at Camp:

1. In a medium-size bowl, combine ground beef with chow mein noodles. Add salt and ground black pepper to taste.

2. Form into four patties.

3. Grill to taste, and serve on buns with toppings of your choice.

Required Equipment:

Medium-size mixing bowl

Donna Pettigrew, Anderson, Indiana
Tanglewood Day Camp Director and Master Trainer, Central Indiana Girl Scout Council, Girl Scouts of the USA

Penn Woods Onion

Servings: 2 / Multiply as Required | Challenge Level: Easy

Preparation at Camp:

1. Place sliced onion on two sheets of heavy-duty aluminum foil wrap.

2. Sprinkle remaining ingredients on top of onion, finishing with the butter.

3. Wrap onion in foil and cook over coals or on a grill over medium heat, about 20–30 minutes or until onion is tender. Turn only once while cooking.

Required Equipment:

Heavy-duty aluminum foil

1 large sweet onion, sliced

⅛ teaspoon salt

⅛ teaspoon ground black pepper

⅛ teaspoon garlic salt

1 tablespoon brown sugar

1 tablespoon butter

Leona Mills, Duncanville, Pennsylvania
District Member at Large / Unit Commissioner, Troop 15, Penn Woods Council, Boy Scouts of America

Tolochee Salsa Chicken

Servings: 1 / Multiply as Required | Challenge Level: Easy

"Credit goes to Kate Hibbeler, who introduced us to this recipe at Leadership Training at Camp Tolochee in Brunswick, Georgia. In freezing cold temperatures, she warmed us up with Tolochee Salsa Chicken."

1 tablespoon butter

½ boneless chicken breast, skin removed

¼ cup salsa

1 carrot, thinly sliced into ovals

1 potato, thinly sliced into ovals

Salt and ground black pepper to taste

Preparation at Camp:

1. Grease a large sheet of heavy-duty aluminum foil with butter.

2. Place chicken breast in foil and coat with salsa.

3. To the foil, add sliced carrots, potatoes, and any remaining butter. Add salt and pepper to taste.

4. Wrap and fold the foil around the chicken and vegetables to create a strong seal.

5. Cook on a grill or over an open fire, about 15 minutes per side. Chicken is ready once meat reaches an internal temperature of at least 170 degrees F.

6. Unwrap chicken and serve.

Required Equipment:

Heavy-duty aluminum foil

Janet Harden, Brunswick, Georgia
Committee Chairman, Pack 224, Okefenokee Area Council, Boy Scouts of America

Kentuckiana Backcountry Pizza

Servings: 1 / Multiply as Required | Challenge Level: Easy

Preparation at Camp:

1. Tear off two sheets of heavy-duty aluminum foil, each slightly larger than a tortilla. Rub one side of both pieces of foil with vegetable oil to prevent tortillas from sticking.

2. Place one tortilla on the greased side of each sheet of foil.

3. Spread half of the pizza sauce on each tortilla along with any optional pizza toppings.

4. Sprinkle half of the shredded cheese on each tortilla.

5. With each tortilla uncovered on top of its foil sheet, place on grill or over campfire and cook until cheese is melted.

Required Equipment:

Heavy-duty aluminum foil

Tips: To cook, tortilla can also be folded in half, placed on a greased pan, then heated until cheese melts, flipping once. Tortilla can also be folded and wrapped with foil before heating.

1 teaspoon vegetable oil

2 flour tortillas

1 (½-cup) pouch Boboli pizza sauce

Your favorite pizza toppings (optional)

½ cup shredded cheese

Melissa Seacat, Salem, Indiana
Troop Leader, Troop 2037, Kentuckiana Council, Girl Scouts of the USA

Go-Go Crab Salad

Servings: 6–8 | Challenge Level: Easy

2 pounds imitation crabmeat

1 cup mayonnaise

6 tablespoons Tabasco sauce, or to taste

½ cup diced green onion

½ cup diced green bell pepper

Box of crackers or loaf of bread

Preparation at Camp:

1. Combine crabmeat, mayonnaise, Tabasco sauce, onion, and green pepper in a large-size mixing bowl. If required, adjust Tabasco sauce to taste.

2. Serve on crackers or bread.

Required Equipment:

Large-size mixing bowl

Charles McKnight, Cambridge, Ohio
Scoutmaster, Troop 526, Muskingum Valley Council, Boy Scouts of America

Blue Heron BLT Wraps

Servings: 5 | Challenge Level: Easy

"My all-time favorite lunch is the BLT. We have enjoyed many of these on Sapelo Beach while on sea kayak High Adventure treks out of Camp Blue Heron in Georgia. By noon, the boys have paddled about four hours and are ready for some serious nourishment. For camping, tortillas and pitas are superior to bread because they travel well, don't get easily smashed in the pack, and can hold together all the wonderful things you throw at them.

This recipe is dedicated to Camp Blue Heron, located near Riceboro, Georgia. This scout camp, like many others in the past, has become surrounded by development and is hosting its final summer program. As disappointing as this is, the good news is that a larger site to service the Savannah area is being pursued, and the Coastal Empire Council looks forward to a brilliant future."

Preparation at Camp:

1. Add to each tortilla or pita your favorite condiment, lettuce, tomato slices, and 3 pieces of bacon.

2. Add black pepper to taste and optional cheese.

3. Wrap and serve.

5 flour tortillas or pitas

Favorite condiment: mayonnaise, yellow mustard, honey mustard, Italian dressing (your choice)

½ head of lettuce

2 fresh tomatoes, thinly sliced

1 (15-slice) pack precooked bacon

Ground black pepper to taste

Cheese (optional)

Options: Where once there were two types of canned tuna at my grocer, there are now foil packages and cans of tuna (10 flavors), salmon (8 flavors), chicken (8 varieties), and even precooked beef. All of these lend themselves to wrapping. I prefer to use the foil packets over the cans because the packaging is lighter and takes up less space.

Max Coles, Richmond Hill, Georgia
Scoutmaster / Sea Kayak High Adventure Staff Member, Troop 486, Coastal Empire Council, Boy Scouts of America

Easy Camp Fruit Salad

Servings: Varies Depending on Quantity of Fruit Used | Challenge Level: Easy

Any mixture of your favorite fruit, which might include:

Apples

Pears

Grapes

Strawberries or other berries

Bananas

Cantaloupe

Honeydew melon

Mandarin oranges

Kiwi

Mangos

Watermelon

Cherries

Papaya

Peaches or nectarines

1 (20-ounce) can crushed pineapple

1 (3-ounce) package raspberry or strawberry Jell-O

Preparation at Camp:

1. Cut fruit into bite-size pieces and place in a large-size bowl or ziplock bag.

2. Add crushed pineapple and Jell-O powder to the fruit pieces. Mix well.

3. Let fruit mix rest for about 20 minutes before serving.

Required Equipment:

Large-size mixing bowl or ziplock bag

Rikki Webb, Hampton, Virginia
Troop Leader, Council of the Colonial Coast, Girl Scouts of the USA

Ticks on a Toilet Seat

Servings: 3 | Challenge Level: Easy

Preparation at Camp:

1. Remove core from apples.

2. Cut apples crosswise into slices about ¼-inch thick to form circles with holes in the middle . . . sort of like toilet seats!

3. Spread peanut butter on apple slices and then decorate with raisins to look like the "ticks" on the "toilet seats"!

3 apples (your choice)

1 (12-ounce) jar peanut butter

3 (1½-ounce) boxes raisins

Katie Salyer Cox, Tucson, Arizona
Leader and Trainer, USA Girl Scouts Overseas and Sahuaro Council, Girl Scouts of the USA

Ants on a Log

Servings: 3 | Challenge Level: Easy

Preparation at Camp:

1. Spread cream cheese into celery grooves.

2. Decorate each piece with raisins to look like "ants on a log"!

6 celery stalks, each trimmed and cut in half

1 (8-ounce) package cream cheese

3 (1½-ounce) boxes raisins

Katie Salyer Cox, Tucson, Arizona
Leader and Trainer, USA Girl Scouts Overseas and Sahuaro Council, Girl Scouts of the USA

Fruit Salad Confetti

Servings: 10–12 | Challenge Level: Easy

1 small seedless watermelon, cut into bite-size pieces

1 pound seedless grapes (your choice)

1 cup sweetened shredded coconut

1 cup multicolored mini marshmallows

1 cup chopped walnuts

1 (15-ounce) can mandarin orange segments, drained

1 (20-ounce) can pineapple tidbits, drained

Preparation at Camp:

1. Combine all ingredients in a large bowl.

2. Chill in a cooler until ready to serve.

Required Equipment:

Large-size mixing bowl

Millie Hutchison, Pittsburgh, Pennsylvania
Girl Scout Trainer, Trillium Council, Girl Scouts of the USA

Zippy Bean Salad

Servings: 8–10 | Challenge Level: Moderate

Preparation at Camp:

1. Pour drained beans and corn into a large bowl. Add onion, celery, bell pepper, and optional mushrooms.

2. In a medium-size bowl, combine all dressing ingredients.

3. Pour dressing over bean salad. Let stand for 2 hours prior to serving.

Required Equipment:

Large-size mixing bowl
Medium-size mixing bowl

Bean Salad:

2 (15-ounce) cans kidney beans, drained

1 (15-ounce) can pinto beans, drained

1 (15-ounce) can garbanzo beans, drained

1 (15-ounce) can great northern beans, drained

1 (15-ounce) can kernel corn, drained

1 medium onion, chopped

2 stalks celery, diced

1 small bell pepper, diced

1 (8-ounce) can mushroom stems and pieces, drained (optional)

Dressing:

1 clove garlic, minced

2 tablespoons lemon juice

1 tablespoon vinegar

1 teaspoon mustard

⅓ cup olive oil

⅓ cup vegetable oil

Salt and ground black pepper to taste

Helen Greymorning, Missoula, Montana
Committee Member, Troop 1911, Montana Council, Boy Scouts of America

Black Bart's Salmagundi

Servings: 6–8 | Challenge Level: Moderate

"During his four-year reign of terror on the high seas, Black Bart captured nearly 400 vessels, making him one of the most notoriously successful pirates of all time. Salmagundi was a general term used for pirate gruel, often including meat pickled to prevent spoilage on long voyages. Black Bart was said to be eating salmagundi when the British Navy overtook his ship and killed him on February 10, 1722, somewhere off the coast of West Africa."

4 eggs

1 head Romaine lettuce or 8 ounces salad greens

2 medium carrots

10 ounces frozen tiny green beans or French-cut green beans

½ cup golden raisins

Option: If it isn't practical to keep the food cool for your trip outdoors, bring canned chicken and vegetables instead.

Preparation at Home:

1. Hard-cook the eggs: Cover with water, bring to a boil, remove from heat and allow to stand covered 23 minutes.

2. Rinse the greens, if necessary, and pat dry in paper towels.

3. Cut the carrots into 2-inch lengths, then quarter the larger pieces lengthwise.

4. Cook the carrots and green beans until barely tender, about 8 minutes.

5. Soak raisins for 10 minutes in hot water, then drain.

6. Keep all ingredients chilled and separated until ready to serve at camp.

Preparation at Camp:

1. Spread layer of greens on a platter and sprinkle with about ¼ cup salad dressing.

2. Place entire cooked chicken in center of greens. Arrange ham strips around chicken.

3. Peel hard-cooked eggs and cut into quarters; arrange around the meat.

4. Place the cooked green beans, carrots, and pickled vegetables on one side of the platter.

5. Place apple and orange slices on the opposite side from the vegetables.

6. Sprinkle raisins and optional croutons over the top, and serve with more salad dressing. Enjoy, matey! Arrrrrrgh!

Required Equipment:

Large serving platter

1 whole precooked rotisserie chicken

4 ounces cooked ham, cut into strips

8 ounces pickled vegetables or three-bean salad, drained

2 apples (Cortland, Gala, Granny Smith, or Red Delicious work well), cored and sliced

1 (8-ounce) can mandarin orange slices, drained

¾ cup Caesar or vinaigrette salad dressing

½ cup croutons (optional)

Option: Other possible ingredients include sliced almonds, corned beef, celery, cheeses, cucumber, pickled herring, mango, olives, cooked onions, green onions, peas, potatoes, spinach, and tomatoes. The meat and vegetables in salmagundi may also be slow-cooked and served hot.

Ken Harbison, Rochester, New York
Former Boy Scout, Washington Trail Council, Boy Scouts of America

Judy Harbison, Rochester, New York
Lifetime Member, Genesee Valley Council, Girl Scouts of the USA

Walking Salad

Servings: 6 | Challenge Level: Moderate

"I made these as a young girl in the 1960s, and they are definitely a Girl Scout tradition. The recipe was once used as an example in the Junior Girl Scout Handbook. The term 'walking salad' originally referred to using fresh fruits and vegetables as a no-cook snack that could be carried with you and eaten while hiking. Here's the version that I use with my troop."

12 very small apples

1 (6-ounce) container vanilla yogurt

½ teaspoon ground cinnamon

1 teaspoon lemon juice

1 teaspoon sugar, or to taste

1 carrot, grated

3 (1½-ounce) boxes raisins

Option: Stuff apples with your favorite gorp mixture instead!

Preparation at Home or Camp:

1. Wash carrots and apples. By cutting from the top, remove core from each apple, leaving the bottom of the apple intact. Also, try not to damage the top of the apple core so that it can be trimmed to plug the apple once it is filled.

2. Mix yogurt, cinnamon, lemon juice, and sugar in a medium-size mixing bowl. Adjust sugar, if necessary, for desired sweetness.

3. Add grated carrot and raisins. Mix all ingredients together.

4. Pack salad mixture into hollowed-out apples. Plug each with top of core.

5. Seal in plastic wrap. Set aside for lunch or toss in your pack for your next hiking adventure.

Required Equipment:

Medium-size mixing bowl
Plastic wrap

Katie Salyer Cox, Tucson, Arizona
Leader and Trainer, USA Girl Scouts Overseas and Sahuaro Council, Girl Scouts of the USA

High Adventure Energy Roll-Ups

Servings: 6 | Challenge Level: Easy

Preparation at Camp:

1. Divide peanut butter and jelly among all 12 tortillas.

2. Fold, roll, and serve.

2 (9-ounce) squeeze containers peanut butter

1 (16-ounce) squeeze container grape jelly (or your choice)

1 (12-count) package flour tortillas

Cap Cresap, Saugus, California
High Adventure Team Member, Venture Crew 220, Verdugo Hills Council, Boy Scouts of America

Genesee Valley Gorp

Servings: 4–6 | Challenge Level: Easy

"This recipe was adapted from an old outdoor cookbook published by the Girl Scouts of Genesee Valley. The concept of gorp continues to change, and it is now embellished by whatever the hiker enjoys snacking on, the only rules being that the ingredients should not melt (as uncoated chocolate would do) nor be greasy (as cheese or pepperoni would be)."

Preparation at Home:

1. In a large-size bowl, combine all ingredients.

2. Store in ziplock freezer bags.

1 cup raisins

1½ cups peanuts or mixed nuts

1 cup M&Ms

1 cup mini pretzels

1 cup dried fruit, such as dates, apricots, or Craisins

1 cup dry cereal, such as Fruit Loops, Wheat Chex, or Cheerios

Ken Harbison, Rochester, New York
Former Boy Scout, Washington Trail Council, Boy Scouts of America

Judy Harbison, Rochester, New York
Lifetime Member, Genesee Valley Council, Girl Scouts of the USA

Fisherman's Backup Plan

Servings: 2 / Multiply as Required | Challenge Level: Easy

"When I was young, my dad would often take me out to sea to go fishing. Once we brought along my Uncle Tommy, who agreed to supply lunch. Uncle Tommy showed up with a large brown grocery bag. 'What did you bring?' I asked. 'It's a surprise,' he replied.

After several hours of trolling in the warm sun without any luck, we pulled into shore for lunch. Uncle Tommy opened the grocery bag and took out bread, deviled ham, and pork and beans. He slapped them together to make sandwiches. Yuck!

'Try it. You'll like it,' he said. I was so hungry that I reluctantly took a bite. It wasn't bad! I actually ate two of the strange sandwiches that day. I don't recall catching any fish, but I'll always remember the tasty, albeit unusual, sandwiches we had for lunch."

1 (4¼-ounce) can deviled ham

1 (16-ounce) can pork and beans

2 large flour tortillas

Option: When preparing this recipe in camp, 4 slices of bread can be used in lieu of the 2 tortillas. Bread won't survive on the trail, and so the durability of tortillas is required if taking this hiking.

Preparation on Trail:

1. Divide deviled ham and pork and beans among the 2 tortillas.

2. Fold, roll, and serve.

Required Equipment:

Can opener for the beans

Greg Miyashiro, Aiea, Hawaii
Former Webelos Scout, Troop 221, Aloha Council, Boy Scouts of America

Wacky Gorp

Servings: Varies Depending on Quantity of Ingredients Used | Challenge Level: Easy

"With the list of ingredients in this recipe, you can use any wacky combination to make your favorite gorp!"

Preparation at Home:

1. A great-tasting mix is usually produced by using three to six ingredients in addition to the granola base. Gather ½ cup granola for each ½ cup of additional ingredients added.

2. Combine in a large-size bowl, store in ziplock storage bags, and hit the trail!

Base:

½ cup granola for each ½ cup of your favorite ingredients—

Your favorite nuts or seeds:

Peanuts
Almonds
Macadamia nuts
Pine nuts
Cashews
Beer Nuts
Sunflower seeds
Pecans
Pumpkin seeds

Your favorite dried fruits:

Blueberries
Bananas
Cherries
Mango
Apples
Raisins
Apricots
Dates
Prunes
Cranberries

Your favorite snacks:

Coconut flakes
Mini marshmallows
Chex cereal
Cheerios cereal
Pretzels
M&Ms

Helen Greymorning, Missoula, Montana
Committee Member, Troop 1911, Montana Council,
Boy Scouts of America

Pine Nut Soup

Servings: 2 / Multiply as Required | Challenge Level: Easy

"On an outing once, I had an adult join us who was a vegetarian. I was asked to make soup for the boys. I prepared this meat-free dish at the last minute using what I had on hand."

1 (1.4-ounce) package vegetable recipe mix (Knorr is preferred)

¼ cup pine nuts

¼ cup walnuts

1 (1½-ounce) box raisins

1 tablespoon honey

3 cups water

Preparation on Trail:

1. Combine all ingredients in a small pot and bring to a boil.

2. Let stand about 5 minutes before serving.

Required Equipment:

Small cook pot

Ken Spiegel, Farmingville, New York
Committee Member, Troop 80, Suffolk County Council, Boy Scouts of America

Old Grumpy Commissioners Cheesy Potatoes

Servings: 6–8 | Challenge Level: Easy

"I have often made this dish for my troop and, more recently, for a bunch of old grumpy commissioners. Never a complaint except when I add broccoli to it. This recipe serves 6–8 hungry campers or one district executive."

Preparation at Camp:

1. In Dutch oven, combine potatoes, ¼ cup melted butter, soup, onion, cheese, sour cream, and evaporated milk.

2. Crush cornflakes in a medium-size bowl and mix with ½ cup melted butter.

3. Evenly spread the buttered cornflake mixture over the potatoes in the oven.

4. Using 17 coals on the lid and 8 briquettes under the oven, bake for about 30 minutes or until the potatoes become soft.

Required Equipment:

12-inch Dutch oven
Medium-size mixing bowl

6 medium potatoes, peeled and diced

¼ cup (½ standard stick) butter, melted

1 (10¾-ounce) can condensed cream of chicken soup

1 small onion, diced

1 cup shredded cheddar cheese

1 cup sour cream

1 (5-ounce) can evaporated milk

3 cups cornflakes

½ cup (1 standard stick) butter, melted

Options: Add chunks of chicken or ham along with some broccoli prior to cooking.

Richard T. Davis, Bangor, Maine
Unit Commissioner, Troop 301 / Rocking Chair Patrol, Katahdin Area Council, Boy Scouts of America

Frontier Pizza

Servings: 4 | Challenge Level: Easy

"The first time I made Frontier Pizza was at our Troop Cracker Barrel at the Webelos Woods weekend campout. I perform living history demonstrations at these events. Using a mountain-man camp setup, I prepared all the pizzas by candlelight. The scouts would devour them as fast as I could bake them. That night, I must have made ten pizzas, saving the last two for the leaders. Since that campout, the troop begs me to bake pizzas at every Cracker Barrel! Frontier Pizza was voted 'Best Cracker Barrel' by Troop 47. It also took second place at Slippery Falls Scout Ranch Scoutmaster Cook-Off, being beat out by barbeque ribs."

2 (6½-ounce) packages dry pizza dough mix

1 cup water

¼ cup olive oil

Extra flour as needed for working dough

1 (14-ounce) can pizza sauce

Pizza toppings (optional, your choice)

1 cup shredded cheese, such as "pizza blend"

¼ cup grated Parmesan cheese

Preparation at Camp:

1. In a medium-size bowl, combine pizza dough mix, water, and olive oil. If dough is too sticky, add additional flour one or two tablespoons at a time. Cover dough and let sit for 5 minutes.

2. Press dough into bottom of greased Dutch oven, pushing crust one inch up the sides of the oven.

3. Pour pizza sauce on middle of the dough and spread outward. Add any optional toppings now. Sprinkle cheese over sauce and toppings.

4. Cover oven and cook using 10 briquettes under the oven and 19 coals on the lid. Bake for about 20–30 minutes or until pizza crust is golden brown.

5. Remove pizza with a spatula. Sprinkle with Parmesan cheese and cut into four equal slices.

Required Equipment:

12-inch Dutch oven
Medium-size mixing bowl

Tip: If preparing many pizzas for large groups, spaghetti sauce can be substituted for prepared pizza sauce as a less costly option.

Erick D. Noah, Oklahoma City, Oklahoma
Assistant Scoutmaster, Troop 47, Last Frontier Council, Boy Scouts of America

Swamped Pig

Servings: 6 | Challenge Level: Easy

Preparation at Camp:

1. Mix soup, milk, rice, onion, celery, garlic, salt, and black pepper to taste in Dutch oven.

2. Add pork chops, thoroughly coating them in the mixture.

3. Using 18 briquettes on the lid and 9 coals under the oven, bake for 1 hour or until the internal temperature of the pork reaches 160 degrees.

Required Equipment:

12-inch Dutch oven

1 (10¾-ounce) can condensed cream of mushroom or cream of chicken soup

1 can whole milk (use empty soup can to measure)

1 cup long-grain rice

1 small onion, finely chopped

1 stalk celery, finely chopped

1 clove garlic, finely chopped or minced

½ teaspoon salt

Ground black pepper to taste

6 pork chops, trimmed of fat and bone left in

Helen Greymorning, Missoula, Montana
Committee Member, Troop 1911, Montana Council, Boy Scouts of America

Texas Firehouse Chili

Servings: 6–8 | Challenge Level: Easy

"This dish comes from a collection of recipes provided by Texan firefighters and EMS workers."

2 pounds lean ground beef

1 small onion, chopped

1 tablespoon garlic powder

1 tablespoon chili powder

2 tablespoons brown sugar

Salt and ground black pepper to taste

1 (15-ounce) can dark kidney beans, drained and rinsed

1 (15-ounce) can light kidney beans, drained and rinsed

1 (15-ounce) can red beans, drained and rinsed

1 (29-ounce) can tomato sauce

Hot sauce to taste

Options: This recipe goes great over rice or pasta or with a side of corn bread.

Preparation at Camp:

1. Brown ground beef and onion in Dutch oven over 25 coals. Drain any excess grease.

2. Add garlic powder, chili powder, brown sugar, and salt and black pepper to taste. Stir.

3. Pour in beans and tomato sauce and stir. Add a few dashes of hot sauce to taste.

4. Relocate 17 briquettes to the lid, leaving 8 coals under the oven. Simmer for 2 hours, refreshing coals as needed.

5. Serve, allowing each scout to add enough hot sauce to set off the Texas firehouse alarms . . . if they dare!

Required Equipment:

12-inch Dutch oven

Eric Notkin, Canton, Massachusetts
Assistant Scoutmaster, Troop 88, Old Colony Council, Boy Scouts of America

Ponderosa Pork Chops

Servings: 4 | Challenge Level: Easy

Preparation at Camp:

1. Trim fat from pork chops, leaving bone in.

2. Combine all additional ingredients in Dutch oven and stir. Add meat, turning to coat each side.

3. Using 9 briquettes under the oven and 18 on the lid, cook for 45 minutes. Flip meat and continue cooking for an additional 15 minutes. Internal meat temperature must be at least 160 degrees F before serving.

Required Equipment:

12-inch Dutch oven

4 pork chops

¼ cup brown sugar

½ cup ketchup

¾ cup water

1 (1.4-ounce) package dried onion soup mix

Option: Eight chicken drumsticks, skin removed, can be substituted for the pork chops, but extend cooking time: Bake for 1 hour, then flip in sauce and continue cooking for approximately 30 additional minutes. Chicken is ready to serve once meat temperature reaches 170 degrees F.

Helen Greymorning, Missoula, Montana
Committee Member, Troop 1911, Montana Council, Boy Scouts of America

Wood Badge Jambalaya

Servings: 8–10 | Challenge Level: Easy

"This recipe originated at a wood badge course taught many years ago. One of the great characteristics of Wood Badge Jambalaya is that the liquid prevents the rice from sticking to the bottom of the oven, so constant stirring is unnecessary."

2 cups Uncle Ben's Converted rice

2 pounds fresh shrimp, shelled

1 (10½-ounce) can condensed French onion soup

1 (10½-ounce) can beef broth

2 (10½-ounce) cans water (use empty soup can to measure water)

1 pound smoked sausage, mild or hot, sliced

1 (8-ounce) can tomato sauce

½ cup (1 standard stick) butter cut into pats

½ cup fresh parsley, chopped

1 bunch green onions and tops, chopped

1 medium green bell pepper, chopped

1 tablespoon ground thyme

1 teaspoon ground black pepper

Minced garlic to taste

Option: Bite-size pieces of boneless chicken breast may be substituted for the shrimp.

Preparation at Camp:

1. Pour all ingredients into Dutch oven and mix thoroughly.

2. Bake using 8 briquettes under the oven and 17 on the lid. Refresh coals as required to maintain heat, and stir once after 45 minutes.

3. The jambalaya is ready to serve once rice becomes tender. Total cooking time should be between 1 hour 15 minutes and 1½ hours.

Required Equipment:

12-inch Dutch oven

Tom Owens, Scranton, Pennsylvania
Assistant Scoutmaster, Troop 81, Northeast Pennsylvania Council, Boy Scouts of America

High Adventure Macaroni

Servings: 10–12 | Challenge Level: Easy

"We served this with chilled peach slices during a recent High Adventure white water rafting trip on the Deschutes River."

Preparation at Camp:

1. Brown ground beef and sausage in Dutch oven over 25 briquettes. Drain grease.

2. Stir in garlic and continue to cook until it becomes golden.

3. Add oregano, spaghetti sauce, water, and uncooked macaroni. Stir, making sure all noodles are saturated.

4. Cover Dutch oven and redistribute briquettes, placing 13 coals on the lid and leaving 12 briquettes under the oven.

5. Bake until pasta is fully cooked, about 45 minutes.

6. Add mozzarella cheese. Once melted, sprinkle with grated parmesan cheese, then serve.

Required Equipment:

12-inch Dutch oven

2 pounds lean ground beef

1 pound ground Italian sausage

2 tablespoons crushed or minced garlic

1 tablespoon dried oregano

1 (26-ounce) can spaghetti sauce

2 (26-ounce) cans water (use empty spaghetti sauce can for measuring)

2 pounds uncooked elbow macaroni

2 cups shredded mozzarella cheese (or your choice)

¾ cup grated Parmesan cheese

Carmen Lohkamp, Gresham, Oregon
Committee Member and Eagle Mentor, Troop 542, Cascade Pacific Council, Boy Scouts of America

Sir George Carteret's Crab Imperial

Servings: 2 / Multiply as Required | Challenge Level: Easy

"In 1664, King Charles II of England granted a substantial portion of his Empire in America to his brother, James, Duke of York, who almost immediately granted the portion that was to become New Jersey to John Lord Berkeley and Sir George Carteret. Sir George straightaway began colonizing his grant, founding the settlement of Elizabethtown. It cannot be said that Sir George did not have some of the colony's abundant blue claw crabs prepared and served as in the following recipe, in this outpost of the British Empire!"

⅓ **green bell pepper, finely chopped**

⅓ **whole pimiento, finely chopped**

⅔ **teaspoon Colman's dry English mustard**

⅔ **teaspoon salt**

1 egg

⅓ **cup mayonnaise**

1 pound crabmeat, drained

Additional mayonnaise to taste

Paprika to taste

Preparation at Camp:

1. Mix bell pepper, pimiento, mustard, salt, egg, and mayonnaise in a 9-inch round aluminum pie pan.

2. Add crabmeat to the pan and smooth over the top.

3. Use a knife to spread the top lightly with additional mayonnaise to taste. Sprinkle with paprika, if desired.

4. Place pan on trivet in Dutch oven.

5. Using 17 coals on the lid and 8 briquettes under the oven, bake for about 15 minutes or until dish is hot and bubbly.

6. Serve hot, or chill to serve cold. Makes an excellent side dish, entree, or dip.

Required Equipment:

12-inch Dutch oven with trivet
9-inch round aluminum pie pan

Tips: If multiplying this recipe by 3, use 2 eggs instead of 1; a deeper pie dish will also be required. Pimiento can be found in the Italian section at your grocer.

William Sheehan, Pitman, New Jersey
Assistant Scoutmaster, Troop 55, Southern New Jersey Council, Boy Scouts of America

Missoula Vegetable Bake

Servings: 6–8 | Challenge Level: Easy

Preparation at Camp:

1. In greased Dutch oven, combine all ingredients except butter and bread crumbs.

2. Toss bread crumbs with butter in a small-size bowl and sprinkle over top of vegetables in the oven.

3. Using 17 coals on the lid and 8 briquettes under the oven, bake for 45 minutes or until cheese has melted throughout.

Required Equipment:

12-inch Dutch oven
Small-size mixing bowl

1 (16-ounce) bag frozen cut broccoli, thawed

1 (16-ounce) bag frozen cut cauliflower, thawed

1 (15-ounce) can creamed corn

1 (15-ounce) can corn kernels, drained

1 (10¾-ounce) can condensed cream of celery soup

1 (4-ounce) can sliced mushrooms, drained

2 cups (8 ounces) shredded cheddar cheese

4 green onions, chopped

1½ cups seasoned bread crumbs

2 tablespoons butter, melted

Helen Greymorning, Missoula, Montana
Committee Member, Troop 1911, Montana Council, Boy Scouts of America

Campfire Potatoes

Servings: 5–6 | Challenge Level: Easy

2 tablespoons olive oil

5 bacon strips

6 large potatoes, sliced into bite-size cubes

1 medium onion, diced

Seasoning salt and ground black pepper to taste

2 cups shredded mild cheddar cheese

Fresh chives (optional)

Preparation at Camp:

1. Heat oil in Dutch oven over 16 coals. Add bacon and fry until crisp. Remove bacon and set aside to drain.

2. Place potatoes and onion in Dutch oven. Add seasoning salt and ground black pepper to taste.

3. Moving 4 briquettes to the lid, with 12 coals remaining under the oven, cook for 20–30 minutes or until potatoes become tender.

4. Crumble bacon over the top and garnish with cheese and optional chives.

Required Equipment:

12-inch Dutch oven

Randi Powell, Shelby, North Carolina
Assistant Scoutmaster, Troop 114, Piedmont Council, Boy Scouts of America

Two-Can Jambalaya

Servings: 6–8 | Challenge Level: Easy

"In June 2002, our troop went to Camp Orr, near Jasper, Arkansas. The leader's manual for the camp had said something about a midweek Scoutmaster's Dutch Oven Cook-off, so we brought along the ingredients for Two-Can. After we arrived, we learned that the competition was to be more specialized than we had assumed: a 'cobbler cook-off'! Creativity ensued. Considering that we were in northwest Arkansas, where a primary staple food is chicken (we had at least one chicken meal every day that week), we decided to give Two-Can a temporary new name: 'World Famous Chicken-Free Two-Can Jambalaya Dump Cake.' (We figured the cook-off judges would appreciate a non-chicken meal even more than we would.) Well, it was an instant hit in the competition. The judges even invented a special category, for which we took top honors: 'Best Cobbler that Wasn't a Cobbler'! An amusing photo commemorating the event was taken and the following caption added:

The Spoon of Might,
The Crossed Batons of the Carriers,
And the Iron Pot of Strength...
These are the symbols of the
Ancient and Mystical Order of the Jambalaya

Ingredients:

- 2 cans (10-ounce each) tomatoes
- 2 cans (10½-ounce each) condensed French onion soup
- 2 cans (10½-ounce each) concentrated beef consommé
- 2 cans (about 1 pound) white rice (measure using empty soup can)
- 2 cans (about 1 pound) cubed kielbasa sausage (measure using empty soup can)
- ½ cup (1 standard stick) butter, cut into pats

Preparation at Camp:

1. Combine all ingredients in Dutch oven.

2. Bake using 8 briquettes under the oven and 17 coals on the lid. Cook for about 1 hour or until rice is tender, refreshing coals as required to maintain heat.

Required Equipment:

12-inch Dutch oven

Tip: Beef consommé is a type of beef stock typically found in your grocer's soup section.

Erich Wolz, Houston, Texas
Assistant Scoutmaster, Troop 505, Sam Houston Area Council, Boy Scouts of America

Scoutcraft Meatloaf

Servings: 4–6 | Challenge Level: Easy

"Scoutcraft Meatloaf was invented the last week of the summer of 2003 at Camp Mountain Run. I was the director of the First-Year Camper Program, and I had gone down to Scoutcraft to hang out with my friend Travis, who was Scoutcraft Director. There was to be a camp-wide Dutch Oven cook-off that evening, and Travis mentioned that there was still food left over from the cooking merit badge class. I'd made meatloaf many times before, but never added anything novel to it. This time, we decided to use up the leftover food and enter the cook-off by jamming whatever we could find into my standard recipe. Scoutcraft Meatloaf was born! We entered the competition, and the leaders, scouts, and staff definitely seemed to like it, because they ate it all. The dish received a large amount of votes. But alas, because we were staff, we were ineligible to win!"

2 pounds ground beef

2 (7-ounce) cans mushroom pieces and stems, drained

½ cup ketchup

¾ cup plain bread crumbs

2 eggs

¾ cup water

1 package Lipton's dried onion soup mix

2 cups shredded mozzarella cheese

½ medium onion, chopped

Preparation at Camp:

1. Combine all ingredients in a medium-size bowl and mix by hand.

2. Mold two loaves out of the meat mixture and place both in the Dutch oven.

3. Bake for about 1 hour 15 minutes using 10 briquettes under the oven and 15 briquettes on the lid. Replenish coals as required to maintain heat.

4. Meatloaf is ready to serve once the center of the loaves is no longer pink.

Required Equipment:

12-inch Dutch oven
Medium-size mixing bowl

Brian Sedgwick, Bellefonte, Pennsylvania
Director–Camp Mountain Run / Advisor–Venture Crew 509, Bucktail Council, Boy Scouts of America

River City Ribs

Servings: 8–10 | Challenge Level: Easy

"We live by the Missouri River, and our historic town is often referred to as the 'River City'. Jack McCall was tried and hung in Yankton in 1877 for shooting Wild Bill Hickok. Also, Lewis and Clark met near here with the Yankton Sioux Tribe in August 1804 on their way through to North Dakota."

Preparation at Camp:

1. Mix Coca-Cola and barbeque sauce together in Dutch oven.

2. Separate ribs between the bones and place in barbeque sauce.

3. Place 15 briquettes under the oven and 10 coals on the lid. Simmer for 1½ hours or until meat is tender, refreshing coals as required.

Required Equipment:

12-inch Dutch oven

¾ **can Coca-Cola (do not use diet soda)**

5 (18-ounce) jars **Sweet Baby James barbeque sauce**

3 racks baby back ribs

Duane D. Kolda, Yankton, South Dakota
Webelos Leader, Pack 259, Lewis and Clark Council, Boy Scouts of America

Spicy Southwestern Chili Soup

Servings: 8–10 | Challenge Level: Easy

"This is a simple recipe, low in fat, and nutritious!"

1 pound lean ground beef

1 medium onion, chopped

2 (14½-ounce) cans diced tomatoes (do not drain)

2 (10-ounce) cans diced tomatoes with green chilies (do not drain)

1 (29-ounce) can corn (do not drain)

3 (15-ounce) cans black beans, drained

1 (1½-ounce) package taco seasoning mix

1 (1-ounce) package ranch dressing mix (such as Hidden Valley)

Preparation at Camp:

1. Brown ground beef and onion in a Dutch oven over 25 briquettes.

2. Add remaining ingredients.

3. Continue to cook, stirring occasionally. Serve once soup is thoroughly heated.

Required Equipment:

12-inch Dutch oven

Large-size cook pot

Tip: As an alternative to the Dutch oven, a frying pan or cook pot can be used to prepare this recipe.

Erin DeGidio, Jacksonville, Florida
Former Webelos Leader, Pack 212, North Florida Council, Boy Scouts of America

Chicken-n-Stuff

Servings: 6–8 | Challenge Level: Easy

Preparation at Camp:

1. Place chicken breasts or tenders in Dutch oven.

2. Cover chicken with Swiss cheese.

3. Pour chicken soup and grape juice over cheese.

4. Spread stuffing over chicken and cheese.

5. Pour melted butter over stuffing.

6. Add black pepper and parsley to taste.

7. Cook for 45 minutes using 8 briquettes under the oven and 17 coals on the lid. Serve once internal temperature of chicken reaches 170 degrees F.

Required Equipment:

12-inch Dutch oven

Tip: Preheat the Dutch oven and use it to melt the butter prior to arranging the chicken and other ingredients for this recipe.

3 pounds chicken breasts or frozen tenders, thawed

1½ pounds Swiss cheese, shredded or cubed

1 (10¾-ounce) can condensed cream of chicken soup

¼ cup white grape juice

1 (6-ounce) box or 2 cups chicken flavored stuffing mix

½ cup (1 stick) butter, melted

Ground black pepper and fresh parsley to taste

Tracy Tuttle, Boise, Idaho
Den Leader, Pack 97, Ore-Ida Council, Boy Scouts of America

Scout Camp Carnitas

Servings: 10–12 | Challenge Level: Easy

"As sold in most supermarkets, 'chili powder' is a mixture of powdered chili peppers, cumin, salt, garlic powder, and, perhaps, oregano. Although chili powder works in this recipe, I've always been a purist and prefer to use powdered chili pepper instead."

3 pounds boneless shoulder pork

1 cup all-purpose flour

1 tablespoon powdered chili pepper

1 teaspoon salt

1 teaspoon ground oregano

1 teaspoon garlic powder

½ cup lard

24 tortillas

3 (15-ounce) cans refried beans

1 (16-ounce) jar salsa

1 (16-ounce) container sour cream

Preparation at Camp:

1. Cut pork into 1 inch cubes.

2. Blend flour, chili pepper, salt, oregano, and garlic powder in a large mixing bowl.

3. Add the pork to the flour mix and thoroughly coat.

4. Place 15 briquettes under Dutch oven and melt lard. Add floured meat mixture.

5. Fry carnitas, occasionally stirring until pork is cooked through and tender, approximately 30–40 minutes depending on heat level. Do not let a hard crust form over the carnitas. This is an indication that the food is overcooking.

6. Serve with tortillas, heated refried beans, salsa, and sour cream.

Required Equipment:

12-inch Dutch oven
Large-size mixing bowl

Tips: The meat can be chopped, coated, and frozen at home prior to your outing. Inexpensive cuts of pork work well in this recipe.

Robert Harrison, Atlanta, Georgia
Den Leader, Pack 550, Atlanta Area Council, Boy Scouts of America

Concho Valley Chicken

Servings: 6–8 | Challenge Level: Easy

Preparation at Camp:

1. Grease Dutch oven with oil, and preheat over 20 briquettes.

2. Chop chicken breasts into small pieces.

3. Sauté meat, along with bell pepper and onion, in hot Dutch oven.

4. Sprinkle chicken with paprika, salt, ground black pepper, and Creole-Cajun seasoning to taste.

5. Drain the cans of diced tomatoes and diced tomatoes with green chilies, and save the liquid. Add drained tomatoes to Dutch oven and mix with the chicken.

6. Once the chicken and tomatoes are thoroughly heated, add chicken broth, rice, and the liquid drained from the tomatoes to the Dutch oven.

7. Mix well, cover, and let simmer until the rice has absorbed the liquid and becomes tender.

8. Sprinkle shredded cheese over top of rice and chicken. Replace the lid on the Dutch oven until cheese has melted.

9. Serve Concho Valley Chicken with warm flour tortillas.

Required Equipment:

12-inch Dutch oven

Ingredients:

1 tablespoon vegetable oil

4 skinless, boneless chicken breast halves

2 green bell peppers, diced

1 medium onion, diced

Paprika, salt, ground black pepper, and Creole-Cajun seasoning to taste

1 (14-ounce) can diced tomatoes

1 (10-ounce) can diced tomatoes with green chilies

1 (32-ounce) container chicken broth

1 (14-ounce) box Kraft Minute Premium Rice

2 cups shredded Monterey Jack cheese

1 (12-count) package flour tortillas

Tony Kieffer, San Angelo, Texas
Assistant Scoutmaster, Troop 22, Concho Valley Council, Boy Scouts of America

Webelos Overnight Camp Beans

Servings: 10–12 | Challenge Level: Easy

"The meal has been an all-time favorite with my Webelos whenever we've gone on an overnight campout."

1 pound bacon

1 large onion, chopped

1 pound kielbasa sausage ring, sliced into chunks

2 (14-ounce) packages cocktail-size smoked sausages (such as Hillshire Farm Lit'l Smokies)

1 (14½-ounce) can butter beans, drained

2 (15-ounce) cans pork and beans

2 (14½-ounce) cans kidney beans (do not drain)

1 (14½-ounce) can black beans, southwestern flavored if available (do not drain)

1 clove garlic, minced

⅔ cup ketchup

¼ cup maple syrup

⅓ cup brown sugar

Option: A loaf of French bread goes great with this dish.

Preparation at Camp:

1. Cut each bacon strip into 1-inch lengths.

2. Brown bacon in Dutch oven over 25 coals. Drain grease.

3. Add chopped onion to bacon and sauté until onion begins to become translucent.

4. Add remainder of ingredients and stir.

5. Reduce heat to a simmer by removing briquettes as required. Cook for 1 hour before serving.

Required Equipment:

12-inch Dutch oven

Duane D. Kolda, Yankton, South Dakota
Webelos Leader, Pack 259, Lewis and Clark Council, Boy Scouts of America

Inside-Out Chicken

Servings: 6–8 | Challenge Level: Easy

"In this recipe, the stuffing is on top!"

Preparation at Camp:

1. In a Dutch oven heated over 20 briquettes, brown chicken, onion, and celery in melted butter.

2. Stir in seasonings, cream of mushroom soup, Worcestershire sauce, and carrots.

3. Cover oven and simmer for 15 minutes.

4. While chicken is simmering, blend stuffing and chicken broth in a medium-size mixing bowl.

5. Spread stuffing mix over top of chicken and vegetables in the Dutch oven. Do not stir. Instead, carefully pat the stuffing mix down.

6. Replace lid and bake about 35 minutes, using 8 coals under the oven and 12 on the lid. The dish is ready once stuffing turns golden brown.

Required Equipment:

12-inch Dutch oven
Medium-size mixing bowl

3 tablespoons butter

2 pounds boneless chicken, cut into small pieces

1 medium onion, diced

1 stalk celery, diced

Lemon pepper, tarragon, parsley, and allspice to taste

2 (10¾-ounce) cans condensed cream of mushroom soup

1 tablespoon Worcestershire sauce

2 carrots, thinly sliced julienne-style

2 (6-ounce) boxes chicken flavored stuffing

1 (14-ounce) can chicken broth

John "The Scout Camp Chef" Jones, North Tonawanda, New York
Scoutmaster, Troop 184, Greater Niagara Frontier Council, Boy Scouts of America

Baldwin Bean Burgoo

Servings: 8–10 | Challenge Level: Easy

"This recipe is named for the town of Baldwin, Michigan, where we go for our annual 10-mile hike along the Muskegon River. The dish is delicious and very easy to prepare."

1 pound lean ground beef

1 pound bacon, chopped

1 onion, chopped

½ cup ketchup

½ cup barbecue sauce

Salt to taste

¼ cup prepared mustard

3 tablespoons molasses

1 teaspoon chili powder

¾ teaspoon ground black pepper

2 (16-ounce) cans kidney beans, drained

2 (16-ounce) cans pork and beans

2 (16-ounce) cans lima butter beans (do not drain)

Preparation at Camp:

1. In a Dutch oven, brown ground beef along with bacon and onions over 25 coals. Drain grease.

2. Add remaining ingredients and stir.

3. Lower heat to a simmer by removing briquettes as required. Continue cooking for at least 2 hours, occasionally refreshing coals.

Required Equipment:

12-inch Dutch oven

Tip: As an alternative to the Dutch oven, a frying pan and cook pot can be used to prepare this recipe.

Shaun Davis, Hastings, Michigan
Den Leader, Pack 175, Gerald R. Ford Council, Boy Scouts of America

Sweet and Sour Wilderness Ham

Servings: 6 | Challenge Level: Easy

Preparation at Camp:

1. Place ham slices in Dutch oven, spreading a thin layer of mustard on each piece.

2. Insert cloves randomly into ham slices.

3. Top ham with bell pepper and pineapple rings.

4. Pour sweet and sour sauce over everything.

5. Cook for about 30 minutes, using 7 briquettes under the oven and 12 coals on the lid.

Required Equipment:

12-inch Dutch oven

6 slices precooked ham (½- to 1-inch thick per slice)

1 tablespoon Dijon mustard

1 tablespoon whole cloves

1 bell pepper, sliced into rings

1 (20-ounce) can pineapple rings, drained

1 (15-ounce) jar sweet and sour sauce

Sherry Bennett, Rochester, New York
Former Den Leader and Merit Badge Counselor, Boy Scouts of America

Three Fires Frito Pie

Servings: 4–6 | Challenge Level: Easy

"This dinner is so good, and the aroma is fabulous! It's a big hit with both kids and adults."

1 tablespoon olive oil

1 onion, diced

1 green or red bell pepper, diced

2 pounds ground beef

1 (1¼-ounce) packet taco seasoning mix

¾ cup water

½ cup salsa

1 (10-ounce) bag Fritos corn chips

8 ounces shredded sharp cheddar cheese

Preparation at Camp:

1. Preheat Dutch oven using 23 briquettes underneath.

2. In Dutch oven, sauté onion and bell pepper in olive oil. Remove from oven and set aside.

3. Brown ground beef in Dutch oven. Drain grease.

4. In a small-size bowl, mix taco seasoning mix with water. Pour into Dutch oven.

5. Return sautéed onion and pepper to Dutch oven and stir.

6. Remove from heat. Stir in salsa. Pour Fritos and cheese over top. Cover and let stand until cheese is melted.

Required Equipment:

12-inch Dutch oven
Small-size mixing bowl

Tip: You can sauté the vegetables and brown the meat at home prior to your trip. Just keep them cold until ready to use.

Don Gross, Roselle, Illinois
Former Cubmaster, Pack 408, Three Fires Council, Boy Scouts of America

Jill Gross, Roselle, Illinois
Former Den Leader, Pack 408, Three Fires Council, Boy Scouts of America

Jacob Gross, Roselle, Illinois
Eagle Scout, Troop 408, Three Fires Council, Boy Scouts of America

Zachary Gross, Roselle, Illinois
Arrow of Light Recipient, Pack 408, Three Fires Council, Boy Scouts of America

Johnny Appleseed Pork Chops

Servings: 6 | Challenge Level: Easy

Preparation at Camp:

1. In Dutch oven over 25 coals, fry pork chops in oil until brown. Remove chops from oven.

2. Prepare stuffing in medium-size bowl according to package directions.

3. Spread pie filling over bottom of the oven.

4. Place pork chops on top of pie filling. Spoon stuffing mix on top of pork chops.

5. Bake for 45 minutes, keeping 12 briquettes under the oven and relocating 13 coals to the lid.

1 tablespoon vegetable oil

6 thick boneless pork loin chops

1 (6-ounce) box stuffing mix, including ingredients required to prepare stuffing

1 (21-ounce) can apple pie filling with cinnamon

Required Equipment:

12-inch Dutch oven
Medium-size mixing bowl

Ed Bedford, Chapel Hill, North Carolina
Scoutmaster, Troop 820, Occoneechee Council, Boy Scouts of America

Not Your Mama's Baked Beans

Servings: 8–10 | Challenge Level: Easy

"This recipe took second place in the 'side dish' category in *Scouting* magazine's 2005 'Camp Food Favorites' recipe contest."

½ cup brown sugar

½ cup 7-Up or Sprite soda

2 (27½-ounce) cans baked beans

1 (20-ounce) can pineapple chunks, drained

1 (8-ounce) can water chestnuts, drained

1 pound summer sausage, sliced and cubed

2 large sweet onions, chopped

3 large bell peppers, chopped

2 large tomatoes, chopped

1 cup chopped fresh mushrooms

Options: Turkey sausage can be used as a lower-fat substitute. Choose a mix of yellow, red, and green bell peppers to add color.

Preparation at Camp:

1. In a small mixing bowl, blend brown sugar and 7-Up until sugar dissolves.

2. Pour baked beans into Dutch oven. Stir in pineapple and water chestnuts. Next add cubed sausage and chopped vegetables.

3. Stir 7-Up mixture into baked bean blend.

4. Cook for 45 minutes to 1 hour using 10 briquettes under the oven and 15 coals on the lid. Stir every 10 minutes or so while cooking.

Required Equipment:

12-inch Dutch oven
Small-size mixing bowl

Tip: This recipe can also be prepared using a large cook pot.

Mark Brown, Ogden, Utah
Committee Member, Troop 236, Trapper Trails Council, Boy Scouts of America

Hoosier Camp Chicken

Servings: 8 | Challenge Level: Easy

"We quickly improvised a weekend campout so that three of our scouts could obtain final cooking requirements for First Class rank. While Hoosier Camp Chicken was heating one evening, the aroma drew other hungry scouts around the Dutch oven. After our group had had their dinner, other patrols, who by then had already eaten as well, hurried over for our leftovers, even pouring the sauce into cups and eating that! Nothing was left. Needless to say, Hoosier Camp Chicken became a favorite."

Preparation at Camp:

1. Preheat Dutch oven over 25 briquettes.

2. In oven, lightly brown both sides of chicken breasts in olive oil. Do not fully cook them!

3. Put a scoop of orange marmalade on each piece of meat.

4. Pour Russian dressing over chicken.

5. Bake for 45 minutes after moving 17 briquettes to the lid and leaving 8 coals under the oven. Before serving, check to ensure that the meat is cooked throughout.

Required Equipment:

12-inch Dutch oven

4 large boneless chicken breasts, each divided in two

1 tablespoon olive oil

1 (8-ounce) jar orange marmalade

1 (8-ounce) bottle Russian salad dressing

Options: Goes great with rice and applesauce or instant mashed potatoes and green beans.

Michael Daniel, Morgantown, Indiana
Assistant Scoutmaster, Troop 218, Crossroads of America Council, Boy Scouts of America

Paddlers Pot Roast

Servings: 6–8 | Challenge Level: Easy

"Before I leave for a backcountry canoe trip, I wrap the frozen roast in two sheets of foil then surround this in layers of newspaper or an insulating bag. After several hours of drive time and one or two hours of paddling time, the roast has thawed enough to cook."

1 pot roast, about 3 pounds

4 potatoes

2 onions

2 pounds baby carrots

Salt and ground black pepper to taste

Preparation at Camp:

1. Place roast in Dutch oven.

2. Peel and slice potatoes and onions into large pieces. Arrange these, along with baby carrots, around the sides of the roast in the oven.

3. Sprinkle on salt and black pepper to taste.

4. Cook roast for 1–1½ hours using 8 briquettes under the oven and 17 on the lid. Refresh briquettes as required. Roast is ready to serve once internal meat temperature reaches at least 145 degrees F.

Required Equipment:

12-inch Dutch oven

Tip: Ensure that neither the roast nor vegetables touch the sides or top of the Dutch oven while the roast is cooking or they will burn. No water needs to be added because the roast and vegetables cook in their own juices.

Sherry Bennett, Rochester, New York
Former Den Leader and Merit Badge Counselor, Boy Scouts of America

Spicy BBQ Texas Chicken

Servings: 5–6 | Challenge Level: Easy

Preparation at Camp:

1. Start 25 briquettes.

2. Mix sauces, raisins, and apricots in Dutch oven. Add chicken, ensuring that all pieces are coated.

3. Place 8 coals under the oven and 17 briquettes on the lid. Cook for 1–1½ hours or until the internal temperature of the chicken reaches 170 degrees F, refreshing briquettes as required.

Required Equipment:

12-inch Dutch oven

2 (28-ounce) bottles mesquite- or hickory-flavored barbeque sauce

6 tablespoons chipotle Tabasco sauce

½ cup raisins

½ cup chopped apricots

5 pounds chicken legs and thighs

Option: Serve in bowls along with a hearty bread to sop up the excess barbeque sauce.

Jeff Boswell, Austin, Texas
Assistant Scoutmaster, Troop 410, Longhorn Council, Boy Scouts of America

Adirondack Ham and Sweet Potatoes

Servings: 4 | Challenge Level: Easy

¼ cup (½ standard stick) butter

¾ cup brown sugar

4 thick slices pre-cooked ham

2 sweet potatoes, peeled and cut into ½-inch slices

Preparation at Camp:

1. Start 23 briquettes and warm the Dutch oven over a few of them.

2. Combine butter and sugar in oven and stir until melted.

3. Place ham slices in oven.

4. Arrange sliced sweet potatoes over and around ham.

5. Cover oven and place 16 coals on the lid, leaving 7 briquettes under the oven. Bake for about 45 minutes or until potatoes are soft.

Required Equipment:

12-inch Dutch oven

Sherry Bennett, Rochester, New York
Former Den Leader and Merit Badge Counselor, Boy Scouts of America

Troop 216 Forty-Clove Garlic Chicken

Servings: 8–10 | Challenge Level: Easy

Preparation at Camp:

1. Combine all ingredients, including the entire bottle of McCormick seasoning, into Dutch oven.

2. Place 8 briquettes under the oven and 17 coals on the lid. Cook for about 1 hour or until internal temperature of the chicken reaches 170 degrees F, refreshing coals as required.

Required Equipment:

12-inch Dutch oven

40 cloves garlic, peeled and crushed, or 4¼-ounce jar crushed garlic

6 skinless, boneless chicken breasts, cut into bite-size cubes

4 (10¾-ounce) cans Campbell's chicken gumbo soup

4 cans water (use empty soup can to measure)

1 (16-ounce) bag frozen mixed vegetables

1 (2¾-ounce) bottle McCormick Salt-Free Garlic and Herb Seasoning

George Brown, Los Osos, California
Former Scoutmaster, Troop 216, Los Padres Council, Boy Scouts of America

Sherry's Backcountry Cornish Game Hens

Servings: 4 | Challenge Level: Easy

4 Cornish game hens

1 (32-ounce) container chicken broth

1 cup white or brown rice

1 pound baby carrots

Preparation at Camp:

1. Clean and prepare hens for baking.

2. Pour chicken broth into Dutch oven.

3. Add rice to broth, placing hens on top of rice.

4. Arrange baby carrots around hens.

5. Using 8 briquettes under the oven and 19 coals on the lid, cook for about an hour or until internal temperature of the chicken reaches 170 degrees F, refreshing coals as required.

Required Equipment:

12-inch Dutch oven

Sherry Bennett, Rochester, New York
Former Den Leader and Merit Badge Counselor, Boy Scouts of America

Finger Lakes Spiced Corned Beef

Servings: 8–10 | Challenge Level: Moderate

"I've received rave reviews every time I've prepared this on a campout. The cooking time may seem long, but it doesn't require much effort to get started. And it's worth the wait: The brisket will melt in your mouth."

Preparation at Camp:

1. Place onions and brisket in a well-greased Dutch oven.

2. Using 23 briquettes under the oven, brown the onions and sear the brisket on all sides.

3. In a medium-size bowl, stir together 1 cup of apple juice, brown sugar, orange peel, mustard, and cloves.

4. Pour apple juice mixture over meat, lifting corners of the brisket to allow juice to coat underneath.

5. Cook, leaving 7 coals under the oven and moving 16 briquettes to the lid.

6. Turn the brisket after 1½ hours. Add more apple juice if the liquid is low. Refresh coals as needed.

7. Continue cooking for another 1–2 hours, then add potatoes about 30 minutes before removing oven from heat. Continue to refresh coals as required.

8. Total cooking time should be between 3–4 hours or until brisket is tender and internal meat temperature is at least 145 degrees F.

9. Slice corned beef diagonal to the grain and serve with potatoes.

Required Equipment:

12-inch Dutch oven
Medium-size mixing bowl

Tom Dooley, Honeoye Falls, New York
Treasurer, Troop 10, Otetiana Council, Boy Scouts of America

3 medium onions, thinly sliced into rings

1 (3- to 4-pound) corned beef brisket

1–2 cups apple juice or cider

¼ cup packed brown sugar

2 teaspoons grated orange peel

2 teaspoons prepared mustard

6 whole cloves

3 (14½-ounce) cans whole new potatoes, drained

Doctor J's Chicken and Dumplings

Servings: 14–16 | Challenge Level: Moderate

"I invented this recipe when our troop went on a winter campout to Hennepin Canal in Northern Illinois. The windchill temperature fell below zero, but this dish kept our bodies and souls warm."

2 tablespoons vegetable oil

2 large onions, peeled and diced

2 cloves garlic, minced

4 pounds boneless skinless chicken breast, cubed

4 carrots, peeled and diced

4 potatoes, peeled and diced

4 (15-ounce) cans mixed vegetables, drained

2 teaspoons salt

1 teaspoon ground black pepper

2 bay leaves

6 (10½-ounce) cans chicken gravy

2 (16.3-ounce) containers Pillsbury Grands! Homestyle Biscuits

Preparation at Camp:

1. Place about 30 briquettes under large Dutch oven.

2. Heat oil, adding onions and garlic, and cook until soft.

3. Add cubed chicken to the hot oven, stirring occasionally until the meat turns white.

4. Add remaining ingredients, except for biscuits.

5. Cover the oven and transfer 10 coals from under the oven to the lid.

6. Stir the stew occasionally, and after 1 hour, lay individual biscuits on top of stew.

7. Replace lid and continue to cook for an additional 15 minutes or until biscuits rise. Refresh coals as needed to maintain heat and to ensure that the biscuits brown.

8. Remove bay leaves before serving.

Required Equipment:

14-inch Dutch oven

Dr. Pamela Jurgens-Toepke, New Lenox, Illinois
Committee Member, Troop 40, Tomahawk Council, Boy Scouts of America

Texas Pioneer Pie

Servings: 8–10 | Challenge Level: Moderate

"Pioneer Pie is a Texas adaptation of an old camp recipe that I first cooked many years ago as a Boy Scout. I named it for the pioneer families that came to this area of Texas with Stephen F. Austin. One of these families commissioned a sugar mill in 1843, which became the foundation of our town, Sugar Land. The sugar mill was the original sponsor of our Boy Scout Troop. As the 'Grub Master' for Troop 148, I think you will find Texas Pioneer Pie to be a simple, hearty meal that captures the Texas pioneering spirit. It has become a favorite of our Scoutmaster corps."

Preparation at Camp:

1. Brown ground beef, sausage, and onion in Dutch oven over 25 coals. Drain excess grease.

2. Add beans, tomato sauce, corn, olives, and chili seasoning. Stir. Simmer for 15 minutes.

3. Mix corn muffin mix with egg and milk in a medium-size bowl.

4. Pour muffin batter evenly over the top of the beef-sausage mixture in oven. Do not stir.

5. Using 8 briquettes under the oven and 17 coals on the lid, bake for 30–40 minutes or until the corn bread topping is golden brown. Refresh coals as needed.

6. Sprinkle corn bread topping with cheddar cheese and replace lid, baking for a few additional minutes until cheese is melted.

7. Remove from heat and let set, uncovered, for 5 minutes before serving.

Required Equipment:

12-inch Dutch oven
Medium-sized mixing bowl

1 pound ground beef

1 pound ground sausage

1 small onion, chopped

2 (15-ounce) cans pinto beans

1 (15-ounce) can tomato sauce

1 (15-ounce) can whole kernel corn, drained

2 (4-ounce) cans sliced ripe olives, drained

1 (1¼-ounce) package dried chili seasoning

1 (8½-ounce) package Jiffy corn muffin mix

1 egg

⅓ cup milk

1 cup shredded cheddar cheese

Allen "Senior Grub Master" Largent, Sugar Land, Texas
Assistant Scoutmaster, Troop 148, Sam Houston Area Council, Boy Scouts of America

Trapper Trails Strawberry Chicken Rollups

Servings: 6 | Challenge Level: Moderate

3 (8-ounce, 8-count) containers refrigerated crescent roll dough

1 (8-ounce) package cream cheese, softened

¼ cup (½ standard stick) butter, softened

3 (5-ounce) cans chicken, drained

1 cup strawberry jam

½ cup light corn syrup

¼ cup sliced almonds

Preparation at Camp:

1. Open crescent roll containers and separate dough into rectangles, creating a total of 12.

2. Mix cream cheese, butter, and chicken pieces in a medium-size bowl.

3. Divide chicken mix over top of 12 dough rectangles. Roll each. When finished, they should have the appearance of enchiladas.

4. Place rollups into Dutch oven and cook for about 15 minutes using 17 coals on the lid and 8 briquettes under the oven. The tops of the rolls should be nicely browned when finished.

5. While rollups bake, mix the strawberry jam and corn syrup in a small pot and heat slightly. The pot can be warmed over the coals on lid of Dutch oven.

6. Generously drizzle rollups with the strawberry topping. Sprinkle with almonds and serve.

Required Equipment:

12-inch Dutch oven
Small-size cook pot
Medium-size mixing bowl

Linda Pfaff, Ogden, Utah
Commissioner, Troop 285, Trapper Trails Council, Boy Scouts of America

Plebian Meatloaf

Servings: 6–8 | Challenge Level: Moderate

"I've had the distinguished honor of seeing my original Plebian Meatloaf recipe reprinted in three other cookbooks: *Retro Ranch: A Roundup of Classic Cowboy Cooking, 2002 Olympic Winter Games Dutch Oven Cooking,* and *Cee Dub's Ethnic and Regional Dutch Oven Cookin'.* The men of E Clampus Vitus, a California historical group that I am a member of, regularly request this dish."

Preparation at Camp:

1. Using Dutch oven warmed over 25 coals, sauté onion in olive oil until well caramelized.

2. In a large bowl, combine onion, ground beef, sausage, cracker crumbs, eggs, and salt. Mix well and form into an oblong loaf.

3. Lay bacon on bottom of Dutch oven. Place meatloaf on top of bacon.

4. Relocate 17 coals to the lid, leaving 8 briquettes under the oven. Bake for 30 minutes, then remove excess fat with a baster.

5. Add thawed vegetables around sides of meatloaf.

6. Replace lid and continue baking for an additional 15 minutes. Once again, remove fat.

7. Bake for a final 15 minutes, again removing any excess fat. Meatloaf is ready to serve once internal temperature exceeds 160 degrees F. Season the vegetables to taste.

Required Equipment:

12-inch Dutch oven
Large-size mixing bowl
Baster

Jim Tanner, Mountain View, California
Former Scout, Great Sauk Trail Council, Boy Scouts of America

2 tablespoons olive oil

1 large yellow onion, finely chopped

1 pound lean ground beef

1 (16-ounce) package spicy hot sausage (Jimmy Dean preferred)

1 sleeve Ritz crackers, well crumbled

2 eggs

1 teaspoon salt

½ pound bacon

2 (16-ounce) bags Santa Fe or California blend frozen vegetables, thawed

Your favorite spice mix to season vegetables

Option: An interesting variation is to bake the meatloaf in the shape of a cake using a smaller 10-inch Dutch oven. Instead of forming an oblong loaf, simply push the meatloaf into the round bottom of the oven. When it comes time to add the vegetables, lay them on top of the meat instead of around the sides.

Darrell's Tomahawk Casserole

Servings: 8–10 | Challenge Level: Moderate

"The first time I made this recipe was at Camp Strake during a Dutch oven cook-off for the adults. We submitted our ingredient request to the mess hall, but when the camp cook delivered the groceries, we found he left out one critical item from each of our lists. I figured it was just a mistake until I discovered he had won the last two cook-offs. Well, we decided that since he knew what we were cooking, he had an unfair advantage, so we turned the tables on him. A few of us left camp for a local grocery store, purchasing items for totally different recipes. Imagine the camp cook's surprise when he brought his dish to the competition and it didn't even place. Tomahawk Casserole won the cook-off, and our troop's other recipes were awarded second, third, and fifth place!"

2 pounds lean ground beef or turkey

2 (1¼-ounce) packages taco seasoning

2 (10-ounce) cans diced tomatoes with green chilies

2 (15-ounce) cans ranch-style beans

2 (10¾-ounce) cans condensed cream of mushroom soup

1 (4¼-ounce) can chopped black olives

2 green onions, diced

10 medium flour tortillas

2 cups shredded cheddar cheese

2 cups shredded Mexican-style cheese

1 jalapeño, sliced

Preparation at Camp:

1. Brown meat in Dutch oven over 27 coals. Drain grease and place meat in large bowl.

2. To the browned meat, add taco seasoning, diced tomatoes, ranch beans, soup, half of the olives, and the green onions. Stir well.

3. Cut tortillas into strips.

4. In Dutch oven, layer ingredients starting with taco mixture, cheese, and then tortilla strips. Repeat, so layers are: mixture, cheese, tortilla strips, mixture, cheese, tortilla strips, mixture, and ending with cheese.

5. On top of the cheese, sprinkle the remaining olives and the jalapeño slices.

6. Moving 18 coals to the lid and leaving 9 briquettes under the oven, cook for 30–45 minutes.

7. Remove from heat and let rest, uncovered, for 15 minutes. Slice and serve.

Required Equipment:

12-inch Dutch oven

Large-size mixing bowl

Darrell Laurence, Austin, Texas
Assistant Scoutmaster, Troop 8787, Capitol Area Council, Boy Scouts of America

Black Swamp Pasta

Servings: 18–20 | Challenge Level: Moderate

Preparation at Camp:

1. Brown ground beef or sausage in large Dutch oven over 39 coals. Remove excess grease.

2. Boil pasta in large cook pot according to package directions. Drain.

3. In Dutch oven, layer the ingredients, including cooked pasta, in order shown in the ingredients list. Try to repeat entire layering sequence two additional times.

4. Relocate 26 coals to the lid, leaving 13 briquettes under the oven. Bake for 1 hour, refreshing coals as required.

Required Equipment:

16-inch Dutch oven

Large-size cook pot

Tip: This recipe can also be cooked in a deep 14-inch / 10-quart Dutch oven, but it's a very tight fit. Pasta may touch lid and burn. If a deep 14-inch is ultimately used, bake with 11 coals under the oven and 21 briquettes on the lid

2 pounds ground beef or sausage

3 (16-ounce) boxes rotini (corkscrew) pasta

5 (14-ounce) cans pizza sauce

3 (3-ounce) packages presliced pepperoni

1 bell pepper, diced

1 onion, diced

2 (4-ounce) cans sliced mushrooms, drained

3 (16-ounce) packages shredded mozzarella cheese

Greg Brown, Hicksville, Ohio
Assistant Scoutmaster, Troop 216, Black Swamp Area Council, Boy Scouts of America

Flaming Arrow Meat Pockets

Servings: 4 | Challenge Level: Moderate

"On one campout, the Flaming Arrow Patrol told me they were going to make a special pie for dinner. I assumed some huge apple or blueberry thing . . . they wouldn't tell me the details. I found out later they had planned to prepare a sort of shepherd's pie without the mashed potatoes, using a piecrust instead. But when they went to work with the crust, it broke into halves. They improvised, deciding to fold the crusts over, creating pockets instead. They were successful as everyone liked the new meat-filled mini-pies. The name 'Flaming Arrow Meat Pockets' stuck, and the scouts have experimented with all kinds of fillings since."

1 pound lean ground beef

1 small onion, chopped

2 cloves garlic, diced

1 small tomato, chopped

1 small bell pepper, chopped

1 tablespoon Worcestershire sauce

¼ teaspoon thyme

¼ teaspoon ground cloves

¼ teaspoon savory

¼ cup seasoned bread crumbs

1 cup grated cheese (optional)

1 (15-ounce) package of 2 Pillsbury refrigerated pie crusts

Preparation at Camp:

1. Brown ground beef in skillet.

2. Add onion, garlic, tomato, and bell pepper. Cook until onion and bell pepper soften.

3. Remove from heat and add Worcestershire sauce, spices, and bread crumbs.

4. Lay pie crusts flat and cut each in half.

5. Spread meat mixture on each half and fold to form wedges that look like a quarter of a pie. Seal edges with a fork, and make two slit vents in each wedge.

6. Line Dutch oven with foil. Grease foil and place all 4 wedges in Dutch oven.

7. Using 19 coals on the lid and 10 briquettes under the oven, bake for 30–40 minutes or until tops of meat pockets turn golden brown.

Required Equipment:

12-inch Dutch oven

Large-size frying pan

Heavy-duty aluminum foil

Tips: Keep pie crusts cold to make them easier to work with. This recipe also works great using a box oven.

Michael Harney, Bolton, Connecticut
Scoutmaster, Troop 73, Connecticut Rivers Council, Boy Scouts of America

Boulder Onion Pudding

Servings: 8–10 | Challenge Level: Moderate

Author's Note: Tim and I had the privilege of serving as judges in *Scouting* magazine's 2005 'Camp Food Favorites' outdoor cooking contest. We awarded this recipe first place in the side dish category. Cutting all of those onions might bring tears to your eyes, but the results are fantastic!—Christine

Preparation at Camp:

1. Melt ¼ cup of the butter in a large skillet. Add onions and garlic. Simmer for 15 minutes. Raise temperature to medium and stir until onions begin to caramelize.

2. Remove onion mixture from heat and transfer to a large-size bowl. Add bread chunks, salt, black pepper, and chicken broth. Mix well.

3. Spread onion-bread mixture in greased Dutch oven.

4. Melt remaining butter and pour over the top of onion-bread mixture. Sprinkle cheese over all.

5. In a medium-size bowl, beat eggs slightly and add half-and-half. Pour the egg-milk mixture evenly over bread-onion-cheese in the oven.

6. Pile 24 coals in a continuous ring around the oven, close to but not quite touching the oven's base. Cook for 30–40 minutes until pudding is puffed and golden.

Required Equipment:

12-inch Dutch oven
Large-size frying pan
Large-size mixing bowl
Medium-size mixing bowl

¼ cup (½ standard stick) butter

8 cups diced onions

1 clove garlic, crushed

6 cups French bread, cut into 1-inch chunks

¼ teaspoon salt

¼ teaspoon ground black pepper

¼ cup chicken broth

¼ cup (½ standard stick) butter

2 cups grated Swiss cheese

3 eggs

2 cups (1 pint) half-and-half

Michael Ryan, Boulder, Utah
Scoutmaster, Troop 678, Utah National Parks Council, Boy Scouts of America

Campin' Dawgs Chili Relleno Casserole

Servings: 12–14 | Challenge Level: Moderate

Casserole:

4 green onions, chopped

⅓ cup diced pickled jalapeños

4 (7-ounce) cans whole green chilies, chopped

2 pounds cheddar cheese, grated

2 pounds Monterey Jack cheese, grated

8 eggs, whites and yolks separated

6 tablespoons all-purpose flour

2 (12-ounce) cans evaporated milk

½ teaspoon salt

½ teaspoon ground black pepper

Topping:

1 (24-ounce) container sour cream

2 cups raisins

Preparation at Camp:

1. In greased Dutch oven over 23 coals, heat green onions, jalapeños, and two cans of the green chilies in their juice. Cook until tender, remove from heat, and drain the juice.

2. Pour the remaining two cans of green chilies into oven, cover with all of the cheddar cheese, and top with the cooked green onions, jalapeños, and chilies.

3. Cover with all of the Monterey Jack cheese.

4. In a medium-size bowl, beat egg whites until stiff. In a separate medium-size bowl, beat yolks with flour, evaporated milk, salt, and black pepper.

5. Fold egg white mixture into yolk mixture and pour over casserole.

6. Moving 16 coals to the lid and leaving 7 briquettes under the oven, bake for 45 minutes or until a knife inserted in the center comes out clean. Refresh coals as required.

7. While casserole bakes, prepare topping by mixing sour cream and raisins together.

8. Serve casserole, covering with topping to taste.

Required Equipment:

12-inch Dutch oven
2 medium-size mixing bowls

Darrell Laurence, Austin, Texas
Assistant Scoutmaster, Troop 8787, Capitol Area Council, Boy Scouts of America

Grand Prize Butter Bake

Servings: 4–5 | Challenge Level: Moderate

"This recipe was the grand-prize winner in *Scouting* magazine's 2001 'Great Tastes in Camp Cooking' outdoor cooking contest!"

Preparation at Camp:

1. Peel squash and remove seeds. Cut into 1/2-inch thick slices.

2. Place squash slices into greased Dutch oven.

3. Core and peel apples. Slice and place over squash.

4. Combine melted butter, flour, brown sugar, and nutmeg in a small-size bowl. Pour over squash and apples.

5. Place a ring of 8 coals just under the edge of the oven base. Use 17 briquettes on the lid. Bake for about 45 minutes until squash becomes tender. Refresh coals as required.

1 butternut squash

2 apples

¼ cup (½ standard stick) butter, melted

1 tablespoon all-purpose flour

½ cup brown sugar

½ teaspoon ground nutmeg

Required Equipment:

12-inch Dutch oven
Small-size mixing bowl

Debbie Moore, Sutton, Massachusetts
Assistant Scoutmaster, Troop 131, Mohegan Council, Boy Scouts of America

Refried Rocket Beans

Servings: 6–8 | Challenge Level: Moderate

"My family loves beans in any way, shape, or form. We are particularly fond of the re-fried version found at Mexican restaurants, a taste that just can't be captured in cans. I adapted this recipe from one I discovered in *Cook's Illustrated*. It's a more healthy variant in that it doesn't call for large amounts of oil or lard, but instead relies on tasty broth for moisture and only a small amount of bacon for a punch of flavor.

1 tablespoon vegetable oil

4 bacon strips

6 garlic gloves, minced

1 large onion, chopped

2 jalapeño peppers, seeds removed and minced

2 poblano peppers, seeds removed and chopped

1 teaspoon salt, or adjust to taste

1 teaspoon ground cumin

4 (15 1/2-ounce) cans pinto beans, drained

1 cup water

1 chicken bouillon cube

2 tablespoons cilantro leaves, chopped

Juice from a fresh-squeezed lime (optional)

Preparation at Camp:

1. Pour oil in Dutch oven and heat over 12 briquettes.

2. Fry bacon in oven until crispy. Remove bacon and set aside. Do not drain grease.

3. Sauté garlic until fragrant, about 1 minute.

4. Add onion, peppers, and salt. Sauté, uncovered, until onion becomes translucent, about 15 minutes.

5. Add cumin and pinto beans to Dutch oven. Stir in water and crushed chicken bouillon cube.

6. With oven over coals, use hand-masher to crush beans in the oven until mixture resembles a coarse paste.

7. Crumble bacon and stir into bean paste.

8. Continue to cook over 12 coals, uncovered, for 20 minutes. Stir occasionally, and refresh briquettes as required.

9. Remove from heat. Stir in cilantro leaves and optional lime juice before serving.

Required Equipment:

12-inch Dutch oven
Hand-masher

Caution: Stabilize the hot Dutch oven with a glove-covered hand to keep the oven from tipping when using the masher.

Tim Conners, Statesboro, Georgia
Former Leader, Coastal Empire Council, Boy Scouts of America

Smoked Sausage Cassoulet

Servings: 8–10 | Challenge Level: Moderate

Preparation at Camp:

1. Fry bacon until crisp in Dutch oven over 25 coals. Remove bacon from oven and set aside to drain.

2. Add onion, thyme, rosemary, and garlic to bacon drippings in Dutch oven. Sauté until tender.

3. Add pork and sausage cubes to oven and fry until pork is fully cooked.

4. Crumble bacon and place in oven. Add salt, black pepper, tomatoes, and beans.

5. Mash about half of the beans against the bottom of the Dutch oven with the back of a large wooden spoon. Stir.

6. Cover oven with lid and relocate 15 of the coals from under the oven to the top, distributing evenly over the lid. Leave 10 briquettes under the oven.

7. Cook for 30 minutes, stirring occasionally to make sure the mixture does not stick to the bottom and burn.

8. Serve, sprinkling Parmesan cheese and parsley over each serving.

Required Equipment:

12-inch Dutch oven

---

5 bacon slices

1 cup chopped onions

1 teaspoon dried thyme

½ teaspoon dried rosemary

3 garlic cloves, minced

1½ pounds lean boneless pork loin, cut into 1-inch cubes

½ pound smoked turkey sausage, cut into 1-inch cubes

1 teaspoon salt

½ teaspoon ground black pepper

2 (14½-ounce) cans diced tomatoes (do not drain)

2 (15-ounce) cans great northern beans with spices (such as Glory) (do not drain)

⅓ cup Parmesan cheese, shredded (use block cheese)

Fresh parsley to taste

Neil "The Cookin' Webmaster" Stillman, Katy, Texas
Assistant Scoutmaster and Webmaster, Troop 209, Sam Houston Council, Boy Scouts of America

Hawkeye Stew

Servings: 10–12 | Challenge Level: Moderate

"My wife found this recipe decades ago. It was a family favorite when we went camping, and my son prepared it many times when he was a Boy Scout. Perhaps the only drawback is that some scouts turn their noses up at it when they discover that it contains cabbage… but they nearly always change their minds once they've tried it!"

2 pounds ground beef

1 head cabbage, cut into ¼ inch thick slices

8 stalks celery, diced

4 medium onions, peeled and thinly sliced

2 (15-ounce) cans stewed tomatoes (do not drain)

2 (15-ounce) cans kidney beans (do not drain)

2 cups water

2 teaspoons salt

½ teaspoon ground black pepper

4 teaspoons chili powder

4 cups Bisquick

1⅓ cups milk

Preparation at Camp:

1. Brown ground beef in a Dutch oven over 25 coals, then drain grease.

2. Stir cabbage, celery, and onions into the ground beef. Continue to cook, stirring occasionally.

3. Once vegetables are semi-transparent, stir in tomatoes, kidney beans, water, salt, black pepper, and chili powder.

4. Bring stew to a boil, then reduce heat by removing some of the briquettes until the stew reaches a simmer. Continue to cook for about 45 minutes.

5. While beef mixture is simmering, prepare dumplings by mixing Bisquick and milk in a gallon-sized ziplock freezer bag or medium-size bowl.

6. Drop dumpling dough by spoonfuls onto the simmering stew at end of 45-minute simmer period.

7. Cover and continue to cook for an additional 10 minutes.

Required Equipment:

12-inch Dutch oven

Gallon-size ziplock freezer bag or medium-size mixing bowl

Tip: A large cook pot or very large skillet can be used instead of the Dutch oven to prepare this recipe.

Jeff Mathewson, Anamosa, Iowa
Scoutmaster, Troop 67, Hawkeye Area Council, Boy Scouts of America

Mama Oldani's Italian Pasta

Servings: 6–8 | Challenge Level: Moderate

"Mama Oldani lives in South St. Louis. She raised her family on ravioli, lasagna, and cannoli. When her son, Ed, went off to college, she was worried that he wouldn't eat properly while away from her table. To ensure he would stay true to his Italian roots, she created this easy and tasty recipe so Ed could feed himself and his friends when they weren't hitting the books. Originally a casserole dish, we adapted Mama Oldani's Italian Pasta for the Dutch oven."

Preparation at Camp:

1. Cook pasta in a medium-size pot according to package directions.

2. Brown ground beef in a Dutch oven that has been preheated over 25 coals.

3. Carefully drain ground beef, and add drained pasta to the meat.

4. Gently blend in thawed spinach, cheeses, and spaghetti sauce.

5. Return oven to the coals, baking for 30 minutes using 9 briquettes under the oven and 16 on the lid or until the sauce is hot and the cheese melted.

Required Equipment:

12-inch Dutch oven

Medium-size cook pot

1 (16-ounce) box pasta shells

1 pound ground beef

1 (10-ounce) package frozen chopped spinach, thawed

2 cups shredded mozzarella cheese

2 cups shredded sharp cheddar cheese

1 (26-ounce) jar Ragu Chunky Garden spaghetti sauce

Options: During Step 4, include mushrooms and coarsely chopped green peppers.

Jim Hauser, Madison, Alabama
Assistant Scoutmaster, Troop 350, Greater Alabama Council, Boy Scouts of America

Troop 44's Grand Prize Seafood Jambalaya

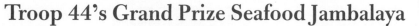

Servings: 10–12 | Challenge Level: Moderate

"Seafood Jambalaya was the 2005 grand-prize winner of *Scouting* magazine's 'Camp Food Favorites' outdoor cooking contest. But this wasn't the first time this recipe won a ribbon. Scoutmaster Kevin Young recalls, 'Seafood Jambalaya originated at a summer camp cook-off. After days of typical camp rations, the fathers and leaders of Troop 44 wanted to impress the judges with something they probably hadn't eaten in quite some time. Not only did the jambalaya win the event, hands-down, we ended up feeding most of the camp staff and other leaders!'"

1 pound boneless chicken breast, cubed

1 pound uncooked mild Italian ground sausage

1 large onion, chopped

2 stalks (about ½ cup) chopped celery

2 small red or green bell peppers, quartered and sliced

⅓ cup vegetable oil

2 medium tomatoes, coarsely chopped

1 (14-ounce) can chicken broth

3 cups sliced okra, fresh or frozen

2 cups fresh sliced mushrooms

½ teaspoon cayenne pepper or dried crushed hot red peppers

1 teaspoon ground black pepper

1 teaspoon ground white pepper

2 cups long-grain white rice

2 cups water

1 tablespoon Worcestershire sauce

½ cup orange juice

1 pound precooked seafood mix (e.g., shrimp, crab, and crawfish)

1 teaspoon gumbo filé (powdered sassafras leaves)

Preparation at Camp:

1. In Dutch oven over 32 coals, heat chicken and Italian sausage until cooked through, but not browned. Drain grease.

2. In Dutch oven lid or another pan, sauté onion, celery, and bell peppers in vegetable oil until tender.

3. Add sautéed vegetables, along with tomatoes, chicken broth, okra, and mushrooms, to the chicken and sausage in the Dutch oven. Mix thoroughly.

4. Stir cayenne powder, ground black and white pepper, rice, and water into the chicken and vegetables.

5. Cover Dutch oven and bring jambalaya to a boil. Add Worcestershire sauce and orange juice, then reduce heat to a simmer. Cover and cook until rice becomes tender, about 20 minutes.

6. Once rice is tender, add seafood mixture. Continue to simmer for an additional 10 minutes. Stir in gumbo filé and serve.

Required Equipment:

Deep 14-inch Dutch oven
Medium-size frying pan (if not using Dutch oven lid)

Tip: A cook pot can be substituted for the Dutch oven in this recipe.

The Members of Troop 44, Heyburn, Idaho
Snake River Council, Boy Scouts of America

Point Lookout Chili Pie

Servings: 12–14 | Challenge Level: Moderate

"Troop 1575 was on a trip to Point Lookout on the Chesapeake Bay. After exploring the Civil War prisoner camp on the point, the Road Runner patrol got together to start dinner. They began to prepare my chili pie but decided to make changes to the list of ingredients. Some wanted to add honey; others wanted cheese on top. One scout proposed adding a surprise. The Road Runners, perhaps the troop's best cooking patrol, finally devised a plan. After working on the meal, they asked me to sample the chili. To my surprise, it was very tasty and I could immediately identify without a doubt the mystery ingredient: Old Bay, the Scoutmaster's favorite seasoning!"

3 pounds lean ground beef or turkey

2 medium onions, chopped

1 bell pepper, chopped

1 hot chili pepper, chopped

½ cup (1 standard stick) butter

4 (15-ounce) cans chili beans

1 (16-ounce) jar medium salsa

1 (16-ounce) bottle hickory smoke flavored barbeque sauce

1 (10-ounce) jar honey

Chili powder and McCormick Old Bay seasoning to taste

3 (7-ounce) packages corn bread mix (including ingredients required by package directions)

2 cups shredded cheddar cheese

Preparation at Camp:

1. Place 32 coals under Dutch oven. Brown meat and onions. Drain excess grease.

2. Add pepper, chili pepper, butter, chili beans, salsa, barbeque sauce, honey, and seasonings. Stir.

3. Mix corn bread in medium-size bowl according to package directions.

4. Pour corn bread mix evenly over chili. Do not stir.

5. Rearrange coals, using 10 briquettes under the oven and 22 on the lid. Bake for about 25–35 minutes until the corn bread becomes golden brown.

6. Sprinkle cheese on top of corn bread and replace lid, baking for a couple of extra minutes to let the cheese melt before serving.

Required Equipment:

14-inch Dutch oven
Medium-size mixing bowl

Bernie Spicer, Upper Marlboro, Maryland
Scoutmaster, Troop 1575, National Capital Area Council, Boy Scouts of America

Hunter's Roast Beast

Servings: 8–10 | Challenge Level: Moderate

Preparation at Camp:

1. Cover bottom of Dutch oven with vegetable oil and preheat over 32 briquettes.

2. Brown the roast on all sides and remove the browned meat from oven.

3. Blend French onion soup mix into the drippings in oven then add just enough water to a depth that matches the height of your trivet.

4. Return roast to the oven and place on trivet. Rearrange briquettes such that 12 coals are under the oven and 20 are on the lid. Refresh the coals as required to maintain heat as the roast is cooking. The roast must not touch the lid or sides of the oven, or it will burn.

5. Roughly 2 hours after starting the roast, wash, peel, and cut the onions, carrots, and potatoes.

6. Add vegetables to oven and refresh coals at this time, the extra heat being necessary to quickly return the oven to roasting temperature.

7. The roast will be ready to serve after about 3–4 hours of total cooking time, but check the meat for doneness with a cooking thermometer before serving, ensuring that the temperature at the center of the roast is at least 145 degrees F.

8. Remove roast and slice thinly across the grain of the meat. Serve with the vegetables and juice from the oven. Add salt and black pepper to taste.

Required Equipment:

14-inch Dutch oven with trivet

Brad Elliott, Dublin, Ohio
Eagle Scout, Troop 200, Simon Kenton Council, Boy Scouts of America

½ cup vegetable oil

1 (3- to 4-pound) venison round roast (for the less fortunate, beef can be substituted)

1 packet French onion soup mix

Water as required

2 onions, thickly sliced

6 carrots, thickly sliced

6 medium potatoes, skin-on and coarsely cubed

Salt and ground black pepper to taste

Pow Wow Lasagna

Servings: 12–14 | Challenge Level: Moderate

"This recipe was inspired by the Orange County BSA Pow Wow Dutch Oven Workshop. It's a great dinner to have your scouts help prepare at camp."

1 (16-ounce) box lasagna noodles

2 pounds ground beef

1 onion, diced

2 cloves garlic, minced

Preparation at Home:

1. Boil lasagna noodles according to package directions.

2. Drain noodles, cool, and place in large ziplock freezer bag.

3. Brown ground beef, onion, and garlic in frying pan.

4. Drain grease, cool, and place mixture in large ziplock freezer bag.

1 (32-ounce) jar spaghetti sauce

1 (24-ounce) container cottage cheese

2 cups grated cheese (mozzarella or your choice)

1 (24-ounce) container sour cream

½ cup grated Parmesan cheese

Option: Serve with fresh garlic bread.

Preparation at Camp:

1. Start 50 briquettes.

2. Divide spaghetti sauce between two Dutch ovens and spread evenly over bottom of each.

3. Two lasagna layers are to be created in each of the two ovens. With this in mind, add a layer of precooked noodles, followed by cottage cheese, browned ground beef from ziplock bag, grated cheese, and sour cream.

4. Begin the second layer in each oven with the noodles and continue by following the same sequence in the previous step. Reserve enough noodles for step 5.

5. Top with remaining noodles followed by Parmesan cheese.

6. Place 12 briquettes under each oven and 13 coals on each lid. Cook until hot and bubbly, about 45 minutes.

Required Equipment:

2 12-inch Dutch ovens

Wendy Harder, Mission Viejo, California
Den Leader, Pack 709, Orange County Council, Boy Scouts of America

Mohegan Spinach and Rice Bake

Servings: 4–6 | Challenge Level: Moderate

"This entree won second place in *Scouting* magazine's 2005 'Camp Food Favorites' recipe contest."

Preparation at Camp:

1. Using medium-size cook pot, bring rice to a boil in 1⅓ cups water, then reduce heat to a simmer. Cover and continue to cook over low heat until water is fully absorbed and rice is tender, about 15 minutes.

2. Pour cooked rice into Dutch oven. Stir in butter until melted, then mix in remaining ingredients.

3. Bake for 45 minutes using 8 coals under the oven and 17 briquettes on the lid.

Required Equipment:

12-inch Dutch oven
Medium-size cook pot

⅔ cup long-grain rice

1⅓ cups water

2 tablespoons (¼ standard stick) butter

2 (10-ounce) packages frozen chopped spinach, thawed and drained

2 cups shredded cheddar cheese

⅔ cup milk

4 eggs, beaten

¼ cup chopped onion

1 teaspoon Worcestershire sauce

1 teaspoon salt

½ teaspoon dried rosemary

Debbie Moore, Sutton, Massachusetts
Assistant Scoutmaster, Troop 131, Mohegan Council, Boy Scouts of America

Sam Houston Spaghetti

Servings: 8–10 | Challenge Level: Moderate

"This dish is named after Sam Houston, one of the most colorful and controversial figures in Texas history."

1 pound spaghetti pasta

2 pounds ground beef

1 (16-ounce) jar mild picante sauce

2 cups spaghetti sauce with mushrooms

⅔ cup grated Parmesan cheese

2 eggs, beaten

2 tablespoons butter

1 (15-ounce) container ricotta cheese

2 cups shredded mozzarella cheese

Tip: Spaghetti noodles can be prepared at home prior to your trip. Store in a ziplock bag and bring them with you to camp.

Preparation at Camp:

1. Cook spaghetti in large-size cook pot according to package directions. Drain water.

2. Preheat Dutch oven using 25 briquettes underneath.

3. Brown ground beef in Dutch oven, stirring to separate meat. Drain grease.

4. Stir in picante sauce and spaghetti sauce. Heat through. Remove ground beef mixture and set aside in a medium-size bowl.

5. Mix cooked spaghetti, parmesan cheese, eggs, and butter in Dutch oven.

6. Form a depression in the center of the spaghetti mixture, and scoop ricotta cheese into it.

7. Top ricotta cheese and spaghetti with the beef mixture set aside in step 4.

8. Cover Dutch oven, keeping 8 briquettes under the oven and placing 17 coals on the lid.

9. Bake for 30 minutes or until thoroughly heated through.

10. Sprinkle mozzarella cheese over top.

11. Remove from heat. Let stand 5 minutes, providing time for mozzarella cheese to melt, then serve by cutting into wedges.

Required Equipment:

12-inch Dutch oven
Large-size cook pot
Medium-size mixing bowl

Ed Bedford, Chapel Hill, North Carolina
Scoutmaster, Troop 820, Occoneechee Council, Boy Scouts of America

Chicken and Varmints

Servings: 6–8 | Challenge Level: Moderate

"During a troop excursion to Pinery Provincial Park, in Ontario, Canada, one evening we began preparing my new chicken recipe. We soon noticed several raccoons in the area. One walked through camp. We were astonished at how bold it was. When we sat down to eat, there were more raccoons, at least eight of them. While we were cleaning up, another raccoon wandered into camp. Then another. And another. They walked among us as if they were house cats! The Scoutmaster had the scouts gather around our campfire and begin singing, figuring that would drive anything away. The raccoons remained unfazed. On their own schedule, they eventually abandoned our camp. Soon after, we heard shrieks from the campsite down the road. The raccoon patrol had apparently found a new home!"

Preparation at Camp:

1. In medium-size cook pot, prepare rice according to package directions.

2. Melt butter in Dutch oven over 25 coals. Add chopped onion and celery. Cook, stirring occasionally, until onion becomes translucent.

3. Add garlic and cook for 1 additional minute.

4. Add thyme and chicken. Sprinkle Cajun seasoning over the chicken and cook, stirring frequently, until meat is no longer pink, about 15 minutes.

5. Push chicken and vegetables to one side, exposing the juice. Sprinkle flour into the juice and stir until no lumps remain. Mix the chicken and vegetables into the resulting flour roux. Add optional bell pepper at this time.

6. Pour broth over chicken and stir. Cover and cook for an additional 5 minutes. Serve over rice.

Required Equipment:

12-inch Dutch oven
Medium-size cook pot

2 cups long-grain or converted rice

½ cup (1 standard stick) butter

2 large onions, chopped

2 celery stalks, chopped

1 clove garlic, minced

½ teaspoon thyme

3 pounds boneless skinless chicken breast, cut into bite-size pieces

1 tablespoon Luzianne Cajun Seasoning or Paul Prudhomme's Poultry Magic

3 tablespoons all-purpose flour

1 bell pepper, chopped (optional)

1 (14½-ounce) can chicken broth

Michael Darnell, Okemos, Michigan
Assistant Scoutmaster, Troop 109, Chief Okemos Council, Boy Scouts of America

Ranger John Ham and Macaroni

Servings: 10–12 | Challenge Level: Moderate

"This dish is named after Ranger John Hankins of Camp Brady Saunders in the Heart of Virginia Council. Ranger John tells great campfire stories, including some about camp cooking. His stories feature recipes that would not make it into any cookbook!"

2 pounds elbow macaroni pasta

½ cup (1 standard stick) butter

½ cup all-purpose flour

¼ cup brown sugar

2 tablespoons prepared mustard

½ teaspoon salt

½ teaspoon ground black pepper

4 cups milk

2 pounds ham, cubed

4 medium apples, peeled and sliced

2 cups shredded cheddar cheese

2 cups bread crumbs

¼ cup (½ standard stick) butter, melted

Preparation at Camp:

1. Cook macaroni in large-size cook pot according to package directions. Drain water.

2. In Dutch oven over 25 coals, melt ½ cup butter. Blend in flour, brown sugar, mustard, salt, and black pepper.

3. Add milk. Continue to heat, stirring until mixture becomes thick and bubbly.

4. Blend in cooked macaroni, ham cubes, apple slices, and cheese.

5. Mix bread crumbs and melted butter in a medium-size bowl. Sprinkle crumbs over top of macaroni.

6. Bake for 35 minutes, keeping 12 briquettes under the oven and moving 13 coals to the lid.

Required Equipment:

12-inch Dutch oven
Large-size cook pot
Medium-size mixing bowl

Tip: Macaroni can be prepared at home prior to your trip. Store in ziplock bags and bring it with you to camp.

Ed Bedford, Chapel Hill, North Carolina
Scoutmaster, Troop 820, Occoneechee Council, Boy Scouts of America

Barbearo Stroganoff

Servings: 8–10 | Challenge Level: Moderate

"The name of this recipe comes from my travels in Central and South America. 'Barbearo' is the name the indigenous Indians from Peru gave me, because my last name was otherwise too difficult to pronounce.

I've tinkered with and tweaked this dish for many years. It is, in fact, a culmination of the unique personal touch of several people throughout the world whom I've had the pleasure of meeting. Who said, 'too many cooks spoil the broth'?"

Preparation at Camp:

1. Preheat Dutch oven over 20 briquettes.

2. Brown ground beef in oven. Drain grease and set ground beef aside.

3. Add onions, bell pepper, garlic powder, lemon pepper, and Worcestershire sauce to the oven. Cook for 5 minutes until onion is tender.

4. Return ground beef to oven. Stir then heat for an additional 5 minutes.

5. In medium-size bowl, dissolve bouillon cubes in hot water and mix with mushroom soup and cornstarch.

6. Spread uncooked noodles over meat in Dutch oven. Do not stir!

7. Pour soup mixture over noodles. Again, do not stir!

8. Cover Dutch oven, placing 8 briquettes on the lid and refreshing the coals underneath. Cook for 20–30 minutes until noodles become tender.

9. Stir then heat for an additional 5 minutes.

10. Blend in sour cream, and simmer for 3 more minutes before serving.

Required Equipment:

12-inch Dutch oven
Medium-size mixing bowl

2 pounds ground beef

2 medium yellow onions, diced

2 medium green bell peppers, diced

2 teaspoons garlic powder

1 teaspoon lemon pepper

¼ cup Worcestershire sauce

6 beef bouillon cubes

3 ½ cups hot water

2 (10¾-ounce) cans condensed cream of mushroom soup

2 tablespoons cornstarch

1 (24-ounce) package extra-wide noodles

8 ounces sour cream

David "Juan Barbearo" Barber, Shasta Lake, California
Assistant Scoutmaster, Troop 122, Golden Eagle Council, Boy Scouts of America

Giskhaquen's Bean Soup

Servings: 18–20 | Challenge Level: Moderate

"I developed this one-pot Dutch oven recipe for a 'pioneer days' reenactment to demonstrate outdoor fire cooking techniques using foods that were ripe and available in the fall season. Giskhaquen is the Vigil Honor name given to me in the Order of the Arrow. It means 'Wood Cutter.'"

1 pound dried soup beans

1 pound dried lima beans

2 pounds smoked sausage, cubed

1 smoked ham hock

4 large white potatoes, peeled and cubed

1 pound baby carrots

1 large sweet onion, chopped

1 (15¼-ounce) can sweet corn, drained

4 large apples, cored and cubed

1 bell pepper, chopped

8 cups apple cider, with extra as required during cooking

1 tablespoon salt

1 tablespoon ground black pepper

1 tablespoon liquid smoke

2 cups water or as needed to cover ingredients in oven

Preparation at Camp:

1. Combine dried beans and soak overnight in about 2 quarts of water.

2. The next day, drain beans and add with all remaining ingredients to large Dutch oven.

3. Add additional water as needed to just cover all vegetables and meat.

4. Place Dutch oven in a wood fire pit containing coals that have ashed over. Oven can also be placed over a standard bed of charcoal briquettes.

5. Occasionally stir soup while it is cooking, adding more cider as needed to keep the vegetables covered.

6. The soup is ready to serve once the lima beans become soft and tender.

Required Equipment:

Deep 14-inch Dutch oven

Tip: This recipe can also be prepared using a large cook pot.

Dennis Straits, Dola, Ohio
Eagle Scout, Silver Beaver Recipient, and Silver Roundtable Chairman, Troop 124, Black Swamp Council, Boy Scouts of America

Los Osos Lasagna

Servings: 6–8 | Challenge Level: Moderate

"Coming to you from Los Osos, The Valley of the Bears, this yummy meal will fill up a whole patrol of hungry scouts on a cool evening."

Preparation at Camp:

1. Brown meat in a Dutch oven over 23 briquettes. Drain excess grease.

2. Add spaghetti sauce, hot water, and oregano to ground beef. Stir and set aside in a medium-size bowl.

3. In a second medium-size bowl, mix mozzarella cheese, cottage cheese, Parmesan cheese, and egg.

4. With the goal of creating several layers of lasagna, place a band of uncooked noodles on the bottom of the oven. Cover noodles with a layer of meat blend, then cover meat blend with a layer of cheese-egg mix.

5. Repeat the process, layering each item in the same order until all ingredients are expended.

6. Cook for about 45 minutes, leaving 10 briquettes under the oven and moving 13 coals to the lid. The lasagna is ready to serve once noodles are soft.

1 pound lean ground beef

1 (26-ounce) jar spaghetti sauce

¾ cup hot water

¼ teaspoon ground oregano

3 cups shredded mozzarella cheese

1 (16-ounce) container cottage cheese

⅓ cup grated Parmesan cheese

1 egg

8 ounces lasagna noodles

Required Equipment:

12-inch Dutch oven
2 medium-size mixing bowls

George Brown, Los Osos, California
Former Scoutmaster, Troop 216, Los Padres Council, Boy Scouts of America

Shawnee Trails Gumbo

Servings: 6–8 | Challenge Level: Difficult

"Scouts and new leaders almost always recoil at the first site of the corn bread batter being poured over the gumbo. 'Gross!' is a typical response. So when preparing this recipe for the uninitiated, I like to tease them a bit. I pretend that I have no idea what I am doing, and after I pour the corn bread on top of the gumbo, I look upon it with feigned horror and say, 'Oh no! It's not supposed to look like that!' While they are busy grumbling about how I ruined dinner, I put the lid on the oven and let the batter work its magic. Our scouts always insist that a 'secret ingredient' must be added. I try to keep spare spices around that will complement what we will be eating so they won't add ants or beetles."

Gumbo:

3 skinless boneless chicken breasts, chopped

1 pound smoked sausage, sliced

⅓ cup vegetable oil

⅓ cup all-purpose flour

1 medium onion, chopped

2 stalks celery, chopped

¼ cup bell pepper, chopped

2 cloves garlic, minced

2½ cups water

3 cubes chicken bouillon

1 tablespoon apple cider vinegar

Salt and crushed red pepper to taste

Preparation at Camp:

1. Place 25 coals under Dutch oven and brown chicken and sausage until chicken is cooked through. Remove meat and set aside.

2. Place oil and flour in Dutch oven. Over low heat, stir constantly until oil-flour mixture (the roux) turns chocolate brown. Be patient; this may take 20–30 minutes.

3. Remove from heat. Stand back and quickly dump the chopped vegetables into the roux. Return to heat and sauté for about 3 minutes.

4. Add water, bouillon cubes, vinegar, optional spices, and cooked meat to the oven. Stir and simmer while you prepare corn bread mixture.

5. To prepare the corn bread, combine flour, cornmeal, sugar, baking powder, milk, vegetable oil, egg, and chopped onion in a medium-size bowl. Mix well.

6. Pour batter evenly over the top of the gumbo. Do not stir!

7. Moving 20 coals to the lid and leaving 5 briquettes under the oven, bake for 20–30 minutes until corn bread is golden brown. Refresh coals as needed.

Required Equipment:

12-inch Dutch oven
Medium-size mixing bowl

Tip: The secret to this recipe is the roux. You have to heat the roux to just shy of burning. Cook it slowly, stirring constantly. If it begins to smoke before it turns dark brown, then your fire is too hot. Remove a coal or two.

Homemade Corn Bread Mix:

1¼ cups all-purpose flour

¾ cup cornmeal

¼ cup sugar

2 teaspoons baking powder

1 cup milk

¼ cup vegetable oil

1 egg

¼ cup chopped onion

Gumbo filé (powdered sassafras leaves) to taste

Marcus Newman, West Paducah, Kentucky
Den Leader, Pack 21, Shawnee Trails Council, Boy Scouts of America

117 Jambalaya

Servings: 10–12 | Challenge Level: Difficult

"The steps in this recipe are designed so that the work can be divided: chopping veggies, cutting meats, stirring the pot, etc. That way, each scout becomes immersed in a portion of the cooking process. Different tasks can be assigned each time they cook.

This is a dish that our scouts love to complain about. They complain that it is 'too spicy,' then come back for seconds and thirds at about 20-minute intervals. The adults who join us in camp keep their mess kits handy and make sure they are at the head of the line. The 'chili heads' pass out hot sauce."

½ **pound spicy andouille sausage**

½ **pound kielbasa smoked sausage**

1 **pound ham, cut into slices ½-inch thick (either precooked or uncooked meat is acceptable)**

1 **pound white meat of chicken (either precooked or uncooked meat is acceptable)**

2 **large red onions**

4 **large stalks celery**

2 **large green bell peppers**

4 **large cloves garlic**

2 **bunches scallions**

1 **bunch parsley**

¼ **cup olive oil**

4 **cups long-grain white rice**

1 **(64-ounce) can chicken broth**

Salt to taste

Coarse ground black pepper to taste

Hot sauce to taste (optional)

Preparation at Camp:

1. Start at least 32 charcoal briquettes.

2. Split sausages in half lengthwise. Cut each sausage piece into ⅛-inch slices. Cut ham into ½-inch cubes. Set sausage and ham pieces aside. Cut chicken into ¾-inch chunks. Place chicken chunks aside, but do not mix with sausage and ham.

3. Coarsely chop red onions, celery, and green bell peppers and set aside. Mince garlic. Chop scallions, including green tops, into ½-inch lengths, and set aside with garlic apart from the onions, celery, and bell peppers. Finely chop parsley, stems and all, and set aside by itself.

4. Put Dutch oven over coals. Once the oven becomes very hot, cover the bottom with a light coating of olive oil. Add sausage and ham, browning well. Add chicken to the sausage and ham and lightly brown the chicken meat. Remove all the meat and set aside in a medium-size bowl, leaving oils in bottom of oven.

140

5. Pour remainder of olive oil into Dutch oven. Add chopped onions, celery, and bell peppers, stirring until onion begins to become translucent. Add garlic and scallions and continue to stir until fragrant, about 2 minutes.

6. Return browned meats to the oven, including any juices that are in bottom of bowl. Mix well with vegetables. Add rice and stir for 2 minutes, ensuring rice is well coated with oil. Add chicken broth and bring to boil, stirring often.

7. Once liquid begins to boil, move 21 briquettes from under the oven to the lid.

8. Put a round of aluminum foil, shiny side up, over the top of the jambalaya. (The foil helps prevent the top layer of rice from burning.) Cover and cook for 30 minutes or until rice is tender.

9. Remove Dutch oven from the coals. If there are any dry bits of rice on the top of the jambalaya, carefully remove them with a spoon. Add parsley and thoroughly stir to fluff the rice. Let stand for about 5 minutes to allow flavors to mellow. Add salt, black pepper, and optional hot sauce to taste.

Options: To make the jambalaya less spicy, use kielbasa sausage exclusively. To make it more spicy, use andouille sausage exclusively.

Required Equipment:

14-inch Dutch oven
Medium-size mixing bowl
Aluminum foil

Tip: If andouille is not available, spicy kielbasa, or any spicy smoked sausage, can be substituted.

Christopher Lange, Warwick, Rhode Island
Committee Chairman and Outdoor Coordinator, Troop 117, Narragansett Council, Boy Scouts of America

Cub-O Soup

Servings: 8–10 | Challenge Level: Easy

"This recipe became surprisingly popular at a Cub-O event held by our council one weekend after Christmas. We planned our menu for the event assuming we'd feed the adults the soup and cook hot dogs for the kids. Instead, we discovered the kids loved the hot soup on that cold weekend just as much as the adults. We've tried to change the menu in the intervening years, but the requests have always been for the soup. They line up with bowls in hand waiting for their meal!"

4 cups (about 20 ounces) precooked boneless turkey, chopped

1 (16-ounce) package frozen mixed vegetables

1 (16-ounce) package frozen cut green beans

4 medium potatoes, peeled and cubed

1 (14½-ounce) can diced tomatoes

1 small onion, peeled and chopped

1 (4-ounce) can green chilies, diced

½ cup fresh cilantro, chopped

2 teaspoons salt

1 teaspoon ground black pepper

2 tablespoons chili powder

1 teaspoon cumin powder

1 teaspoon ground oregano

6–7 cups water

Preparation at Camp:

1. Place all ingredients in a large-size cook pot.

2. Add enough water to cover vegetables.

3. Cover and cook, stirring occasionally. Add water as needed. Soup is ready once potatoes are tender.

Required Equipment:

Large-size cook pot

Tip: Cub-O Soup can also be prepared in a Dutch oven.

Loyl and Melinda Bussell, Burleson, Texas
Webelos Leaders, Pack 627, Longhorn Council, Boy Scouts of America

Otetiana Chicken Erin

Servings: 10 | Challenge Level: Easy

"I've used this recipe at home for years and recently adapted it to serve more than 20 people at the Cub-Parent weekend at Camp Cutler. Both kids and adults love it. I serve it with Near East Rice Pilaf and a vegetable side. The recipe is an easy and tasty one-pot alternative to the standard fare found on weekend campouts."

Preparation at Camp:

1. Add salt and black pepper to taste to both sides of chicken breasts.

2. Apply oil or nonstick spray to bottom of large pre-heated stockpot or frying pan. Place chicken breasts inside pot.

3. Combine ranch dressing with water or broth and pour over chicken breasts, making sure all chicken is coated. The chicken does not need to be submerged in the dressing.

4. Cover pot or pan, and cook on medium-high heat for 5–8 minutes.

5. Remove cover and rearrange chicken breasts, swapping those on bottom with those on top. Cover and cook for an additional 4–6 minutes. Chicken is ready to serve once internal temperature reaches 170 degrees F.

Required Equipment:

Large-size cook pot or frying pan

Tip: One half of a chicken breast per child is often sufficient, but hungry adults who have stomped in the woods chasing their kids all day usually devour both halves.

Salt and ground black pepper to taste

10 boneless chicken breast fillets, each split into two

1 tablespoon oil or nonstick vegetable spray

1 cup ranch dressing

1 cup water or chicken broth

Option: For Otetiana Chicken Brendan, briefly pound breasts, then sprinkle with Herbs de Provence spice mix. Roll chicken breasts with 2 or 3 shrimp inside, securing the meat with toothpicks before continuing with step 2 above.

Christopher V. Taffe, Rochester, New York
Cubmaster, Pack 171, Otetiana Council, Boy Scouts of America

Swedish Alpine Baked Beans

Servings: 8–10 | Challenge Level: Easy

"This is an excellent side dish to accompany any entree. Goes great with corn bread or other breads."

2 pounds dry northern beans

1 large onion, chopped

2 bay leaves

2 cups packed brown sugar

1 cup molasses

1½ pounds uncooked ham or bacon, cut into small pieces

1 tablespoon ground mustard powder

½ cup Worcestershire sauce

1 teaspoon ground ginger

1 teaspoon ground cloves

2 teaspoons salt

Water sufficient for covering beans

Preparation at Camp:

1. Soak beans for at least 8 hours.
2. Combine beans and all remaining ingredients in a large cook pot. Use enough water to cover beans ½ inch deep.
3. Cook over medium heat 3–4 hours, stirring every 30 minutes or so. Add water as required to maintain ½ inch deep layer of liquid over beans.
4. Dish is ready once beans are tender. Remove bay leaves before serving.

Required Equipment:

Large-size cook pot

Tip: This recipe can also be prepared in a large-size Dutch oven over medium heat.

Mark Case, Sr., Randleman, North Carolina
Cubmaster and Chaplain, Old North State Council, Boy Scouts of America

Porcupine Ball Soup

Servings: 6–8 | Challenge Level: Easy

"This is a great 'first-time' recipe we used for both the Girl Scout and Boy Scout troops my children were involved in."

Preparation at Camp:

1. Combine beef, onion, rice, salt, and egg in a medium-size mixing bowl.

2. Form beef mixture into bite-size balls.

3. In a large cook pot, combine tomato soup and water and bring to a boil.

4. Gently drop porcupine balls into boiling soup. Cover and simmer over low heat for 30 minutes or until meatballs are cooked through.

Required Equipment:

Medium-size mixing bowl
Large-size cook pot

2 pounds lean ground beef

1 medium onion, chopped

2 cups Minute Rice

½ teaspoon salt

1 egg

3 (10¾-ounce) cans condensed tomato soup

3 (10¾-ounce) cans water (use empty soup can to measure)

Options: Top with shredded cheese or croutons when serving.

Kathleen Kirby, Milltown, New Jersey
Cooking Merit Badge Counselor, Troop 33, Central New Jersey Council, Boy Scouts of America
Former Leader, Troop 12, Delaware-Raritan Council, Girl Scouts of the USA

Paul Bunyan Barbeque Beans

Servings: 6–8 | Challenge Level: Easy

1 (15-ounce) can baked beans (Bush's preferred)

1 (15-ounce) can navy beans, drained

1 (15-ounce) can kidney beans, drained

1 (15-slice) package precooked bacon, chopped

2 cups smoked ham, chopped

1 large yellow onion, chopped

1 small chili pepper, chopped

1 cup light brown sugar

½ cup barbeque sauce

1 clove garlic, chopped

Preparation at Camp:

1. Thoroughly mix all ingredients in a large-size pot.

2. Cover and simmer over medium heat for several hours, stirring often.

Required Equipment:

Large-size cook pot

Robert Rainwater, Brookwood, Alabama
Scoutmaster, Troop 3, Black Warrior Council, Boy Scouts of America

Bear Canyon Tuna Noodle Casserole

Servings: 3 / Multiply as Required | Challenge Level: Easy

Preparation at Camp:

1. In a medium-size cook pot, boil macaroni and cheese noodles until soft. Drain water.

2. To the noodles, add cheese powder from macaroni and cheese box, along with tuna, peas, and condensed cream of chicken soup. Stir until well mixed.

3. Serve, sprinkling crushed potato chips over the top.

Required Equipment:

Medium-size cook pot

Tip: This recipe is also suitable for short backpacking trips.

1 (7¼-ounce) box macaroni and cheese (Kraft Original preferred)

2 (3-ounce) pouches tuna fish

1 (15-ounce) can baby peas, drained

1 (10¾-ounce) can condensed cream of chicken soup

1 (single-portion) bag potato chips

David Brown, Tucson, Arizona
Committee Chairman, Troop 141, Catalina Council, Boy Scouts of America

Susan Brown, Tucson, Arizona
Former Den Leader, Pack 141, Catalina Council, Boy Scouts of America

Chicken Fajita Soup Even the Most Finicky Scout Will Love

Servings: 12–14 | Challenge Level: Easy

2 pounds precooked chicken fajita meat, cut into bite-size pieces

5 (14-ounce) cans chicken broth

1 (16-ounce) jar mild picante sauce

1 bunch green onions, diced

2 bell peppers, diced

1 medium onion, diced

1 (15-ounce) can whole kernel corn, drained

1 (15-ounce) can kidney beans, drained

1 (6.8-ounce) box Spanish-flavored Rice-a-Roni (including seasonings)

6 flour tortillas, cut into 1/4-inch strips

1 pound shredded 4-blend Mexican-style cheese

1 (8-ounce) container sour cream

Crackers

Preparation at Camp:

1. Add all ingredients, except tortillas, shredded cheese, sour cream, and crackers, to a large-size cook pot. Bring to a low boil. Cook until onions and bell peppers are tender.

2. Mix in all tortilla strips, a few at a time.

3. Slowly blend in cheese and sour cream, a little at a time.

4. Serve warm with crackers.

Required Equipment:

Large-size cooking pot

Michael Trdy, Cameron, Texas
Scoutmaster, Troop 752, Longhorn Council, Boy Scouts of America

Campout Pasta Pizza

Servings: 6–8 | Challenge Level: Easy

Preparation at Camp:

1. In a medium-size pot, cook egg noodles according to package directions. Drain.

2. Add spaghetti sauce and sliced pepperoni. Stir and simmer until warm.

3. Dish into bowls and top with cubed cheese.

Required Equipment:

Medium-size cook pot

1 pound wide egg noodles

2 (26-ounce) jars spaghetti sauce (your choice)

1 (6-ounce) package sliced pepperoni

1 (16-ounce) package Velveeta cheese, cubed

Bernice Holly, Bellevue, Nebraska
Committee Chair, Troop 351, Mid-America Council, Boy Scouts of America

South Sioux City Public Library
2121 Dakota Avenue
South Sioux City, NE 68776

Mulligan Stew

Servings: 4–6 with more to share | Challenge Level: Easy

"I recall with fondness the stories from my grandmother about Irish immigrant farmers making a stew of this sort on days they came together for a barn raising, each contributing what they could. It's a special story I share with my scouts."

1 tablespoon vegetable oil

1 pound stew meat per each group of four to six people

1 onion, chopped

1 (46-ounce) can tomato juice

1 chopped fresh vegetable from each adult (potatoes, carrots, cabbage, celery, etc.)

1 can vegetables from each scout, labels removed

Preparation at Camp:

1. In a large-size pot, add vegetable oil and brown the meat slightly along with the onion.

2. Add can of tomato juice and the chopped fresh vegetables donated by each adult. Cover the pot and simmer.

3. Once the fresh vegetables are fully cooked, have each scout open a can of vegetables. With the labels having been removed from the cans previously, the intent is to make it a mystery as to what the contents are. Depending on how much liquid is in the stew at this point, some of the canned vegetables may need to have the juice drained from them.

4. Have each scout add their can of vegetables to the pot while taking a turn stirring the stew.

5. Continue cooking until the stew is thoroughly heated.

Required Equipment:

Large-size cook pot

Note: This recipe is perfectly suited for accompanying the Stone Soup fable in the Epilogue!

Julie Lewis, Irving, Texas
Rank Advancement Chair, Troop 166, Circle Ten Council, Boy Scouts of America

Eagle Scout Macaroni and Cheese

Servings: 10–12 | Challenge Level: Easy

"My father, David Yount, was a professor at the University of Hawaii. He served as Chair of the Department of Physics and Astronomy, Vice President for Research and Graduate Education, and author of many ground-breaking papers on such diverse topics as high-energy physics, diving medicine, acoustics, and surface chemistry.

My father passed away several years ago. He had much to be proud of during his life. But one of his greatest sources of pride had nothing to do with his research as an adult. Instead, it had everything to do with what he accomplished as a teenager: My dad was an Eagle Scout.

This is one of the scout recipes he taught me when I was a child."

Preparation at Camp:

1. In a large-size pot, boil macaroni until tender.

2. While the macaroni cooks, cut hot dogs into circular slices.

3. Drain water from macaroni. Add sliced hot dogs, cubed cheese, and peas to the hot pasta.

4. Stir, adding small amounts of water as necessary to maintain moisture. Serve once cheese is melted.

Required Equipment:

Large-size cook pot

2 pounds shell macaroni pasta

1 pound turkey hot dogs

2 pounds Velveeta, cubed

1 (16-ounce) bag frozen peas, thawed

Christine Conners, Statesboro, Georgia
Former Girl Scout, Hawaii Council, Girl Scouts of the USA

Mister S's Sweet Beans

Servings: 6–8 | Challenge Level: Moderate

"Having the job of mixing ingredients with bare (clean) hands is always a popular and coveted task in our troop. New scouts will respond with equal amounts of 'yuck!' and 'cool!' to the assignment. But in the end, all will agree it's delicious."

½ **pound bacon**

1 pound ground beef

1 (28-ounce) can pork and beans

1 (15-ounce) can kidney beans, drained

1 (15-ounce) can butter beans, drained

1 cup light brown sugar

1 cup barbecue sauce

1 (1-ounce) envelope dry onion soup mix

Preparation at Camp:

1. Fry bacon in skillet until crisp. Drain, crumble, and set aside.

2. Brown ground beef in skillet, draining off excess fat.

3. Combine and thoroughly mix cooked beef, bacon, and remaining ingredients in a large-size pot.

4. Reduce heat and simmer, uncovered, for 30–40 minutes, stirring occasionally.

Required Equipment:

Medium-size frying pan

Large-size cook pot

Tips: This recipe can also be prepared in a Dutch oven. The ingredients list makes it easy to double the number of servings.

Ron Schagrin, Palatine, Illinois
Committee Member, Troop 335, Northwest Suburban Council, Boy Scouts of America

Dancing Dog Skins

Servings: 4–5 | Challenge Level: Moderate

"This dish was originally created to provide a way to use the skin of potatoes and yams. It evolved to include the whole yam or potato along with dipping sauces, which scouts always have fun with. This is an original recipe from Troop 1467."

Preparation at Camp:

1. Wash unpeeled potatoes and dry thoroughly.

2. Slice potatoes into ⅛-inch thick sections. Lengthwise cuts are preferred, but cross-section cuts on a slight diagonal work as well.

3. In a small-size bowl, combine eggs with milk or water. Set aside.

4. In another small-size bowl, combine flour, garlic salt, Mrs. Dash seasoning, and Italian herbs.

5. Pour canola oil into medium-size pot or wok. Heat until oil is very hot, but do not let it over-heat and smoke. A drop of water will sizzle and dance on the surface when ready.

6. Using tongs, dip potato slices in egg wash and then dust slices in flour mix.

7. Place a few slices at a time in the hot oil. Do not add too many at one time as this will overly cool the oil!

8. Deep-fry until golden brown. Drain for a few minutes on paper towels, and serve with your choice of dipping sauces.

Required Equipment:

Medium-size cook pot or wok

Tongs

2 small-size mixing bowls

1 small-size mixing bowl for each of the selected dipping sauces

2 large sweet potatoes or 3 large white potatoes

3 eggs

1 tablespoon milk or water

1 cup all-purpose flour

1 teaspoon garlic salt

1 tablespoon Mrs. Dash Original seasoning

1 teaspoon Italian herb mix (parsley, basil, sage, and oregano)

4 cups canola oil

Dipping Sauces (combine ingredients according to the option selected):

a) **½ cup barbeque sauce, 1 tablespoon honey, ½ teaspoon Worcester-shire sauce**

b) **½ cup mayonnaise, 1 teaspoon horseradish, 1 teaspoon spicy brown mustard**

c) **½ cup soy sauce, 1 tablespoon honey**

d) **½ cup ketchup, 1 teaspoon Worcester-shire sauce**

Curt "The Titanium Chef" White, Forks, Washington
Scoutmaster, Troop 1467, Chief Seattle Council, Boy Scouts of America

Goober Soup

Servings: 6–8 | Challenge Level: Moderate

1 teaspoon vegetable oil

1 medium onion, diced

1 pound sweet potatoes, peeled and diced

½ pound (2–3 medium-size) carrots, diced

2 cloves garlic, diced, or ¼ teaspoon garlic powder

1 (14-ounce) can vegetable or chicken broth

1½ cups water

2 teaspoons curry powder

1 teaspoon hot pepper sauce or ¼ teaspoon cayenne pepper powder

½ cup peanut butter

1 cup sour cream, plain yogurt, soy milk, or milk

1 (14½-ounce) can petite diced tomatoes, with juice

⅓ cup peanuts, coarsely chopped

Preparation at Camp:

1. In a large-size cook pot, lightly sauté diced onion in oil until softened.

2. Add diced sweet potatoes, carrots, garlic, and broth. Add water until vegetables are just covered, about 1½ cups.

3. Bring to a boil, then reduce heat and simmer until vegetables are soft.

4. Remove from heat and stir in curry powder, hot pepper, and peanut butter.

5. Using a potato masher or hand mixer, blend until fairly smooth.

6. Mix in sour cream and diced tomatoes. Cook until heated through.

7. Stir in chopped peanuts, and serve.

Required Equipment:

Large-size cook pot
Potato masher or hand mixer

Ken Harbison, Rochester, New York
Former Boy Scout, Washington Trail Council, Boy Scouts of America

Judy Harbison, Rochester, New York
Lifetime Member, Genesee Valley Council, Girl Scouts of the USA

Devil's Postpile Hot and Sour Soup

Servings: 6–8 | Challenge Level: Moderate

"This recipe is a bit involved, but it's so good on a cold fall campout! When the tofu slices are stacked together on the cutting board, they remind me of Devil's Postpile National Monument in the Sierra Nevada."

Preparation at Camp:

1. Soak mushrooms in water until soft, about 15 minutes. Cut away tough stems and slice into small strips.

2. Cut bamboo shoots, tofu, and chicken into juliennes (thin strips).

3. Pour chicken broth into a large pot and add mushrooms, bamboo, tofu, chicken, and ginger. Bring to a boil.

4. Mix cornstarch with water in a cup, stir, and add to pot. Next, add soy sauce and stir.

5. Continue to boil until chicken is cooked through, then reduce heat to bring soup to a simmer.

6. While stirring soup, dribble in beaten egg so it forms streamers. Add green onion.

7. Combine black pepper and vinegar in a cup, adding about three-quarters of mixture to the soup. Sample soup, adding more pepper-vinegar until desired hotness or sourness is achieved.

8. Remove from heat. Mix in sesame oil and serve.

Required Equipment:

Large-size cook pot

6 dried shitake mushrooms (about 2 inches in diameter)

4 ounces sliced bamboo shoots, drained

1 (16-ounce) tofu cake, medium or firm

1 large boneless chicken breast

6 cups chicken broth

1 tablespoon fresh ginger, peeled and minced

1 tablespoon cornstarch

3 tablespoons water

2 tablespoons soy sauce

1 large egg, beaten

1 green onion, finely chopped

½ teaspoon ground black pepper

1 tablespoon rice or cider vinegar

1 tablespoon sesame oil

Mark Leifer, Boulder, Colorado
Assistant Scoutmaster, Troop 72, Longs Peak Council, Boy Scouts of America

Tony's Camp Chili

Servings: 10–12 | Challenge Level: Moderate

3 (28-ounce) cans whole tomatoes

3 pounds ground beef

3 tablespoons chili powder

1 teaspoon ground cayenne pepper

1 teaspoon paprika

2 medium onions, chopped

2 green bell peppers, chopped

3 tablespoons garlic powder

3 tablespoons Worcestershire sauce

1 teaspoon crushed basil leaves

2 (40-ounce) cans kidney beans, drained

1 pound shredded cheddar cheese

Preparation at Camp:

1. Drain tomatoes, reserving liquid for later. Chop tomatoes into bite-size pieces and set aside.
2. In a large frying pan, blend chili powder into ground beef and brown the meat. Carefully drain grease.
3. Add ground beef, chopped tomatoes, tomato liquid, and all remaining ingredients, except for kidney beans and cheese, to a large-size cook pot.
4. Simmer chili for 2 hours.
5. Blend in drained kidney beans and continue to simmer for 1 additional hour.
6. Serve chili topped with cheddar cheese.

Required Equipment:

Large-size cook pot

Large-size frying pan

Tip: A large Dutch oven can be used instead of the cook pot to prepare this recipe.

Tony Neubauer, Piscataway, New Jersey
Committee Chairperson, Troop 67, Central New Jersey Council, Boy Scouts of America

Eileen's High-Demand Italian Spaghetti

Servings: 14–16 | Challenge Level: Moderate

"If you don't mind me bragging a little, my Mom, Eileen Conners, makes outstanding Italian sauce and meatballs. I would even go so far as to call them the best. Her recipe has always been in high demand, and for good reason. Once you and your scouts try it, you'll understand why!"

Preparation at Camp:

1. In a large pot, sauté 2 large onions in oil.

2. Combine sautéed onions with remainder of sauce ingredients and mix thoroughly. Bring sauce to a simmer.

3. Combine all meatball ingredients in a large bowl and mix well.

4. Roll meat mixture into approximately 30 meatballs. Be sure meatballs are tightly packed, or they will fall apart during cooking.

5. Gently drop meatballs into the simmering spaghetti sauce.

6. Cook uncovered for 3–4 hours over low heat, occasionally stirring to prevent sauce from burning and sticking to bottom of pot.

7. Approximately 30 minutes prior to serving, prepare the spaghetti pasta according to package directions.

8. Pour sauce and meatballs to taste over each serving of pasta.

Required Equipment:

Large-size cooking pot
Large-size mixing bowl

Sauce:

2 tablespoons olive oil

2 large onions, chopped

3 (12-ounce) cans Contadina tomato paste

9 (12-ounce) cans water

1½ teaspoons salt

½ teaspoon black pepper

1 tablespoon ground oregano

3 tablespoons sugar

1 tablespoon parsley flakes

1 tablespoon garlic powder

Meatballs:

3 pounds lean ground beef

1 large onion, chopped

1½ teaspoons salt

½ teaspoon black pepper

1 tablespoon garlic powder

¼ cup grated Parmesan cheese

1 tablespoon parsley flakes

4 slices stale bread, cubed

3 eggs, beaten

2 pounds spaghetti pasta

Tim Conners, Statesboro, Georgia
Former Leader, Coastal Empire Council, Boy Scouts of America

Longhorn Chicken Curry

Servings: 8–10 | Challenge Level: Moderate

"When we lived in Colorado Springs, my young teenage son and I discovered a few very good Indian restaurants near Academy Boulevard. It was always a great treat to pick him up from school and take him out to lunch. This dish tries to re-create our favorite chicken curry meals from those restaurants. It is very satisfying on cold winter nights and great at the Courts of Honor too!"

4 cups basmati rice

7 cups plus 1 cup water

1 (14-ounce) can coconut milk

2 tablespoons vegetable oil

1 large onion, diced

1 large green bell pepper, diced

2 medium carrots, peeled and diced

1 (3½-ounce) package S&B Golden Curry, broken into pieces

1 bunch cilantro, chopped

1 (15-ounce) can green peas

2 (7-ounce) packages precooked chicken, crumbled

Preparation at Camp:

1. In a medium-size pot, combine rice, 7 cups of water, and ½ of the can of coconut milk. Stir and bring to a vigorous boil.

2. Reduce heat, cover, and let rice sit for about 15 minutes, or until rice is soft.

3. In a large-size skillet or medium-size cook pot, sauté the onion, bell pepper, and carrots in oil.

4. Once the vegetables soften, add 1 cup of water, the remaining coconut milk, the curry, cilantro, and peas. Crumble the chicken into the mix. Stir until curry completely dissolves.

5. Serve curried chicken over rice.

Required Equipment:

Medium-size cook pot

Large-size frying pan or second medium-size cook pot

Option: This recipe is easily modified to make a really fine chicken curry soup by adding one or two cups of chicken broth.

Andy Stokes, Fort Worth, Texas
Assistant Scoutmaster - Troop 151 / Associate Advisor - Venture Crew 151, Longhorn Council, Boy Scouts of America

Pine Burr Pasta

Servings: 8–10 | Challenge Level: Moderate

Preparation at Camp:

1. Cook egg noodles in medium-size pot according to package directions.

2. Meanwhile, slice onion and bell pepper into thin strips.

3. In a large skillet, mix olive oil, sliced onion and bell pepper, and minced garlic. Sauté. Stir frequently and do not let garlic burn.

4. Once onion and pepper begin to soften, add sausage, spices, and shrimp. Stir occasionally until shrimp is cooked (opaque).

5. Add sour cream and stir. Cover with cheese and let melt.

6. Serve over egg noodle pasta.

Required Equipment:

Medium-size cook pot

Large-size frying pan

1 pound egg noodles

1 medium onion

1 medium bell pepper

¼ cup olive oil

4 cloves garlic, minced

1 pound kielbasa sausage, cut into chunks

1 teaspoon McCormick Salad Supreme seasoning

Louisiana-type hot sauce to taste

2 pounds uncooked shrimp, peeled

1 pint (2 cups) sour cream

1 cup shredded cheddar cheese

1 cup shredded Italian cheese blend

Lyman Fite, Columbia, Mississippi
Scoutmaster, Troop 77, Pine Burr Area Council, Boy Scouts of America

Venison Stew

Servings: 8–10 | Challenge Level: Moderate

"This recipe is very old, very straightforward, and very good!"

4 pounds venison, cubed

2 (10¾-ounce) cans condensed cream of mushroom soup

2 cups chopped onions

4 cups peeled and cubed potatoes

1 (12-ounce) jar grape jelly

1 (12-ounce) can 7-Up soda

1 cup chopped celery (optional)

Preparation at Camp:

1. In a large-size frying pan, brown venison.

2. Place meat and remainder of ingredients in a large-size covered pot. Stir.

3. Simmer for 4–6 hours until meat is tender.

Required Equipment:

Large-size frying pan
Large-size cook pot

Tip: As an alternative to the frying pan and cook pot, a Dutch oven can be used to prepare this recipe.

Shaun Davis, Hastings, Michigan
Den Leader, Pack 175, Gerald R. Ford Council, Boy Scouts of America

Flambeau River Jambalaya

Servings: 8–10 | Challenge Level: Moderate

"We prepared this dish for the first time while on a canoe trip down the Flambeau River in Northern Wisconsin. Our boys were used to eating simple foods on the trail, so some were very reluctant to try something this adventurous. But the scouts loved it. My son's patrol prepared the food and had leftovers, and the other patrols ended up arguing over who would finish it off! The scouts now request it for all our campouts. It also helps that they are always actively involved in cooking this dish, which makes it taste so much better!"

Preparation at Home:

1. Mix the spices and store for your camping trip in a ziplock bag.

Preparation at Camp:

1. In a large-size cook pot, add onion, bell pepper, bay leaves, sausage, turkey, and half of the seasoning mix previously prepared at home.

2. Cook over medium high heat, stirring frequently, until the onions are transparent, about 10 minutes.

3. Add tomatoes, water, and bouillon cubes. Stir, cover pot, and bring to a boil.

4. Stir in rice and remaining spice mix. Reduce heat to a simmer and cover.

5. Continue cooking for 15 minutes or until all the liquid is absorbed and the rice is tender. Remove bay leaves and serve.

Required Equipment:

Large-size cook pot

1 tablespoon paprika

1 tablespoon onion powder

2 teaspoons garlic powder

1 teaspoon white pepper

1 teaspoon black pepper

1 teaspoon mustard powder

1 teaspoon dried thyme leaves

½ teaspoon cumin

½ teaspoon cayenne powder

2 onions, chopped

2 bell peppers, chopped

3 bay leaves

1 pound andouille sausage, cut into ¼-inch slices

1 pound smoked turkey, cut into ¼-inch cubes

1 (15-ounce) can diced tomatoes (do not drain)

6 cups water

3 chicken bouillon cubes

3 cups uncooked long-grain white rice

Karen Henneghan, Plover, Wisconsin
Adult Leader, Troop 201, Samoset Council, Boy Scouts of America

Gossipin' Chili

Servings: 25–30 | Challenge Level: Moderate

"This dish won two awards at the 2005 Chili Cook-Off in Roosevelt, Utah. The judges gave it first place; then the spectators at the event had a chance to sample the chili, and they awarded it first place for people's choice.

How did Gossipin' Chili acquire its name? It's nice to your face, but it talks behind your back!"

2 pounds lean ground beef

Salt, ground black pepper, and chili powder to taste

3 pounds bacon, chopped

3 large onions, diced

1 green bell pepper, diced

1 red bell pepper, diced (save a few whole, round rings for garnish)

1 orange bell pepper, diced

2 Anaheim peppers, diced

3 jalapeño peppers, diced

1 cayenne pepper, diced

1 (6-pound 12-ounce) can ranch beans

2 (16-ounce) cans baked beans (Bush's preferred)

2 (15-ounce) cans great northern beans (drained)

2 (16-ounce) cans dark kidney beans (drained)

2 (15-ounce) cans light kidney beans (drained)

2 (15-ounce) cans white kidney beans (drained)

2 (14½-ounce) cans French-style green beans (drained)

2 (16-ounce) cans small red beans (drained)

¾ cup brown sugar

¼ cup chili powder

1 (24-ounce) jar picante sauce

¼ cup chipotle Tabasco sauce

1 tablespoon garlic powder

1 tablespoon onion powder

1 teaspoon jalapeño pepper powder (such as Texas Gunpowder)

8 ounces shredded Monterey Jack cheese

Preparation at Camp:

1. Brown ground beef in large skillet with a little salt, black pepper, and chili powder. Drain grease and set aside in a medium-size bowl.

2. Brown the chopped bacon in skillet and drain off nearly all the grease, reserving a small amount by pouring it in a large-size cook pot.

3. Add onion and bell peppers to the skillet, sautéing for a few minutes.

4. Transfer browned ground beef to the cook pot. Stir in all remaining ingredients except cheese.

5. Finish low and slow, cooking for 3 hours and occasionally stirring the chili.

6. Serve, garnishing with Monterey Jack cheese and rings of red bell pepper.

Required Equipment:

Very large-size cook pot (approximately 5-gallon capacity)
Large-size frying pan
Medium-size mixing bowl

Tip: This recipe makes about 3 gallons of chili, so a very large–size cook pot is a requirement!

John Foster, Duchesne, Utah
Committee Chair, Commissioner, and Cubmaster, Troop 268, Utah National Parks Council, Boy Scouts of America

Hunter's Chili

Servings: 10–12 | Challenge Level: Difficult

"As a farmer, I often trade fresh organic potatoes and squash for wild and exotic meats that I use in my chilies. A recurring positive comment I often receive about Hunter's Chili is that it is interesting because the meat and vegetables are cut to similar-size pieces. This recipe won first place in a local Michigan chili cook-off."

1 (14½-ounce) can stewed tomatoes

3 large bell peppers (1 green, 1 yellow, and 1 red), chopped

2 cloves garlic, minced

2 teaspoons parsley flakes

¼ cup (½ standard stick) butter

1 whole bunch celery, chopped

2 teaspoons dill seed

2 large Vidalia onions, chopped

2 teaspoons dill weed

1½ to 2 pounds venison loin (or similar cut)

1 pound thin-sliced prime steak cuts

1 pound coarse ground lean sirloin or buffalo

1 teaspoon coarse ground black pepper

¼ teaspoon cayenne pepper

2–6 dried hot chili peppers with seeds, diced (select number to suit taste)

2 quick shakes oregano

2 teaspoons sugar

1 (15-ounce) can tomato sauce

1 (6-ounce) can tomato paste

1 (15-ounce) can dark red kidney beans, drained

1 (15-ounce) can light red kidney beans, drained

2 tablespoons ground cinnamon

4 large dried bay leaves, each broken in half

Preparation at Camp:

1. Chop stewed tomatoes into ¾-inch cubes, pouring both the liquid and chopped tomatoes into a large cook pot.

2. In a large-size frying pan, sauté bell peppers with garlic and parsley, using about ⅓ of the butter. Place sautéed peppers in cook pot. Note that none of the vegetables in this recipe should be thoroughly cooked when sautéed as most of the cooking will occur once all the ingredients are simmered in the pot.

3. In the frying pan, sauté the celery along with the dill seed using an additional ⅓ of the butter. Place sautéed celery in cook pot.

4. Using the remainder of the butter, sauté the onions along with the dill weed. Transfer sautéed onions to the cook pot.

5. In the frying pan, sear and partially quick-cook the whole venison loin.

6. Set venison on a cutting board to cool for a few minutes then cut into ¾-inch cubes. Add seared venison to the vegetables in the pot.

7. In the frying pan, sear and partially quick-cook the steak.

8. Cut steak into ¾-inch cubes. Add steak to the pot.

9. Sear the coarse ground sirloin in the frying pan along with black pepper and cayenne pepper. Keep ground meat chunks to the same size as the other meats and vegetables during this step. Drain grease.

10. Add the remainder of the ingredients to the cook pot, reserving the bay leaves for last.

11. Cover and cook chili over medium-low heat for at least 3 hours. Stir every 15 to 30 minutes. Remove bay leaves and serve.

Options: When serving, chili toppings can include grated cheese, fresh cut onions, sour cream, and hot pepper powder or sauce. This recipe goes great served with a side of fresh corn bread and apple butter. Orange habañeros, dark red thin Thais, and a few green jalapeños make an intimidating garnish for this recipe.

Required Equipment:

Large-size cook pot
Large-size frying pan

Spencer Rife, Southfield, Michigan
Assistant Scoutmaster, Troop 1677, Detroit Area Council, Boy Scouts of America

Mystery Meat Parmesan

Servings: 8 | Challenge Level: Moderate

"Mystery meat carries a bad reputation from summer camps. But in this dish, while the meat might be a mystery to those enjoying it, it tastes great. The turkey is much like veal, but much more affordable. See if anyone can guess what kind of meat was used! This recipe turns everyday spaghetti into a special meal."

1 cup herb-flavored Stove Top stuffing

2 pounds ground turkey

1 small onion, diced

1 tablespoon vegetable oil

1 pound spaghetti pasta

2 (26-ounce) jars spaghetti sauce

1 cup grated Parmesan cheese

Preparation at Camp:

1. In a medium-size bowl, smash stuffing into course crumbs. Set aside half of the stuffing.

2. To the stuffing that remains in the bowl, mix ground turkey with diced onion.

3. Form 8 patties from the turkey mix. Use remaining stuffing that had previously been set aside to coat each patty.

4. In a large-size pan, fry patties in vegetable oil until turkey meat is cooked through.

5. Meanwhile, in a large-size pot, cook spaghetti pasta according to package directions. Drain water.

6. In a medium-size pot or the frying pan, heat the spaghetti sauce.

7. On each plate, add a base of spaghetti noodles topped by a turkey patty. Over both, pour spaghetti sauce followed by a sprinkling of Parmesan cheese.

Required Equipment:

Large-size frying pan
Large-size cook pot
Medium-size cook pot
Medium-size mixing bowl

Tip: Some patrols dip the turkey patties in beaten eggs before breading. Doing so can help the stuffing mix better adhere to the turkey meat.

Ed Bedford, Chapel Hill, North Carolina
Scoutmaster, Troop 820, Occoneechee Council, Boy Scouts of America

Tommy's Supply Failure

Servings: 4–5 | Challenge Level: Easy

"This dish is an adaptation of one handed down to me by my father, who was a Scout-master in Colorado. His troop suffered a supply failure on an expedition and found it-self attempting to prepare dinner with only a few ingredients remaining on its last day out. A Second Class by the name of Tommy was on cooking detail and came up with the base dish, hence this recipe's name. I added the onions, garlic, garlic salt, cayenne, and French bread. (I'm generally well-prepared, but hail Tommy anyway!)

This dish is just about the perfect camp food. It is hearty, easily prepared, and requires minimal utensils. It is also easy to scale: I have prepared it for as few as four or as many as 40."

Preparation at Camp:

1. Cut bread into cross sections. Lightly toast, if desired.

2. Roughly chop the garlic and onion.

3. Brown ground beef in a skillet.

4. Add garlic and onions and cook until translucent. Drain fat and add seasoning to taste.

5. Stir in the soup. Do not add additional water.

6. Simmer the dish for 10 to 15 minutes and adjust seasonings as required.

7. Serve over French bread sections.

Required Equipment:

Large-size frying pan

Tip: Go easy on the cayenne pepper for non-Cajun scouts.

1 loaf French bread

1 clove garlic

1 small onion

1 pound ground beef

Garlic salt to taste

Cayenne pepper to taste

2 (10½-ounce) cans condensed vegetar-ian vegetable soup

John Spencer, Slidell, Louisiana
Assistant Cubmaster, Pack 360, Southeast Louisiana Council, Boy Scouts of America

Spam-O-Rama

Servings: 4–5 | Challenge Level: Easy

"This is an original recipe, created by Troop 1467."

¼ cup canola oil

2 red potatoes, diced

2 carrots, diced

1 onion, diced

1 cup diced fresh green beans or 1 (15-ounce) can green beans, drained and diced

2 garlic cloves, diced

2 (12-ounce) cans Spam, cut into ½-inch cubes

¼ teaspoon red pepper flakes, or to taste

¼ teaspoon chili powder, or to taste

1 teaspoon Mrs. Dash seasoning

Salt and ground black pepper to taste

Options: Eggs can be scrambled along with the Spam. For a spice variation, use Worcestershire sauce, tomato ketchup, or steak sauces.

Preparation at Camp:

1. In a large-size skillet, stir-fry potatoes, carrots, onion, green beans, and garlic in canola oil.

2. When vegetables become tender, add diced Spam and fry until browned.

3. Stir in spices and serve.

Required Equipment:

Large-size frying pan

Curt "The Titanium Chef" White, Forks, Washington
Scoutmaster, Troop 1467, Chief Seattle Council, Boy Scouts of America

Campfire Beef Stew

Servings: 4–6 | Challenge Level: Easy

"I acquired this recipe from Troop 830 out of Clinton, Pennsylvania. I found this an easy dish to teach to my Webelos who were about to cross over to Boy Scouts. This is also a good recipe for scouts to use when working on the cooking merit badge."

Preparation at Camp:

1. In a large-size frying pan, brown beef in the olive oil.

2. Sprinkle meat with garlic salt, add flour, then toss the beef to coat.

3. Add vegetables, crumbled bouillon cubes, water, and black pepper to taste. Stir to mix.

4. Continue to cook over medium heat until vegetables are tender.

Required Equipment:

Large-size frying pan

Tip: A Dutch oven can be used instead of the frying pan to prepare this recipe.

2 tablespoons olive oil

1½ pounds beef stew meat, cubed

⅛ teaspoon garlic salt

⅛ cup all-purpose flour

2 (14½ ounce) cans new potatoes, drained and cubed

1 stalk celery, chopped

3 medium carrots, sliced

1 medium onion, chopped

2 beef bouillon cubes

3 cups water

Ground black pepper to taste

Robert Ward, Clinton, Pennsylvania
Assistant Scoutmaster, Troop 830, Greater Pittsburgh Council, Boy Scouts of America

Pioneer Chow

Servings: 12–14 | Challenge Level: Easy

"This recipe is from Girl Scouts Peacepipe Council, which serves southwestern Minnesota. It is named for our annual outing, Pioneerland, which takes us across southern Minnesota along the same routes that pioneer and author Laura Ingalls Wilder once traveled."

4 pounds ground beef

2 medium onions

1 large (29-ounce) can tomato sauce

1 (11-ounce) can condensed tomato bisque–flavored soup

1 (53-ounce) can pork and beans

4 (12-ounce) packages corn chips (such as Fritos)

Optional toppings:

4 cups shredded cheddar cheese

2 (16-ounce) containers sour cream

Preparation at Camp:

1. In a large-size skillet, brown ground beef and onions. Drain grease.

2. Blend in tomato sauce, tomato soup, and pork and beans.

3. Heat thoroughly, and serve over corn chips using optional toppings, if desired.

Required Equipment:

Large-size frying pan

Jeanie Haas, Redwood Falls, Minnesota
Membership and Marketing Specialist, Peacepipe Council, Girl Scouts of the USA

Granny's Chicken

Servings: 6–8 | Challenge Level: Easy

"Our troop attends one of the last patrol cooking camps in America. On Thursday nights at Camp Bowman, in Goshen, Virginia, the dinner is always fried chicken, mashed potatoes, vegetable, and pie. I've found that the scouts have a hard time coating and frying the chicken without burning it, and they often overheat the oil. Using the method in Granny's Chicken, no cooking oil is used. During the last few minutes of frying, once the water is mostly evaporated, the oil from the meat crisps the chicken. The flavor can be adjusted by using different spices, such as a Cajun mix."

Preparation at Camp:

1. Place chicken legs side-by-side in a large-size cast iron skillet.

2. Add water to cover the bottom 1-inch deep.

3. Place a lid on the skillet and cook chicken over medium heat. If you have no lid, aluminum foil can be used.

4. Occasionally check to make sure that water remains in the skillet, replenishing as necessary.

5. After 30 minutes, sprinkle chicken with seasoned salt. Turn chicken, and add seasoned salt to the other side of the meat.

6. Cover again and continue cooking for an additional 20 minutes. Remove cover from the skillet to allow moisture to evaporate, maintaining just enough water to prevent the chicken from burning.

7. Brown chicken on all sides and serve.

Required Equipment:

Large-size cast iron frying pan
Aluminum foil (if frying pan has no lid)

16 chicken drumsticks (with or without skin)

Lawry's seasoned salt

Water

Linda Nosalik, Upper Marlboro, Maryland
Assistant Scoutmaster / Venture Crew Activities Chairman, Troop 1575,
National Capital Area Council, Boy Scouts of America

Santa Fe Stew

Servings: 6 | Challenge Level: Easy

2 pounds boneless skinless chicken breasts

1 (1¼-ounce) packet McCormick Grill Mates Southwest Marinade spice mix

2 tablespoons water

2 tablespoons white vinegar

¼ cup vegetable oil

2 large green bell peppers

2 large red bell peppers

1 medium red onion

1 (15¼-ounce) can Del Monte fiesta corn

6 flour tortillas

Preparation at Home:

1. Cut chicken into bite size pieces and place in a gallon-size ziplock freezer bag.

2. Using water, white vinegar, and vegetable oil, follow Grill Mates package directions to prepare marinade.

3. Add marinade to the chicken in the ziplock bag. Knead and refrigerate, allowing to rest at least overnight to reduce grittiness of sauce.

Preparation at Camp:

1. Trim and chop peppers and onion.

2. Brown marinated chicken in large frying pan. Keep covered when not stirring.

3. Add peppers and onion. Stir to avoid burning.

4. Once peppers and onion are cooked to taste, add corn, liquid and all.

5. Simmer for 5–10 minutes then serve with tortillas.

Required Equipment:

Large-size frying pan

Aluminum foil (if frying pan has no lid)

Mark Doiron, Midwest City, Oklahoma
Committee Member, Troop 275, Last Frontier Council, Boy Scouts of America

Troop 60 Pony Express Chili

Servings: 8–10 | Challenge Level: Easy

"When we make this recipe, there are never any complaints. Nor is there any lack of energy after the scouts have demolished the chili!"

Preparation at Camp:

1. In a large-size frying pan, brown ground beef and drain.

2. Add beans, refried beans, corn, chili, Spam, and Vienna sausages to the ground beef. Heat until bubbling, stirring occasionally.

3. Blend in Colby cheese cubes.

4. Serve once cheese melts.

Required Equipment

Large-size frying pan

½ pound ground beef

2 (15-ounce) cans spicy or Mexican-style beans

1 (16-ounce) can refried beans

1 (15-ounce) can corn, drained

2 (15-ounce) cans chili without beans

1 (12-ounce) can Spam, drained and cut into ¼-inch cubes

1 (5-ounce) can Vienna sausages, drained and sliced

¼ pound Colby cheese, cubed

Jim Lehr, St. Joseph, Missouri
Committee Member, Troop 60, Pony Express Council, Boy Scouts of America

Super Hot Dog Stew

Servings: 8–10 | Challenge Level: Easy

"This recipe has become a favorite among our children, grandchildren, and friends."

2 pounds hot dogs

8 medium white potatoes

2 tablespoons vegetable oil

2 large onions, chopped

6 cups water

1 teaspoon salt

½ teaspoon ground black pepper

Preparation at Camp:

1. Cut hot dogs into round ¼-inch slices. Peel and slice potatoes into ½-inch cubes.

2. Heat oil in frying pan. Cook hotdogs and onions until dark brown.

3. Add cubed potatoes and enough water to just overlay all ingredients. Cover and simmer, stirring occasionally until potatoes are soft. Lightly mash potatoes in the pan.

4. Add salt and black pepper and any additional water as needed. Stir to make a thick brown gravy. Serve hot.

Required Equipment:

Large-size frying pan
Aluminum foil (if frying pan has no lid)

Tip: To make the most tasty Super Hot Dog Stew, ensure that the hot dogs and onions are browned long enough to leave a dark residue on the bottom of the pan. (Scouts shouldn't have a problem making a dark residue.) A slight burnt finish to the hot dogs and onions adds extra flavor, sort of like hot dogs taste when roasted on a wooden stick over an open fire.

Gene Lent, Longwood, Florida
Eagle Scout and Executive Board Member, Central Florida Council, Boy Scouts of America

Ravenous Scout Leader's Steak Au Gratin

Servings: 3–4 | Challenge Level: Easy

Preparation at Camp:

1. In large-size skillet, melt butter and brown sirloin steak strips. Set aside.

2. Add onion and garlic to frying pan, cooking until onion becomes translucent.

3. Stir in vinegar, bouillon water, caraway seeds, marjoram, and black pepper. Bring to a boil, cooking for 1 minute.

4. Return meat to the skillet. Stir, cover, and simmer for 40 minutes.

5. In medium-size mixing bowl, blend flour and sour cream.

6. Add sour cream blend to meat and stir until thickened.

7. Top with shredded cheese. Cover and heat for an additional 5 minutes or until cheese melts.

Required Equipment:

Large-size frying pan
Aluminum foil (if frying pan has no lid)
Medium-size mixing bowl

3 tablespoons butter

2 pounds sirloin steak, cut into bite-size strips

1 large onion, chopped

1 teaspoon minced garlic

⅓ cup white vinegar

1 beef bouillon cube, dissolved in 1 cup hot water

1½ teaspoons caraway seeds

¼ teaspoon marjoram

¼ teaspoon ground black pepper

2½ tablespoons all-purpose flour

½ cup sour cream

8 ounces mild shredded cheddar cheese

Beth Ann Ast, Michigan City, Indiana
Advancement Chair and Cooking Merit Badge Counselor, Troop 871, La Salle Council, Boy Scouts of America

Barracuda Stroganoff

Servings: 8–10 | Challenge Level: Moderate

"This recipe has won our troop cooking awards more often than any other. Barracuda Patrol member Ben Mosteller is the originator of the dish."

1 (16-ounce) package egg noodles

2 pounds lean ground beef

2 medium onions, diced

½ cup (1 standard stick) butter

¼ cup all-purpose flour

2 teaspoons salt

2 cloves garlic, minced

½ teaspoon ground black pepper

1 (8-ounce) can mushroom stems and pieces, drained

2 (10½-ounce) cans condensed cream of chicken soup

1 pint (16 ounces) sour cream

Snipped parsley (optional)

Preparation at Camp:

1. In a medium-size cook pot, prepare noodles according to package directions.

2. In a large-size skillet, brown ground beef and onion in butter.

3. Once onion is tender, stir in flour, salt, garlic, black pepper, and mushrooms. Heat for 5 minutes, stirring constantly.

4. Reduce heat. Stir in cream of chicken soup and simmer, uncovered, for 10 minutes.

5. Blend in sour cream and heat through.

6. Serve over noodles. Sprinkle with optional snipped parsley if desired.

Required Equipment:

Medium-size cook pot

Large-size frying pan

Ed Bedford, Chapel Hill, North Carolina
Scoutmaster, Troop 820, Occoneechee Council, Boy Scouts of America

Dragon Lo Mein

Servings: 3–4 | Challenge Level: Moderate

"Our troop has cooking competitions just about every campout. Daniel Acker, Leader of the Dragon Patrol, asked me about my favorite meals. When he discovered I liked Chinese food, particularly lo mein, he prepared this dinner. It won the award for the weekend!"

Preparation at Camp:

1. Thinly slice meat across the grain. Trim into strips, each about 1 to 2 inches long. Meat is easier to slice if it is partially frozen.

2. In a small bowl or quart-size ziplock freezer bag, combine ginger, green onions, cornstarch, sugar, and soy sauce. Add meat strips and cover with the marinade. Set aside for at least 30 minutes.

3. While meat marinates, cook and drain noodles in a medium-size pot following package directions. Mix in a few drops of oil to keep the noodles from sticking and set aside.

4. Place 1 tablespoon oil in a wok or heavy skillet and heat at medium-high. When oil just begins to smoke, add meat mixture and stir fry for about 3 minutes or until meat is cooked through. Set the cooked meat aside.

5. Pour 1 tablespoon of oil in the wok or skillet and stir fry the vegetables until slightly tender.

6. Combine vegetables, meat, noodles, and salt in the wok or skillet and cook until heated through.

Required Equipment:

Wok or large-size frying pan
Medium-size cook pot
Small-size bowl or quart-size ziplock freezer bag

Ed Bedford, Chapel Hill, North Carolina
Scoutmaster, Troop 820, Occoneechee Council, Boy Scouts of America

---

1 pound flank steak or chicken breast

1 teaspoon dried ginger or 2 slices fresh ginger root, minced

5 green onions, chopped

4 teaspoons cornstarch

1 teaspoon brown or white sugar

2 tablespoons soy sauce

8 ounces lo mein stir-fry noodles

2 tablespoons peanut oil

16 ounces frozen stir-fry vegetables or 4 cups diced fresh vegetables (chosen from cabbage, carrots, celery, green beans, mushrooms, peppers, and snap peas)

½ teaspoon salt

Option: Linguini pasta can be substituted for the lo mein.

Mighty 468 Klondike Chili

Servings: 10–12 | Challenge Level: Moderate

"This recipe's name comes from our council's annual Klondike Campout, where all the scouts rough-it by spending the entire weekend outdoors… in the snow. During the day, there are arctic-themed games to keep the boys warmed up, but at night they must sleep in tents. One year, the temperature dropped to -13 degrees F, and all my kids came through. At the Klondike Campout, there is an adult chili cooking competition, which we have won every year using this recipe.

I attempt to convince my scouts to try non-typical meats, but to do so, I have to get creative. Once we camped outside of Ellicottville, New York, near a huge buffalo ranch. Unbeknownst to the boys, I arranged in advance to purchase several pounds of meat from the ranch for the campout. Buffalo meat tastes like beef, but has almost no fat, so it is correspondingly tougher. To tenderize the meat, I made a stew with wild leeks and home grown garlic. Well, it disappeared fast. After dinner, I told my scouts what kind of meat I used. By their reaction, you'd have thought I served them poison, even though they eventually were able to admit it was very good. After that, they always made a point to ask what kind of meat they were eating!"

½ (20-ounce) package 15-bean soup beans (including seasoning packet)

½ pound each of three of the following (1½ pounds total):
pheasant, rabbit, duck, goose, buffalo, venison, ostrich, or boar

2 pounds ground beef

1 pound ground turkey

2 cloves garlic, minced

1 large onion, chopped

2 (15-ounce) cans crushed tomatoes

2 (16-ounce) cans kidney beans, drained

1 teaspoon lemon balm

1 teaspoon savory

1 teaspoon basil

1 teaspoon chili powder

1 teaspoon horseradish

Dash of Worcestershire sauce or liquid smoke

2 cups shredded cheese (your choice)

Preparation at Camp:

1. Soak ½ package of soup beans (10 ounces total) overnight. Parboil in a medium-size cook pot the day they are to be served.

2. Cube meat from the wild game.

3. Place all meats in a very large–size skillet. Add garlic and onion. Simmer until meat is cooked through. Drain grease.

4. Add tomatoes, kidney beans, soaked soup beans, and half of the contents of the bean soup seasoning package. Stir in lemon balm, savory, basil, chili powder, and horseradish.

5. Simmer for 1 hour, stirring frequently. Just before serving, add Worcestershire sauce, then top with your favorite cheese.

Required Equipment:

Medium-size cook pot
Large-size frying pan

Tip: Do not completely cook the soup beans in the second step. By allowing the beans to finish once added to the chili, they will better absorb the sauce and spices.

Brian Engler, Lancaster, New York
Scoutmaster, Troop 468, Greater Niagara Frontier Council, Boy Scouts of America

Yibin Chinese Stir Fry

Servings: 8–10 | Challenge Level: Moderate

3 cups long-grain rice

½ cup soy sauce

¼ cup sugar

2 tablespoons cider vinegar

2 tablespoons ketchup

1 teaspoon ground ginger

4 cloves garlic, minced

1 teaspoon cornstarch or flour

2 pounds boneless, skinless chicken breasts, cut into strips

4 tablespoons vegetable oil

1 (16-ounce) package frozen stir-fry vegetables

2 (16-ounce) cans unsweetened pineapple chunks, drained

Preparation at Camp:

1. In a medium-size cook pot, prepare rice according to package directions.

2. While rice is cooking, combine soy sauce, sugar, cider vinegar, ketchup, ginger, garlic, and cornstarch in a small-size mixing bowl. Set aside.

3. In a large-size frying pan, stir-fry the chicken in vegetable oil until meat is cooked.

4. Add the frozen vegetables and stir-fry for an additional 3–4 minutes.

5. Add soy sauce mixture prepared in step 2 and drained pineapple. Stir and heat thoroughly.

6. Serve over rice.

Required Equipment:

Large-size frying pan

Medium-size cook pot

Small-size mixing bowl

Ed Bedford, Chapel Hill, North Carolina
Scoutmaster, Troop 820, Occoneechee Council, Boy Scouts of America

Nantucket Scallops

Servings: 6 | Challenge Level: Moderate

"Scallops are best when bought from the fish market at the end of the road by Boy Scout Camp Richard Nantucket!"

Preparation at Camp:

1. In a large skillet, sauté garlic and shallots in 1 table-spoon of butter and the olive oil. Cook until translucent, about 2 minutes.

2. Add scallops and heat until slightly brown. Set scallops, garlic, and shallots aside in a medium-size bowl.

3. Add another tablespoon butter and the mushrooms to the skillet. Cook until mushrooms release their liquid, about 5 minutes.

4. Add remaining ingredients to frying pan, except for rice/pasta and about 1 tablespoon of cilantro. Stir.

5. Let sauce simmer for about 20 minutes, stirring often. Don't let it burn!

6. While sauce is simmering, prepare either rice or pasta in large-size cook pot according to package instruc-tions, then set aside.

7. When sauce has become thick, slowly sliding from spoon, return scallops to the frying pan along with any liquid that may have collected in bowl. Gently stir.

8. Once scallops have warmed, serve over rice or pasta. Sprinkle with remaining cilantro.

Required Equipment:

Large-size frying pan
Large-size cook pot
Medium-size mixing bowl

Tip: If you must use frozen scallops, thaw and remove excess liquid before adding to the frying pan in step 2.

3 large garlic cloves, chopped

2 large shallots, chopped

1 tablespoon butter

1 tablespoon olive oil

3 pounds fresh scallops

1 tablespoon butter

8 ounces sliced fresh mushrooms

1 pint heavy cream

½ teaspoon celery seeds

½ teaspoon ground black pepper

2 tablespoons Dijon mustard

½ cup white grape juice

½ cup fresh cilan-tro, chopped

6 servings of either rice or pasta

Options: Basil or chives can be substi-tuted for the cilantro.

Gregg Shupe, Framingham, Massachusetts
Assistant Scoutmaster, Troop 12, Knox Trail Council, Boy Scouts of America

Blade Blackie's Poison Peppers

Servings: 6–8 | Challenge Level: Moderate

"In 1999, three reporters from Westsylvania Magazine came to the Appalachian Mountains to write a story in honor of the 20th anniversary of the friendly 'over-the-mountain feud' between the counties of Huntingdon and Blair. I graciously offered them a bite of Blade Blackie's Poison Peppers. Two of the reporters stood back as if frightened of the dish. But the other, a petite blonde-haired lady, bravely stepped forward to give it a try. I pulled my favorite spoon from my back pocket, blew the pocket fuzz from it, and gave her a taste of the 'sauce' from the top of the pan between the spokes of hot peppers. While the other two reporters looked on with notable concern, the woman's eyes suddenly opened wide, and she let out a long 'mmmmm,' whereupon she turned her face toward heaven as if to thank God himself for this incredible dish. It seemed the clouds miraculously parted and a ray of sunlight illuminated her glorious face. Along with the little lady, the two hangers-back then stepped forward, thrusting plates at me. The rest is Poison Pepper history.

This dish was awarded first place in the entree category in *Scouting* magazine's 2005 'Camp Food Favorites' recipe contest."

1½ **pounds thick-sliced or chunked bacon, chopped into squares**

1 **medium head of cabbage, chopped into ½-inch strips**

½ **cup water**

1 **softball-size onion, finely chopped**

2 **bell peppers, finely chopped**

1 **pound dried beef, cut into 1-inch squares**

1 **(10¾-ounce) can condensed cream of mushroom soup**

Salt, ground black pepper, and garlic to taste

12 **whole hot peppers (more or less depending on your tolerance of heat)**

Options: This dish is mildly spicy when the hot peppers are left whole and unbroken. They will provide some zing without the burn. If you want the dish to have a little more kick, chop 1 or 2 of the peppers before adding, leaving the rest whole. If you like it really hot, cut up all the peppers and stir the pieces, but keep the antacid handy. Poison Peppers is great by itself or when served on bread or rolls.

1. Fry bacon in a very large–size skillet until golden brown, leaving grease in the pan.

2. Break apart cabbage strips and add to skillet along with ½ cup water.

3. Cover the skillet, but stir occasionally. Cook until cabbage becomes limp.

4. Add chopped onion and bell peppers followed by dried beef squares and the condensed mushroom soup. Add more water as needed to maintain a broth that allows soup to blend easily and that prevents the stock from clinging together.

5. Add salt, black pepper, and garlic to taste, mixing well. Cook until sauce thickens.

6. Add whole hot peppers. Stir carefully to avoid breaking the peppers open.

7. Cook until sauce returns to a smooth and thick consistency, stirring occasionally, then reduce heat, simmering for an additional 15 minutes before serving.

Required Equipment:
Very large–size frying pan
Aluminum foil (if frying pan has no lid)

Tip: This recipe can also be prepared in a Dutch oven.

Stephen D. "Blade Blackie" Black, Spring Mills, Pennsylvania
Council Chair, Troop 381, Juniata Council, Boy Scouts of America

Cincinnati Chili

Servings: 8–10 | Challenge Level: Moderate

"If you haven't had it before, don't expect Cincinnati-style chili to resemble the southwest kind. It's nothing of the sort. And one look at the ingredients list will tell you why. With roots tracing back to the Mediterranean region, this chili style has found a surprisingly passionate following in a region of the United States of predominantly German and Irish ancestry.

Tim is from Cincinnati and could survive solely on the stuff. Being on his top-ten list of important items of heritage to pass along to his posterity, he introduced our kids to this spicy chili when they were babies. They loved it then, and they love it now. In fact, most people do once they get used to the thought of chocolate and cinnamon in their chili. Of course, there is also the strange bit about ladling the concoction over spaghetti and encasing the entire pile in a shell of cheese. For the more robust, the volcanic ensemble continues by adding beans and raw onions.

Odd as it may seem, it all leads to an amazing array of aromas and flavors. It will be the talk of camp, guaranteed. And don't be alarmed by the length of the ingredients list: Once you have your spice kit in order, Cincinnati Chili is straightforward to prepare."

2 tablespoons vegetable oil

2 onions, finely diced

1 garlic clove, minced

2 tablespoons chili powder

1 tablespoon ground oregano

1½ teaspoons cinnamon

1 teaspoon salt

¾ teaspoon ground black pepper

½ teaspoon nutmeg

½ teaspoon thyme

¼ teaspoon allspice

1 (14-ounce) can low sodium chicken broth

1 (29-ounce) can tomato sauce

2 tablespoons white vinegar

1½ tablespoons brown sugar

½ square (½-ounce) unsweetened baking chocolate

1½ pounds lean ground beef

1 pound spaghetti noodles

1 pound shredded mild cheddar cheese (optional)

1 (15-ounce) can kidney beans, drained (optional)

1 onion, chopped (optional)

Preparation at Camp:

1. Heat oil in a large-size skillet. Cook 2 diced onions until soft.

2. Stir in garlic, chili powder, oregano, cinnamon, salt, black pepper, nutmeg, thyme, allspice, chicken broth, tomato sauce, vinegar, brown sugar, baking chocolate, and ground beef.

3. Break up beef into small pieces while bringing the sauce to a boil.

4. Reduce heat and let simmer until sauce thickens.

5. In the meantime, cook spaghetti noodles in large-size cook pot according to package directions. Drain.

6. Serve chili over spaghetti.

7. Top with optional cheddar cheese (called a 'Three-Way'), plus kidney beans (called a 'Four-Way'). For the extra daring, add onions (you guessed it, a 'Five-Way').

Required Equipment:

Large-size frying pan
Large-size cook pot

Tim Conners, Statesboro, Georgia
Former Leader, Coastal Empire Council, Boy Scouts of America

Christine Conners, Statesboro, Georgia
Former Girl Scout, Hawaii Council, Girl Scouts of the USA

Los Padres Picadillo

Servings: 4–5 | Challenge Level: Moderate

"Picadillo is a type of hash ubiquitous throughout Latin America. Roughly translated from Spanish, it means 'little minced meat'. Every nationality has its own version. In Mexico, they might add cinnamon and almonds and use it as a filling for chile rellenos, tacos, or burritos; while Cubans might add cumin, green peppers, green olives, or capers and serve it with rice and black beans. Although the combination of raisins and olives may seem wild, give it a try. I think you'll be pleasantly surprised by the taste.

This entree took third place in *Scouting* magazine's 2005 'Camp Food Favorites' recipe contest."

1 pound ground beef

2 tablespoons vinegar

1 teaspoon garlic, minced

1 teaspoon cumin powder

1 onion, sliced into slivers

1 red bell pepper, chopped

1 tablespoon vegetable oil

1 (8-ounce) can tomato sauce

¼ cup raisins

¼ cup green olives, sliced

Salt and ground black pepper to taste

2 cups instant brown rice

Preparation at Camp:

1. Thoroughly mix ground beef, vinegar, garlic, and cumin in medium-size bowl. Cover meat mixture and let rest for about 15 minutes.

2. In a large-size frying pan, sauté onion and bell pepper in vegetable oil.

3. Once onion and pepper are soft, add the marinated ground beef and cook until the pink disappears.

4. Stir in all remaining ingredients, except for rice, and simmer for 5–10 minutes.

5. While simmering, prepare rice in a medium-size cook pot according to package directions.

6. Serve ground beef mixture over rice.

Required Equipment:

Large-size frying pan
Medium-size cook pot
Medium-size mixing bowl

Tip: Prior to an overnight camping trip, at home freeze marinated ground beef into a thin, flat block, or into a thicker block for longer-term storage in an ice chest.

Pat Brown, Los Osos, California
Former Committee Chairperson, Troop 216, Los Padres Council, Boy Scouts of America

Max's Award Winning Salmon Bake

Servings: 4–6 | Challenge Level: Easy

"I prepared this salmon bake a couple of years ago and won first place in a summer camp cooking competition. It's a great recipe, but I remember it mainly because I cooked it outside in a torrential downpour. Five minutes into the bake, the heavens opened. I frantically dragged our neighboring troop's camp gadget, a tripod, over the fire pit and threw a tarp over the whole thing. For 30 minutes, I diverted rain from the charcoal and periodically checked the fish. I was thrilled to win first place, but glad just to finish cooking!"

Preparation at Camp:

1. Establish a hot bed of coals.

2. Place the salmon, skin-side down, in a half-size aluminum steam table baking pan.

3. Drizzle salmon with olive oil.

4. Cover salmon with all remaining ingredients, ending with the beans on top.

5. Use heavy-duty aluminum foil to cover and seal the baking pan.

6. Place pan directly on coals. Cook for 20–30 minutes or until the edge of the fish flakes easily with a fork and internal temperature is at least 145 degrees F.

Required Equipment:

Half-size aluminum steam table pan
Heavy-duty aluminum foil

1½ to 2 pounds salmon fillet

2 tablespoons olive oil

1 pinch basil

3 cloves garlic, diced

1 spring (small) onion, sliced into circles

1 (14-ounce) can diced tomatoes with zesty mild green chilies (such as Del Monte)

1 (15-ounce) can lima beans or green beans

Option: Your favorite fish can be substituted for the salmon.

Max Coles, Richmond Hill, Georgia
Scoutmaster / Sea Kayak High Adventure Staff Member, Troop 486, Coastal Empire Council, Boy Scouts of America

Corn on the Coals

Servings: 1 / Multiply as Required | Challenge Level: Easy

1 corn on the cob, with husks

Butter and salt to taste (optional)

Preparation at Camp:

1. Peel back the corn husk without tearing it off. Remove corn silks. Pull the husk back up to thoroughly cover the kernels.

2. Place corn in water and soak for 15 minutes or more.

3. Cook directly on coals or grill for 10 minutes, rotating occasionally. Keep a close eye on the husk to be sure it doesn't catch fire. Do not cook over open flame!

4. Carefully remove corn from coals and add optional butter and salt to taste.

Required Equipment:

Container to soak corn

Millie Hutchison, Pittsburgh, Pennsylvania
Girl Scout Trainer, Trillium Council, Girl Scouts of the USA

Pizzaritos

Servings: 4–8 | Challenge Level: Easy

Preparation at Camp:

1. Spread approximately 3 tablespoons pizza sauce onto each tortilla.

2. Sprinkle each tortilla with ¼ cup shredded cheese and top with pepperoni slices.

3. Tuck tortilla sides in and roll like burritos.

4. Wrap each pizzarito in two layers of heavy-duty aluminum foil, and bake over coals for approximately 10 minutes or until cheese is melted.

Required Equipment:

Heavy-duty aluminum foil

Tip: Pizzaritos can also be cooked together in a covered steam table pan on a grill.

Blennie Danielson, Arcadia, California
Troop Volunteer, Troop 111, Lucky Baldwin Council, Boy Scouts of America

1 (14-ounce) jar pizza sauce

8 flour tortillas

2 cups shredded mozzarella cheese

8 ounces sliced pepperoni

Chicken in a Can

Servings: 2 / Multiply as Required | Challenge Level: Easy

½ boneless chicken breast

1 medium potato

1 medium carrot

1 small onion

1 (16-ounce) can corn (do not drain)

2 tablespoons barbeque sauce

½ cup water

Preparation at Camp:

1. Cut chicken into bite-size pieces. Wash potato and remove eyes, but do not peel, then chop into pieces. Wash carrot and slice into ¼-inch lengths. Remove skin and base from onion, and chop.

2. Place all ingredients in large clean coffee can and stir. Seal top of can with heavy-duty aluminum foil, and carefully set can in campfire embers.

3. Using tongs to steady the can, occasionally stir contents, adding more water if ingredients begin to dry out.

4. Cook for 30 minutes or until vegetables are tender. Remove can from fire with tongs, and allow to cool for a few minutes before serving.

Required Equipment:

28-ounce empty coffee can (or equivalent food-grade metal container), label removed

Heavy-duty aluminum foil

Tongs

Ken Harbison, Rochester, New York
Former Boy Scout, Washington Trail Council, Boy Scouts of America

Judy Harbison, Rochester, New York
Lifetime Member, Genesee Valley Council, Girl Scouts of the USA

Trailblazer Roast

Servings: 10–12 | Challenge Level: Moderate

"Some have been hesitant to try this roast because of the ingredients in the sauce, but I've never had leftovers! The meat is very tender, with a mild flavor and a sweet aftertaste."

Preparation at Camp:

1. In a medium-size bowl, create marinade by combining pickle relish, Worcestershire sauce, Italian dressing, and Coca-Cola.

2. Place roast in half-size aluminum steam table pan and pour marinade over roast.

3. Cover steam table pan by wrapping two layers of heavy-duty aluminum foil across the top of the meat, sealing tightly around the edges of the pan.

4. Plan pan in a cooler and allow meat to marinate for 1 hour.

5. Place pan on grate over campfire coals that have burned down and are no longer flaming. Use medium heat within the pan (300–350 degrees F) for the first hour.

6. By raising pan or rearranging coals, drop temperature in pan to medium-low (250–300 degrees F) and continue roasting for an additional 2–3 hours. Meat is safe to serve once internal temperature reaches 160 degrees F.

1 (10-ounce) jar sweet pickle relish

¾ cup Worcestershire sauce

1 (16-ounce) bottle Italian salad dressing

1 (12-ounce) can Coca-Cola

6 pounds beef or venison roast

Required Equipment:

Medium-size mixing bowl
Half-size aluminum steam table pan
Heavy-duty aluminum foil

Tip: Instead of the campfire, a grill or large Dutch oven can also be used to cook the roast.

Kevin Joiner, Columbus, Georgia
Treasurer, Troop 98, Chattahoochee Council, Boy Scouts of America

Backcountry Over-Stuffed Fish

Servings: 4–5 | Challenge level: Moderate

"When I travel in the backcountry, I always take a variety of spices with me. You never know when one of your companions will catch a fish along the way. This is a recipe modified from my dad's Charles Sommers Canoe Base wilderness cooking pamphlet, passed on to me and used on many of my own canoe trips."

2–3 pounds whole fresh fish

Salt to taste

1 plain bagel, crumbed

2 tablespoons butter, melted

¼ cup raisins

1 teaspoon allspice

Salt and ground black pepper to taste

2 teaspoons milk (reconstituted powdered milk can be substituted)

1 tablespoon vegetable oil or melted butter

6 bacon strips

Preparation at Camp:

1. Clean fish, leaving head and bones attached. If using a large fish, or one with large scales, remove scales by scraping with a knife toward the head. Rinse the fish, inside and out, with water and pat dry. Rub the empty inner cavity of the fish with salt.

2. In a medium-size bowl, combine crumbled bagel, 2 tablespoons melted butter, raisins, allspice, and salt and pepper to taste. Soften the dressing with milk until just moistened.

3. Rub the skin of the fish with oil or melted butter. Lightly salt and pepper the skin to taste.

4. Place fish on heavy-duty aluminum foil and stuff with the dressing. Place bacon strips on both sides of fish.

5. Wrap foil around fish and pinch edges of foil to seal tightly.

6. Place foil in the embers of a fire or on a grill for about 30 minutes, turning once after the first 15 minutes. Low cooking heat works best.

7. Check for doneness. Meat should be flaky when tested with a fork, the internal temperature about 145 degrees F. Bake longer if needed.

8. When ready, either flake the meat from the bones or, for heftier fish, cut into sections.

Required Equipment:

Medium-size mixing bowl

Heavy-duty aluminum foil

Tips: Cooking time and the amount of stuffing should be adjusted according to the weight, size, and number of fish. Fish can also be baked inside a Dutch oven on top of an inverted metal pan to keep from burning or sticking to the bottom.

Options: Bagel crumbs can also be mixed with apples, raisins, dried onion, nuts, and brown sugar. Precooked rice can be substituted for the bagel. Whole salmon goes well with this recipe, but any fish of this general shape will work, including trout and bass.

Curt "The Titanium Chef" White, Forks, Washington
Scoutmaster, Troop 1467, Chief Seattle Council, Boy Scouts of America

Pusch Ridge Volcano Potatoes

Servings: 8 | Challenge Level: Moderate

"When hiking near Pusch Ridge in the Catalina Mountains north of Tucson, we used to see bighorn sheep, now near extinction because of growth in the Tucson metropolitan area. My brother's Eagle Scout project involved assisting with the study of the sheep in this area, so I used to think about them a lot. As a leader, I was wondering how to encourage my scouts to eat more vegetables on campouts. I came up with the idea of placing those 'bighorn sheep' (cauliflower) on potato 'mountains'. Before long, Volcano Potatoes was born. It's a great way to add vegetables to a young scout's diet (and to talk to them about endangered species)!"

8 medium potatoes

Butter or vegetable oil to taste

1 large bunch broccoli

1 large bunch cauliflower

4 carrots, grated

½ pound sharp cheddar cheese, grated

1 bottle ketchup

Preparation at Camp:

1. Wash and dry potatoes, then lightly rub with butter or oil.

2. Put one large nail, no longer than potato, all the way into each. The nail point must not protrude from the potato, otherwise it will pierce the foil.

3. Wrap each potato in heavy-duty aluminum foil, cover the foil with a wet paper towel, then wrap in foil once more.

4. Place potatoes directly on hot coals, turning occasionally while they cook.

5. While potatoes are baking, cut broccoli into bite-size pieces that look like small "trees." Place cut broccoli in a medium-size bowl. Do the same with the cauliflower, making small "sheep." Place these in a separate bowl.

6. The potatoes should be finished baking about 35–45 minutes after setting in the coals. Remove from fire and carefully discard foil and paper towels. Place the nails in a safe location.

7. Slice open each potato lengthwise and lightly mash the inside with a fork.

8. To create the "volcano," carefully mound up the mashed potato. Add trees (broccoli pieces) and sheep (cauliflower pieces) to the white "mountainside."

9. Now make the volcano erupt by adding grated carrots, grated cheese, and ketchup to the potato "peak." Serve.

Required Equipment:

Heavy-duty aluminum foil
8 large steel nails, clean and free of coating
8 wet paper towels, white with no dyes
2 medium-size mixing bowls

Tip: The wet paper towel delays burning of the potato skin while the nail helps transfer heat to the center of the potato, reducing cooking time. Use white paper towels to avoid transferring dye from the towel to the potato.

Katie Salyer Cox, Tucson, Arizona
Leader and Trainer, USA Girl Scouts Overseas and Sahuaro Council, Girl Scouts of the USA

Camp Tres Ritos Grilled Sweet Potatoes

Servings: 5–6 | Challenge Level: Moderate

"My troop was enjoying their summer at Camp Tres Ritos in New Mexico when this recipe was born. Exhausted by an overabundance of white potato recipes, my scouts were desperate to try something new. I had brought along the ingredients for this dish to try at camp, but was hesitant to test its exotic flavors on the boys. As I watched my troop suffering from DPC (i.e., desperate potato conditions), I decided to take the risk. Much to my surprise, everyone enjoyed Grilled Sweet Potatoes so much that none was left over. My boys went on to adapt the dish for the Dutch oven for a Camporee contest later in the year and received rave reviews from the judges. The recipe ultimately took third place in the 'side dish' category in *Scouting* magazine's 2005 'Camp Food Favorites' outdoor cooking contest!"

2 pounds sweet potatoes, peeled and cut into ½-inch thick slices

1–2 sweet onions, peeled and cut into ½-inch thick wedges

2 mangos, peeled, seeded, and cut into ½-inch thick slices

1 red bell pepper, cut into ½-inch thick slices

¼ cup olive oil

2 teaspoons lime juice

½ teaspoon ground cinnamon

½ teaspoon ground cumin

¼ teaspoon ground nutmeg

¼ teaspoon salt

Pinch cayenne pepper

¼ cup fresh chopped cilantro

⅓ cup chopped walnut pieces

Preparation at Camp:

1. Combine sweet potatoes, onions, mangos, and bell pepper in a large-size bowl.

2. In a small-size bowl, mix olive oil, lime juice, cinnamon, cumin, nutmeg, salt, and cayenne pepper.

3. Pour juice-oil-spice blend over potato mixture. Toss and fold to coat evenly.

4. Lay out and stack two large pieces of heavy-duty aluminum foil. Mound sweet potato mixture onto the middle of top sheet.

5. Wrap in the double layer of foil, turning up edges and folding tightly to form a sealed package.

6. Place directly on thin layer of coals or on a grate over a hot fire. Cook for 45 minutes–1 hour until potatoes become fork tender.

7. Remove from fire. Let cool slightly before unwrapping to avoid getting burned by escaping steam.

8. Transfer mixture back to large-size bowl and toss with chopped cilantro and nuts before serving.

Required Equipment:

Large-size mixing bowl

Small-size mixing bowl

Heavy-duty aluminum foil

Jon Gresham, Lubbock, Texas
Scoutmaster, Troop 505, South Plains Council, Boy Scouts of America

Zealand Falls Apple Pork Loin

Servings: 10–12 | Challenge Level: Moderate

"I like to make this recipe for the troop when we go up to New Hampshire each summer. We stay at the state-owned Dolly Copp Campground in White Mountains National Forest. Some in our group hike the Daniel Webster Scout Trail while others climb the Zealand Falls Trail to the Appalachian Mountain Club hut. When we return, we go for a swim in the Peabody River swimming hole, and afterwards, I prepare the fire and meal. The last time we went to the White Mountains, the air temperature was in the 80s but the river was at 48 degrees and Tuckerman's Ravine on Mount Washington still had 6 feet of snow at the end of June!"

1 pork loin, approximately 5 pounds

2 apples

1 bunch fresh rosemary

10 carrots

10 small red potatoes

2 red onions

Salt and ground black pepper to taste

Preparation at Camp:

1. Tear off seven large sheets of heavy duty aluminum foil, each sheet long enough to wrap completely around the pork loin and vegetables. Stack the sheets of foil.

2. Place meat, fat-side up, on stack of foil. Butterfly the loin by cutting the meat lengthwise from end-to-end but not all the way through.

3. Cut apples into ¼-inch slices and lay them inside the butterflied portion of the loin. Pull sprigs of rosemary off the bunch and lay them inside the pork loin as well.

4. Peel the carrots and place them alongside the loin. Arrange the potatoes around the loin with the carrots. Slice the onions and lay them over the meat. Sprinkle salt and black pepper over the top.

5. Wrap the foil, one sheet at a time, completely around the entire meal. Carefully seal each sheet of foil tightly around the edges. A tight seal is necessary for the loin to cook evenly throughout.

6. Place the foil package, loin fat-side up, directly onto the hot embers of your charcoal or wood fire, but not on the flames.

7. Cook for 10–15 minutes per pound. Note that the actual cooking time can vary considerably depending on the size and type of campfire. About the time you expect the meal to be ready, measure meat temperature using a thermometer. Check the temperature only as the loin approaches completion, as each hole poked through the foil package by the thermometer will permit steam to escape, slowing the cooking process.

8. Once the internal temperature of the loin reaches 160 degrees F, turn the package over to brown the fat-side for the last 5 minutes of cooking time.

9. Remove package from embers, carefully open foil to avoid escaping steam, and let the feast begin!

Required Equipment:

Heavy-duty aluminum foil

Jim Quirk, Charlestown, Rhode Island
Assistant Scoutmaster, Troop 15, Narragansett Council, Boy Scouts of America

Camp Kootaga Chicken Stix

Servings: 12 (2 sticks per serving) | Challenge Level: Easy

"Kootaga is Allohak Council's summer camp. 'Kootaga' means 'good friends,' and was the name given by a Kiowa Indian who helped with the camp program in 1929."

24 chicken thighs (about 10 pounds)

1 (12-ounce) bottle soy sauce

1 cup water

½ cup canola oil

1 cup brown sugar

¼ cup minced fresh ginger

¼ cup minced fresh garlic

1 teaspoon cinnamon

1 teaspoon Chinese spice mix

1 teaspoon crushed hot chili peppers

Preparation at Camp:

1. Remove skin and bones from chicken thighs. Cut meat into 1-inch cubes. Set aside.

2. In a large-size container or extra-large ziplock freezer bag, mix all remaining ingredients into a marinade.

3. Place meat cubes into the marinade. Ensure that chicken is well-coated.

4. Seal container and chill, marinating meat for at least 4 hours, stirring occasionally.

5. Slide meat onto bamboo skewers.

6. Cook for 10–15 minutes on grill or over open fire, turning as required to prevent burning. Meat is ready to serve once it becomes white throughout, with no hint of pink.

Required Equipment:

Large-size covered container of shape that will fit in cooler, or extra-large ziplock freezer bag

24 9-inch bamboo skewers

Tips: This is a great meal to prepare at home in advance. Cube the meat at home and place in ziplock bags with marinade sauce. Set bags in cooler. The longer the meat marinates, the better the flavor. Skewer the chicken cubes at camp when ready to cook. Note that Chinese spice mix can be found in the spice rack at your grocer.

Michael Zorn, West Union, West Virginia
Scoutmaster, Troop 1030 / Cubmaster, Pack 4030, Allohak Council, Boy Scouts of America

Cornell Barbecued Chicken

Servings: 12 | Challenge Level: Easy

"This is a classic dish used for fundraising by volunteer fire departments and church groups throughout Central New York. The recipe was developed in the Department of Poultry Science at Cornell University. It is usually served with baked potatoes, corn, and macaroni salad."

Preparation at Camp:

1. In a medium-size bowl, beat the egg, and add remaining ingredients except chicken. Blend well.

2. Cover the chicken with the egg marinade in gallon-size ziplock plastic bags or in a large-size covered bowl. Allow the chicken to absorb the marinade for at least 1 hour, preferably longer, in a chilled cooler or refrigerator.

3. Remove the chicken pieces from the marinade and arrange on grill over high heat. Every 5–10 minutes, turn chicken with tongs and baste with more marinade sauce.

4. Cook until a fork can easily pierce the flesh, revealing no remaining trace of pink meat. This will typically take 25 minutes to 1 hour, depending on the cooking temperature and height of chicken above the flames.

1 egg

1 cup vegetable oil

2 cups cider vinegar

3 tablespoons salt

1 tablespoon poultry seasoning

1 teaspoon ground black pepper

12 chicken quarters, with or without skin

Required Equipment:

Medium-size mixing bowl
Gallon-size ziplock plastic bags or large-size covered bowl

Ken Harbison, Rochester, New York
Former Boy Scout, Washington Trail Council, Boy Scouts of America

Judy Harbison, Rochester, New York
Lifetime Member, Genesee Valley Council, Girl Scouts of the USA

Sleeping Giant Maple Chicken Kabobs

Servings: 4 | Challenge Level: Easy

"This recipe won the Sleeping Giant District Scoutmaster Cook-Off in May 2002. Caution: When I first prepared these, they were an instant hit. Keep a spatula handy to fend off hungry scouts!"

2 pounds chicken breasts

1 cup pure maple syrup

⅔ cup chili sauce

½ cup minced onion

2 tablespoons spicy brown mustard

2 teaspoons Worcestershire sauce

¼ teaspoon red pepper flakes

Preparation at Home:

1. Slice chicken breasts into strips.

2. In a large-size ziplock freezer bag, combine remaining ingredients.

3. Reserve and refrigerate about 3/4 cup of mixture in its own ziplock freezer bag or container for eventually basting the kabobs at camp.

4. Add chicken to main bag of mixture. Seal and shake to ensure chicken is coated in the marinade. Refrigerate, occasionally turning the bag to allow mixture to coat and absorb into chicken.

Preparation at Camp:

1. Thread marinated chicken onto bamboo skewers.

2. Grill chicken kabobs over medium heat, turning occasionally for 10 minutes.

3. Coat kabobs with more marinade mixture prepared earlier at home.

4. Cook for an additional 5–8 minutes, spreading more sauce onto chicken and turning frequently. Serve once juice runs clear and chicken is no longer pink inside.

Required Equipment:

4 12-inch bamboo skewers

Michael Gagne, Wallingford, Connecticut
Scoutmaster, Troop 1, Connecticut Yankee Council, Boy Scouts of America

Poor Man's Chicken Cordon Blue

Servings: 1–2 / Multiply as Required | Challenge Level: Moderate

Preparation at Camp:

1. In a small-size bowl, whisk egg and set aside.

2. Place bread crumbs on a small piece of aluminum foil and set aside.

3. Pound chicken until soft.

4. Lay slice of cheese and slice of ham on the inner side of the chicken breast. Roll the chicken around both.

5. Dip the chicken in the whisked egg, then roll in bread crumbs.

6. Grease a second sheet of aluminum foil with vegetable oil. The foil sheet must be large enough to wrap and tightly seal the meat. Place chicken on foil.

7. Scoop cream of mushroom soup over top of chicken, and pour any remaining egg over chicken as well.

8. Close foil so that chicken is sealed tightly.

9. Cook chicken on grill or over coals for 20–30 minutes. Chicken is ready to serve once internal temperature reaches 170 degrees F.

Required Equipment:

Small-size mixing bowl
Heavy-duty aluminum foil

1 egg

2 tablespoons Italian flavored bread crumbs

1 boneless skinless chicken breast

1 slice Swiss cheese

1 slice ham

1 teaspoon vegetable oil

3 tablespoons condensed cream of mushroom soup

Paula Perry, Richmond Hill, Georgia
Former Brownie, Girl Scouts of Southwest Georgia Council, Girl Scouts of the USA

Puyallup Planked Salmon

Servings: 1 / Multiply as Required | Challenge Level: Moderate

"The rugged Puyallup River in Washington takes its name from the Native Americans who live near the river to this day. Long ago, the Puyallup natives of the Northwest taught Europeans how to cook fish on sticks or planks, instead of boiling. This remains a popular method of cooking salmon in the area."

6- to 8-ounce salmon fillet or steak

½ teaspoon olive oil

½ teaspoon powdered barbecue, jerk, or Cajun seasoning

Preparation at Camp:

1. Wash and rinse the wood shingle or plank, then soak it in water for at least 1 hour.

2. Prepare salmon by lightly rubbing both sides with olive oil and heavily sprinkling one side with seasoning. Add seasoning to the skinless side if using fillets.

3. Heat one side of the plank or shingle over flame or coals until it smokes lightly, about 3 minutes.

4. Remove plank from the grill using tongs, turn hot-side up, and immediately place salmon on the browned side of the wood, with the seasoning side of the fish facing up. If using fillets, the skin side would be placed on the wood, with the thickest part of the fillet on the thinnest end of shingle.

5. Return the plank immediately to the grill and cover with lid. If your grill does not have a cover, an aluminum steam table pan can be placed upside down over the fish. The pan reflects the heat back onto the top of the fish, allowing it to properly bake.

6. Cook until the fish meat is opaque and easily flaked with a fork. As an example, about 10 minutes is required for 1-inch meat thickness cooked over high heat. If using a thermometer, cook until internal temperature is at least 145 degrees F.

Required Equipment:

Untreated cedar wood shingle or plank
Aluminum steam table pan (if grill has no lid)

Caution: In the unlikely event that the plank catches fire, carefully spray wood with water to douse, being careful to stay far enough away from the flames to avoid flare-up. Lower grill temperature to prevent reoccurrence.

Tips: Be certain that the wood has not been treated with preservatives. If shingles are not available, planks may be cut in 10- to 12-inch lengths from 1x6 cedar lumber. Do not use other types of wood, such as pine, which will impart a turpentine flavor to your fish. Prepackaged cedar grilling planks may be found at grocery stores.

Ken Harbison, Rochester, New York
Former Boy Scout, Washington Trail Council, Boy Scouts of America

Judy Harbison, Rochester, New York
Lifetime Member, Genesee Valley Council, Girl Scouts of the USA

Scout Leader's Casserole

Servings: 6–8 | Challenge Level: Moderate

"This foil dinner can be made using a variety of different cuts and types of meat, including bacon, hamburger, ham, or sirloin steak. The vegetables can also be substituted with nearly any other variety. The possibilities are endless!"

1 pound meat (your choice)

1 large onion, sliced into ¼-inch thick circles

2 green chili peppers, seeds removed and sliced into long strips

4 large potatoes, cut into ¼-inch slices

4 yellow squash, cut into ¼-inch slices

2 cups grated cheese (your choice)

Salt and ground black pepper to taste

Preparation at Camp:

1. Stack two large pieces of heavy-duty aluminum foil, each about 3x1½ feet in size.

2. Place meat in center of foil and cover with onions, chili peppers, potatoes, and squash. Top with cheese. Occasionally sprinkle salt and black pepper on vegetables while they are being layered.

3. Fold foil over the ingredients, tightly rolling the edges together, but forming a large air pocket over the top of the meat and vegetables.

4. Grill using medium heat for about 25 minutes or until potatoes are soft. If thick slices of meat are used, ensure doneness with a food thermometer.

Required Equipment:

Heavy-duty aluminum foil

Sheila Cook, Midland, Texas
Former Committee Chair, Troop 19, Buffalo Trail Council, Boy Scouts of America

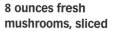

Hilltop Juicy Chicken Packets

Servings: 6 | Challenge Level: Moderate

"This recipe makes super-moist chicken. It's easy to eat from its own packet after cooking and makes little mess. The name originates from the school that our Pack has adopted for our ongoing service project: Hilltop Elementary of Argyle, Texas."

Preparation at Camp:

1. Cut heavy-duty aluminum foil into six sheets, each approximately 12x18 inches in size.

2. Layer mushrooms, beans, and minced garlic in the center of each foil sheet, dividing equally among each.

3. Lay one chicken breast over the mushrooms and beans on each sheet, sprinkling meat with seasoning to taste.

4. Finally, top each piece of chicken with two orange slices, and drizzle with butter and orange juice concentrate.

5. Bring edges of each foil packet together, sealing the ends well. Place packets on a grill over medium to high heat.

6. Cook for about 20–25 minutes or until meat is no longer pink and the juices run clear. Internal temperature of chicken must reach 170 degrees F before serving.

Required Equipment:

Heavy-duty aluminum foil

8 ounces fresh mushrooms, sliced

2 (15-ounce) cans pinto beans, drained

1½ teaspoons minced garlic

6 boneless, skinless chicken breast halves

Grill seasoning or salt and pepper to taste

12 orange slices (approximately 1 orange)

2 tablespoons butter, melted

6 tablespoons frozen orange juice concentrate, thawed

Option: Goes great with grilled garlic bread!

Susanne Fillhart, Argyle, Texas
Den Leader, Pack 192, Longhorn Council, Boy Scouts of America

Sky Meadow Teriyaki Kabobs

Servings: 12 (2 kabobs per serving) | Challenge Level: Moderate

12 boneless chicken breasts (about 6 pounds), cut into 1-inch cubes

1 (10-ounce) bottle teriyaki sauce

3 bell peppers, cut into 1-inch squares

3 zucchini, sliced into 8 rounds each

1 pint cherry tomatoes

2 red onions, with thick slices further cut into 1-inch squares

1 large pineapple, cut into 1-inch cubes

½ cup olive oil

Preparation at Camp:

1. In a gallon-size or larger ziplock freezer bags, combine cubed chicken and teriyaki sauce. Marinate in an ice chest for at least 2 hours.

2. Placed drained marinated chicken in a large-size bowl. Add sliced vegetables to a medium-size mixing bowl and cubed pineapple to another.

3. Allow each scout to carefully assemble their own kabob on a bamboo skewer using meat, vegetables, and pineapple.

4. Spread a thin coat of olive oil over each kabob.

5. Place kabobs on grill approximately 4–6 inches over flames or coals. Grill at medium heat for approximately 15–20 minutes or until chicken is thoroughly cooked.

Required Equipment:

Gallon-size or larger ziplock freezer bags
1 large-size mixing bowl
2 medium-size mixing bowls
24 12-inch bamboo skewers

Millie Hutchison, Pittsburgh, Pennsylvania
Girl Scout Trainer, Trillium Council, Girl Scouts of the USA

Jones 828 Chicken Vegetable Rice

Servings: 4–5 | Challenge Level: Easy

"My friend, Vicki Jones of Troop 828 in Sugar Land, Texas, created this dish."

Preparation at Home:

1. Package dry rice and parsley in small-size ziplock freezer bag.

2. Dehydrate chicken and vegetables.

3. Place dried chicken, dried vegetables, and remainder of ingredients in separate gallon-size ziplock freezer bag.

Preparation on Trail:

1. Add water to gallon-size ziplock bag containing chicken, vegetables, and seasonings. Reseal bag and knead contents. Set aside for about 30 minutes while food rehydrates.

2. Pour rehydrated chicken and vegetable mixture into medium-size cook pot. Bring to a boil while stirring.

3. Reduce heat to a simmer then continue to cook for an additional 5 minutes or until tender.

4. Stir in rice and parsley mixture from small-size ziplock bag. Cover and cook for an additional 5–10 minutes or until rice is tender.

Required Equipment:

Medium-size cook pot

1½ cups Minute Rice

1 tablespoon dried parsley

1 pound canned chicken

2 pounds frozen soup vegetables (such as Bird's Eye)

2 tablespoons dried onion flakes

3 cubes chicken bouillon

¼ teaspoon ground black pepper

5½ cups water

Katie Salyer Cox, Tucson, Arizona
Leader and Trainer, USA Girl Scouts Overseas and Sahuaro Council, Girl Scouts of the USA

Trinchera Peak Noodles Alfredo

Servings: 3–4 | Challenge Level: Easy

"This recipe can be cooked with or without the chicken and is quick to prepare on a backpacking trip. I invented it for an excursion in Colorado near Trinchera Peak."

2 (4.7-ounce) packages fettuccine Alfredo–flavored Pasta Roni

1 pound canned chicken, dehydrated

½ pound frozen peas, dehydrated

½ pound grated carrots, dehydrated

¼ cup low-fat powdered milk

2 tablespoons Butter Buds

6 cups water

Preparation at Home:

1. Pour fettuccine noodles in a small-size ziplock freezer bag.

2. Place dried chicken, dried vegetables, seasoning mix from Pasta Roni packages, powdered milk, and Butter Buds in a gallon-size ziplock freezer bag.

Preparation on Trail:

1. Add water to the gallon-size ziplock bag, then knead. Set aside to rehydrate for about 30 minutes.

2. Pour rehydrated chicken and vegetable mixture into a medium cook pot.

3. Bring contents to a boil, then reduce heat to a simmer. Continue to cook for an additional 5 minutes or until chicken and vegetables are tender.

4. Add noodles. Continue cooking 5–10 minutes until pasta is slightly firm, stirring frequently.

5. Do not overcook. The sauce for the noodles will be thin. Remove from heat and let stand 3–5 minutes for the sauce to thicken before serving.

Required Equipment:

Medium-size cook pot

Katie Salyer Cox, Tucson, Arizona
Leader and Trainer, USA Girl Scouts Overseas and Sahuaro Council, Girl Scouts of the USA

Backpacker's Beef Stew

Servings: 4–6 | Challenge Level: Moderate

Preparation at Home:

1. Cut beef into small pieces, roll in gravy mix powder, and seal in ziplock freezer bags. (Putting the beef in small ziplock bags will allow it to thaw more rapidly when cooking, and you'll find it easier to pack in an insulated bag.)

2. Pour stewed tomatoes with their juice along with the drained mushrooms into a single ziplock freezer bag. Place butter in its own ziplock bag.

3. Freeze the ziplock bags of meat, vegetables, and butter until solid.

4. As you leave for your backpack trip, pack your frozen ingredients in an insulated bag, filling any extra space with small ziplock freezer bags filled with ice. (Using this method, meat can stay frozen until the second night on a two-day backpacking trip, even during summer.)

5. Pack the remainder of the items separately.

Preparation on Trail:

1. Cut potatoes into cubes and chop onion.

2. Melt butter in a pot at least 2½ quarts in size. Sauté onions in melted butter, then brown the meat.

3. Add potatoes, mushrooms and tomatoes, beef stew seasoning to taste, and 1½ cups water.

4. Bring to a boil, then cover and lower heat to a simmer.

5. Stir often to keep from burning. Stew is ready to serve once potatoes soften and meat is cooked through.

Required Equipment:

Cook pot, with a minimum capacity of 2½ quarts, and preferably with nonstick coating

1 pound stew beef

1 (1-ounce) package beef gravy mix

1 (14½-ounce) can stewed tomatoes

1 (13¼-ounce) can cut mushrooms, drained

¼ cup (½ standard stick) butter

4 medium potatoes

1 small onion

1 (1½-ounce) packet powdered beef stew seasoning (use to taste)

1½ cups water

Option: Refrigerated biscuits make a great addition to this recipe. They can be added to the top of the stew inside the covered pot for the last 15 minutes of cooking time, or they can be divided into dough balls and dropped into the stew to cook as dumplings.

Frederick Smith, Lynchburg, Virginia
Assistant Scoutmaster, Troop 10, Blue Ridge Mountain Council, Boy Scouts of America

Clingmans Dome Pasta Primavera

Servings: 2 / Multiply as Required | Challenge Level: Moderate

"My backpacking buddy, Will, and I once pulled an 8-mile climb up Sugarland Mountain to the Mount Collins shelter, north of Clingmans Dome in Great Smoky Mountains National Park. While the other hikers endured the jet-engine drone of their gasoline burners, we retired to a peaceful site away from the shelter and fired up our silent alcohol stove. As dusk gathered, Will watched while I simmered the primavera. We then ate like kings!"

1 (4.3-ounce) package Lipton Alfredo Pasta Sides

⅔ cup nonfat powdered milk

¼ teaspoon garlic salt

½ teaspoon dried oregano

2 cups dehydrated vegetable mix (see directions)

2 tablespoons olive oil

2 cups water

½ head of broccoli, cut into florets

½ sweet red pepper, cut into thin 1-inch strips

½ red onion, thinly sliced

1 medium yellow squash, sliced into thin rounds

½ pound fresh mushrooms, sliced

Preparation at Home:

1. Empty the noodle mix into a quart-size ziplock bag, and add the powdered milk, garlic salt, and dried oregano.

2. Store the dehydrated vegetables in a separate quart-size ziplock bag, and place both bags inside a gallon-size freezer bag to keep the meal organized.

3. Package the olive oil in a small, unbreakable plastic bottle with screw-top lid.

Three options for preparing the vegetables for this recipe:

A. Dry fresh vegetables per the ingredients list.

B. Dehydrate a 1-pound bag of mixed vegetables, such as a California or Oriental stir-fry blend, adding 2 tablespoons of dried onion flakes once dehydrated.

C. Purchase the vegetables already dehydrated.

Preparation on Trail:

1. At your lunch break, begin rehydrating the vegetables by pouring the bag of dried vegetables into a wide-mouthed watertight bottle, adding water to cover. Alternatively, cover the vegetables in the ziplock bag with water, using a double-bag to ensure it doesn't leak.

2. When ready to eat later in the day, place the vegetables and the water used for rehydration into a small-size cook pot. Add additional water to bring total to approximately 2 cups. Pour in olive oil and bring mixture to a boil.

3. Add the noodle mix, then stir well. Reduce heat to a simmer. Continue cooking for an additional 8–10 minutes, stirring frequently. The mixture should still be a little soupy.

4. Cover the pot and set aside for about 10 minutes, if you can stand to wait that long!

Required Equipment:

Small-size cook pot

Bill Griffin, Elkin, North Carolina
Treasurer, Troop 654, Old Hickory Council, Boy Scouts of America

Horgan's Hiking Chicken Ramen

Servings: 4–5 | Challenge Level: Moderate

"Debbie Horgan, of Troop 828 in Sugar Land, Texas, was the originator of this delicious backpacking recipe."

1 (10-ounce) can condensed cream of chicken soup

1 pound canned chicken

1 pound frozen green beans or peas

1 (1-ounce) envelope Lipton's onion soup mix

⅓ cup nonfat powdered milk

2 (3-ounce) packages ramen-style noodles (discard the seasoning packets)

1 tablespoon slivered almonds

5 cups water

Preparation at Home:

1. Dry cream of chicken soup in a food dehydrator on either parchment paper or a plastic dehydrator tray.

2. Package dehydrated soup in a small ziplock freezer bag.

3. Dry canned chicken and vegetables in food dehydrator.

4. Package dehydrated chicken meat and vegetables along with onion soup mix and powdered milk in a gallon-size ziplock freezer bag.

5. Place ramen noodles in a separate quart-size ziplock freezer bag.

6. Store almonds in a snack bag.

Preparation on Trail:

1. Empty the dehydrated chicken soup into the gallon-size ziplock bag containing chicken and vegetables.

2. Add water to the gallon-size bag, then knead. Set aside for about 30 minutes to rehydrate.

3. Pour the rehydrated mix into medium-size cook pot. Bring to a boil, stirring constantly.

4. Reduce heat to a simmer and continue to cook for an additional 5 minutes.

5. Add ramen noodles to the pot. Stir and cook for an additional 5 minutes or until mixture is thick and tender.

6. Garnish with slivered almonds and serve.

Required Equipment:

Medium-size cook pot

Katie Salyer Cox, Tucson, Arizona
Leader and Trainer, USA Girl Scouts Overseas and Sahuaro Council, Girl Scouts of the USA

Best Darned Corn Bread

Servings: 10–12 | Challenge Level: Easy

"This recipe earned its name by winning awards at both Camp Yawgoog and Camp Cachalot. So infamous has this corn bread become, rangers will stop by for a slice when they know our unit is camping. My scouts insist on having this on every outing because they know it's the Best Darned Corn Bread!"

Preparation at Camp:

1. Mix all ingredients in a well-greased Dutch oven.

2. Using 17 coals on the lid and 8 briquettes under the oven, bake for about 45 minutes. Once the top of the bread turns golden brown, it is ready to serve.

Required Equipment:

12-inch Dutch oven

4 (6½-ounce) packages Betty Crocker corn bread mix

8 eggs

1 (14-ounce) can sweetened condensed milk

1 (15-ounce) can sweet creamed corn (do not drain)

Option: When camping in an area where wild blueberries are ripe and plentiful, gather about a cupful and add to the mix, baking as usual. This brings the taste to new heights!

Michael Thomas, Rehoboth, Massachusetts
Scoutmaster, Troop 13, Narragansett Council, Boy Scouts of America

Sweet Oregon Trail Corn Bread

Servings: 6–8 | Challenge Level: Easy

1 cup coarse ground cornmeal

2 cups all-purpose flour

1 tablespoon baking powder

¾ cup sugar

¾ teaspoon salt

¾ teaspoon baking soda

¼ cup powdered buttermilk or powdered milk

2 tablespoons pumpkin pie spice

2 eggs

6 tablespoons shortening

1½ cups water

Preparation at Camp:

1. Combine all dry ingredients in a large bowl. Add eggs and cut in the shortening, then stir in the water. Mix well.

2. Pour corn bread mixture into Dutch oven.

3. Place 11 coals under the oven in a ring, just inside the edge of the base. Place 20 briquettes on the lid in a ring along the outer edge. Add 2 more to middle of the lid near the handle.

4. Bake for 35–45 minutes, about the time you should begin to notice the aroma.

5. Insert a toothpick or fork in the center of bread. If dough sticks, replace lid and bake for an additional 10 minutes. If toothpick or fork comes out clean, bread is ready to serve.

Tip: Three tablespoons cornstarch can be substituted for the two eggs.

Optional Cooking Methods:

The following are inexact methods, but good for kids as this is a bread forgiving of youthful mistakes, and the use of unusual cooking utensils appeals to kids' sense of self-sufficiency.

Pie-Pan-Over-Coals Method: Fill an aluminum pie pan with ⅔ of the above corn bread mix. Cover with a second inverted pie pan and fasten together with two clips. Use a grate to keep coals about one inch from bottom of pan. Add as many coals on the top pan as it will hold. Refresh top coals every 20 minutes or so as a lot of heat is required to brown the corn bread. The bread will take about 1 hour to bake.

Pot Method: The above pie-pan method can be adapted to any style pot. While a top heat source is not absolutely necessary to cook corn bread, a top lid is.

Johnny Cake Method: Dough can be cooked like pancakes over a hot buttered griddle.

Required Equipment:

12-inch Dutch oven
Large-size mixing bowl

Will Satak, Dallas, Oregon
Former Guidance and Merit Badge Counselor, Baden-Powell Council, Boy Scouts of America

Hungry Hunter's Basic Bread Recipe

Servings: 8–10 | Challenge Level: Moderate

"About twenty years ago, I was at my hunting spot in an old gold claim camp in Eastern Washington, cooking in anticipation of the arrival of my sons. We were to go hunting the next morning. I was baking bread in a 12-inch Dutch, and it was to last us the entire trip. I had camped close to the road so as to be easier for my sons to find after the sun set.

It was getting on about dark and I saw a hunter coming up the road. He asked what I was cooking. 'Bread,' I replied. 'You don't say?' he said. 'By the looks of that oven, that may be the biggest loaf I'll ever see.' I had just started the bread on its baking journey, so I told him he would have to wait about half an hour. He said he would go to his camp to clean up and then come back. Well, he did return, and by the time he did, the bread was starting to smell pretty good. And then, wouldn't you know, a few more hunters had come down out of the bush and were walking along the road to their camp. 'Hey!' they shouted to me, 'That smells just like homemade bread!' 'Come on over and see for yourself,' I replied. I put on my gloves and turned the loaf out on the camp grill. It was 12 inches in diameter and about four inches tall, brown and crunchy. I said it would have to cool some, but they were welcome to a slice. They left, promising to be back, as three more men hove into camp asking what that great aroma was. I said, 'I think you know what it is, so come on in and, yes, you too can have a slice when it cools a bit more.'

All were present as I prepared the bread for serving. Each had a knife and a plate. We talked about the prospects of hunting the next day and made other polite conversation. I remember it as polite because hunt camp discussions can be fairly rough. However, you would have thought these men were sitting in church, such was their reverence for a homemade loaf. Shortly, the bread was deemed cool enough. What followed was awe inspiring. The men with butter shared with those who had none, and all were very quiet. The slices were gently buttered. Each bite was very carefully chosen, slowly chewed and savored. Of course, I had to offer a second slice after they showed such respect. It goes without saying that we ate all of that loaf, and, in the process went through a pound of butter. On top of that, I believe we all made some new friends.

I went hunting the next morning to no avail. I probably smelled like yeast. Early that afternoon, I made two loaves. One of the hunters went to town and bought 5 pounds of butter and 25 pounds of flour as a gift for me. We, ten of us, ate bread together after the hunt, each night, for four days. I have never met a more polite and circumspect group of men, in a hunt camp, or anywhere else."

Preparation at Camp:

1. Mix dry ingredients in a large bowl.

2. Add water. Stir until too stiff to mix, then knead by hand for 10 minutes. When finished, dough should be soft and a bit sticky. Add small amounts of flour, while kneading, to adjust as required.

3. Form dough into a smooth-skinned ball and place in a greased 12-inch Dutch oven. It is important that the Dutch oven isn't cold. Preheat, if required, but only enough to take the chill out of the metal.

4. Turn the ball over so entire dough ball becomes oiled.

5. Cover oven and place two coals on lid near edge.

6. Let the dough rise until doubled in bulk, about 45–60 minutes. During this time, keep the oven warm but not hot. The dough ball should fill the oven.

7. Once the dough ball doubles, gently press it down to de-gas it. Remove the dough, and carefully form it back into a smooth ball.

8. Return the dough to the warm oven, and gently press it down to help the dough fill the oven evenly.

9. Replace lid, setting 2 hot coals on lid near edge.

10. Allow the dough to again rise to about twice its bulk. It should now fill the oven nearly to the lid. This will take an additional 30–45 minutes, depending on the temperature of the dough and oven. Don't add too much heat in an effort to hurry the process.

11. Once dough has nearly reached the lid, place 11 fresh hot coals under the oven in a ring, just inside the edge of the base. Place 21 briquettes on the lid in a ring along the outer edge. Place 2 more in the middle of the lid near the handle.

12. Once you can smell the bread, it is almost finished baking, about 35–45 minutes. Take a peek at 35 minutes to see if top is browned.

8 cups all-purpose flour, loosely filled, plus extra for working

3 teaspoons salt

5 teaspoons (two standard packets) rapid-rise yeast

3 cups water, warmed to between 120 and 130 degrees F

Butter to taste

13. Bread is finished baking once inside temperature reaches 185 degrees F, but even then, the top may not be as brown as you like. If this is the case, add more coals to the lid and bake for a few more minutes to darken the crust.

14. Tip the bread out of the oven onto a rack or grate that will allow air circulation under the loaf.

15. Let bread cool for about 45 minutes to improve the flavor.

16. Slice and serve with copious amounts of butter.

Required Equipment:

12-inch Dutch oven
Cooling rack or grate
Large-size mixing bowl

Bread Rising Tips: Getting dough to rise can be tricky business. Yeast likes warmth. The fast-rise yeasts won't activate properly if cold liquids, cold pans, cold flour, or a cold oven is used. Start by using water that is between 120 and 130 degrees F. In the woods, you can expect to need to pre-warm everything. Very hot water should be used to preheat the mixing bowl; and if the flour is cold, it should be mixed with the hot water before adding the yeast. Do not use a cold table or board for kneading the dough. Kneading with cold hands will also cool the dough. And, of course, if left in a cool place to rise, the yeast will hibernate and the dough will rise very slowly, if at all. Make sure your oven is warm before placing dough in it. If it is hot outside, you may not need any coals to preheat the oven. If it is windy, a windbreak may be required to keep the dough from becoming cool while it is rising.

Will Satak, Dallas, Oregon
Former Guidance and Merit Badge Counselor, Baden-Powell Council, Boy Scouts of America

Grandma's Sweet Hungarian Orange Bread

Servings: 8–10 | Challenge Level: Moderate

"Grandma was an amazing cook, and no one could duplicate her recipes. At the age of ten, I asked her how she made my favorite dishes and she explained it to me. As I wrote down her instructions, I realized I had a lot to learn. I later compiled the recipes into a handwritten book as a fifth-grade homework project. I saved that book. Her Magyar Hungarian words I translated many years ago, but it has taken all this time for me to mostly decipher the measurements. Grandma did not know the English words for everything—or maybe she was just testing how badly I wanted those recipes."

Preparation at Camp:

1. In a large-size bowl, combine flour, baking powder, baking soda, salt, sugars, poppy seeds, eggs, and powdered milk. Mix well.

2. Add orange extract and shortening. Cut in the shortening with forks, fingers, or a pastry blender.

3. Add zest, orange juice, and water. Mix well.

4. Preheat a lightly greased Dutch oven for a few minutes using 19 coals on the lid and 8 briquettes in a ring just under the edge of the base of the oven.

5. Pour bread batter into the oven.

6. Arrange coals on the lid in a ring around the raised edge rim. Do not place coals in the center of the lid unless required for browning.

7. Bake for 30–40 minutes or until top of bread becomes golden brown.

Required Equipment:

12-inch Dutch oven
Large-size mixing bowl

Tip: Six tablespoons cornstarch can be substituted for the four eggs.

4 cups all-purpose flour

1 tablespoon baking powder

½ teaspoon baking soda

1 teaspoon salt

1 cup granulated sugar

⅔ cup brown sugar

¼ cup poppy seeds

4 eggs

¼ cup powdered milk

1 tablespoon orange extract

1 cup solid shortening

Zest from 2 oranges (shred outer, colored rind before juicing)

1⅓ cups orange juice (about 4–5 oranges)

1 cup water

Will Satak, Dallas, Oregon
Former Guidance and Merit Badge Counselor, Baden-Powell Council, Boy Scouts of America

Prospector's Sourdough Starter

"I recently introduced my scouts to the art of sourdough cooking. Authentic sourdough requires a yeast and bacteria culture known as a 'starter.' It's what gives the baked goods their unique and great taste. The boys love it because they can watch the starter grow and turn bubbly during the course of the week. It's like a science project in the kitchen. It freaks the scouts out when they contemplate eventually eating something that has sat on the counter so long, rising and falling in the container several times as if it were alive. The strong sour odor certainly doesn't help!

The art of sourdough baking is deeply rooted in American history. Chuck wagon cooks were often judged by the quality of their sourdough starter. (For fun, I usually embellish this story a little, adding that a bad starter could get a cook shot.) This type of cooking was so popular during the gold rush of the 1800s that 'sourdough' was a common nickname for prospectors. That explains why the mascot for the San Francisco 49ers professional football team is a prospector named 'Sourdough Sam'!"

The following forms the foundation for all sourdough recipes in this book. The starter can be prepared at home and then brought to camp.

2½ cups all-purpose flour

2½ cups warm water

½ package active dry yeast

1 teaspoon sugar

Preparation at Home:

1. Combine flour, water, yeast, and sugar in a non-metallic bowl.

2. Let stand in a warm (room temperature) area, covered with a dish towel, for 24 hours.

3. Next, loosely cover the container with plastic wrap and allow the starter to stand, unrefrigerated, until sour. This should take 4 or 5 days. Stir down the bubbles occasionally.

4. The starter can now be used according to your specific recipe. As the starter is expended, replenish it with equal parts of flour and water. No additional yeast is required.

Important Starter Tips:

If the sourdough starter is used frequently, two or more times each week, it is unlikely to require refrigeration. Replenish the starter as required, using equal parts water and flour, and add 1 teaspoon of sugar each week. Keep it loosely covered.

If you plan on using the sourdough starter on a less frequent basis, keep it covered in the refrigerator. When time to use the starter, remove it from the refrigerator the night before to allow the culture to begin growing again. At this point, there are two choices. The first is to add ½ cup of flour and an equal amount of warm water to the starter, stir it, and allow to double in size, about 12 hours, before using. The second is to stir the starter once it is removed from the refrigerator; in a separate bowl, mix flour and water in amounts specified by your recipe, using the required amount of starter; let rest until it reaches room temperature. The first method will usually tone down the sourdough flavor, whereas the second tends to produce a much stronger flavor. A sourdough starter can be stored in the freezer for up to six months.

When a starter rests for an extended period of time on the counter or in the refrigerator, it may separate, developing a large top layer of liquid called "hooch." As long as the liquid doesn't indicate spoilage, by off-color or foul odor, then stir it back in.

Note that water with high chlorine content should be filtered before use, and metal containers should be avoided. Both chlorine and metal can harm the beneficial yeast and bacteria.

Jamison Yardley, Centerville, Utah
Varsity Scout Coach, Team 6989, Great Salt Lake Council, Boy Scouts of America

Picturesque Lake Sourdough Corn Bread

Servings: 8–10 | Challenge Level: Easy

"Named for the little lake with the best campsite at Camp Steiner!"

¾ cup sourdough starter (see recipe for Prospector's Sourdough Starter)

2 cups all-purpose flour

2 cups cornmeal

½ cup sugar

½ teaspoon baking soda

1 teaspoon salt

2 teaspoons baking powder

3 eggs

1 cup milk

½ cup vegetable oil

½ cup chopped green chilies (optional)

1 cup shredded cheese (optional)

Preparation at Camp:

1. In a large-size bowl, mix together sourdough starter, flour, cornmeal, sugar, baking soda, salt, and baking powder.

2. Mix in eggs, milk, vegetable oil, and optional chilies and shredded cheese.

3. Pour batter into greased Dutch oven.

4. Using 17 coals on the lid and 8 briquettes under the oven, bake for 30–40 minutes or until top becomes golden brown.

Required Equipment:

12-inch Dutch oven
Large-size mixing bowl

Jamison Yardley, Centerville, Utah
Varsity Scout Coach, Team 6989, Great Salt Lake Council, Boy Scouts of America

Cooking brings scouts together.

Learning the fine points of cooking at the fire pit.

Cooking teaches thoroughness.   **Can't find your cook pot? Use the can!**

A roaring fire drives the chill away deep in the High Sierra.

Be prepared . . . to cook in the rain.

Cooking teaches patience.

Cooking teaches resourcefulness.

Cooking teaches creativity.

Salmagundi—a feast fit for a pirate!

Scout Camp Cake—birthday style.

Baking fish the old-fashioned way.

A camp kitchen to be proud of.

Cooking teaches cooperation.

The art of building a campfire.

Be prepared   for smoke in your face!

Dinnertime at 13,000 feet.

Baking cake in a cardboard box.

Dutch oven, 25 buck campsite, and a million dollar view.

High Uintas Sourdough Chocolate Cake

Servings: 6–8 | Challenge Level: Easy

"Named for the Uinta Mountains, the only East-West running mountain range in the United States. It has some of the best backpacking in Utah and is home to several Boy Scout summer camps."

Preparation at Camp:

1. Cream sugar and butter in a large-size bowl.

2. Add and mix other ingredients in the order listed. Beat and stir until smooth.

3. Pour batter into a 9-inch round greased cake pan.

4. Preheat Dutch oven using 17 coals on the lid and 8 briquettes under the oven.

5. Place cake pan on a trivet in the oven and bake for 30–40 minutes or until a knife inserted into the cake comes out clean.

6. Allow to cool. Frost with optional icing or serve with ice cream.

Required Equipment:

12-inch Dutch oven with trivet
Large-size mixing bowl
9-inch round cake pan

1 cup sugar

¼ cup (½ standard stick) butter

2 eggs

1 cup sourdough starter (see recipe for Prospector's Sourdough Starter)

1 cup milk

1 teaspoon vanilla extract

1 teaspoon ground cinnamon

½ cup unsweetened cocoa powder

½ teaspoon salt

1½ teaspoons baking soda

2 cups all-purpose flour

Frosting or ice cream (optional)

Jamison Yardley, Centerville, Utah
Varsity Scout Coach, Team 6989, Great Salt Lake Council, Boy Scouts of America

Bear Lake Sourdough Berry Muffins

Servings: 5–6 | Challenge Level: Easy

"Bear Lake is a scout camp in Utah famous for its wild berries."

2 cups all-purpose flour

½ cup (1 standard stick) butter, melted

½ cup sugar

½ cup milk

¾ cup sourdough starter (see recipe for Prospector's Sourdough Starter)

1 egg

1 cup blueberries

¾ teaspoon baking soda

Preparation at Camp:

1. In a large-size bowl, mix ingredients together in order listed.

2. Over 25 coals, preheat greased Dutch oven for a few minutes.

3. Drop batter, about ¼ cup at a time, in blobs adjacent to each other in bottom of oven. The muffins will touch and bake together, but the indentation lines that form between them will allow easy separation once they've finished baking.

4. Relocate 17 coals to the lid, leaving 8 briquettes under the oven. Bake for 20–25 minutes or until top of muffins become golden brown.

Required Equipment:

12-inch Dutch oven
Large-size mixing bowl

Jamison Yardley, Centerville, Utah
Varsity Scout Coach, Team 6989, Great Salt Lake Council, Boy Scouts of America

Camp Steiner Hot Rock Sourdough Biscuits

Servings: 4–5 | Challenge Level: Moderate

"At 10,300 feet above sea level, Steiner is the highest Boy Scout camp in the United States. And here's a little Old West trivia for you: 'Hot rocks' is cowboy slang for biscuits!"

Preparation at Camp:

1. Combine flour, baking powder, baking soda, salt, and sugar in a large-size bowl. Mix well.

2. Form a crater in center of the flour mix, and pour in the shortening, sourdough starter, and eggs. Mix dough in bowl for several minutes.

3. Roll or press dough out to about ½ inch thickness. Cut the dough using a mason jar lid or other such cutter.

4. Dip cut biscuits in the melted butter, and place close together in warm Dutch oven. Begin on the outside edge and work in toward center of oven.

5. Set aside and let biscuit dough rise for 30–60 minutes.

6. Using 16 coals on the lid and 7 briquettes under the oven, bake for 20–30 minutes or until biscuit tops become a light brown. Rotate oven frequently during cooking to prevent biscuit bottoms from burning.

Required Equipment:

12-inch Dutch oven

Large-size mixing bowl

Biscuit cutter

---

2 cups all-purpose flour, plus extra to work the dough

2 teaspoons baking powder

¼ teaspoon baking soda

½ teaspoon salt

1 tablespoon sugar

¼ cup shortening, melted

1 cup sourdough starter (see recipe for Prospector's Sourdough Starter)

2 eggs, beaten

¼ cup (½ standard stick) butter, melted

Option: If deep golden brown biscuit tops are preferred, remove all the coals from under the oven and place on lid for the last 5 minutes of baking.

Jamison Yardley, Centerville, Utah

Varsity Scout Coach, Team 6989, Great Salt Lake Council, Boy Scouts of America

Hart's Sourdough Apple Dumplings

Servings: 8–10 | Challenge Level: Moderate

"Named for Hart Bullock, longtime Scouter."

Biscuit dough (see recipe for Camp Steiner Hot Rock Sourdough Biscuits)

Extra flour as required to work the dough

1 (21-ounce) can apple pie filling

1 cup sugar

1 teaspoon ground cinnamon

¾ cup water

Preparation at Camp:

1. Prepare biscuit dough according to steps 1 and 2 in Camp Steiner Hot Rock Sourdough Biscuits.

2. Roll biscuit dough into a sheet about 16x10 inches and about ¼ inch thick.

3. Spread apple filling evenly over dough, leaving margin near the edges.

4. Combine sugar and cinnamon, and sprinkle half over the apple filling.

5. From a long end, roll the sheet of dough, jellyroll style, forming a cylinder.

6. Slice dough cylinder into 1 inch-thick slices.

7. Place dough slices side-by-side in Dutch oven.

8. Combine remaining sugar-cinnamon mix with water and pour over dough.

9. Using 17 coals on the lid and 8 briquettes under the oven, bake for 30 minutes or until the water evaporates and the tops are lightly browned.

Required Equipment:

12-inch Dutch oven

Large-size mixing bowl

Jamison Yardley, Centerville, Utah
Varsity Scout Coach, Team 6989, Great Salt Lake Council, Boy Scouts of America

Bear Sign Sourdoughnuts

Servings: About 12 Donuts | Challenge Level: Moderate

"'Bear sign' is cowboy slang for donuts. A 'dough puncher' (i.e., camp cook) who could make bear sign was always held in high esteem."

Preparation at Camp:

1. Prepare biscuit dough according to steps 1 and 2 in Camp Steiner Hot Rock Sourdough Biscuits.

2. Pour canola oil in Dutch oven to a depth of 1 inch.

3. Heat oven over 25 briquettes. If oil begins to smoke, reduce heat by removing some of the coals.

4. Roll dough on a clean floured surface into a sheet about ½ inch thick.

5. Cut circles of dough with the clean open end of a can or glass jar. Cut smaller donut holes inside the circles of dough using a bottle cap or small jar opening.

6. Deep-fry the dough in hot canola oil, turning once.

7. Once dough is cooked through, coat donuts with sugar and cinnamon and serve.

Caution: Frying oil becomes very hot. Do not drop dough into the oven as the hot oil can splatter dangerously. Use sturdy tongs to gently place donuts in oil and to remove them once finished frying.

Required Equipment:

12-inch Dutch oven
Large-size mixing bowl
Large- and small-size cans or jars for cutting donut dough
Tongs

Tips: A large, sturdy cook pot can be used in lieu of the Dutch oven. Used canola oil can be cooled and poured into a large glass jar with a tight fitting lid for later disposal.

Biscuit dough (see recipe for Camp Steiner Hot Rock Sourdough Biscuits)

4 to 6 cups canola oil

1 cup sugar

1 teaspoon cinnamon

Jamison Yardley, Centerville, Utah
Varsity Scout Coach, Team 6989, Great Salt Lake Council, Boy Scouts of America

Dem Thar Hills Sourdough Bread

Servings: 4–5 | Challenge Level: Moderate

"A simple sourdough bread recipe that any prospector can make."

2 cups bread flour, plus extra flour to work the dough

1½ cups sourdough starter (see recipe for Prospector's Sourdough Starter)

½ teaspoon salt

Vegetable oil for greasing bowl and dough ball

Preparation at Camp:

1. In a large bowl, combine the flour, sourdough starter, and salt. Knead well for about 10 minutes.

2. Place dough ball in a lightly oiled bowl and rub with oil. Cover the bowl with plastic wrap and place in a warm place. Let rise for about 1½ hours.

3. Remove dough and gently knead on a lightly floured surface, removing any bubbles.

4. Shape dough into a small flat circle, then form a tight ball by pulling the dough over itself and pinching the seams together underneath.

5. With the dough seam-side down, cover with a dry kitchen towel and allow it to rise a second time in a warm place, about 1 hour.

6. Preheat oven using 17 coals on the lid and 8 briquettes under the oven.

7. With a serrated knife, cut a cross-hatch pattern into the top of the dough.

8. Place dough in oven and bake for about 50–60 minutes or until the bread turns a golden brown. Refresh coals as required.

9. Remove bread from oven and let cool for 30 minutes before serving.

Tip: Periodically rotate the lid and oven base to prevent the bread from developing hot spots.

Required Equipment:

12-inch Dutch oven

Large-size mixing bowl

Plastic wrap

Jamison Yardley, Centerville, Utah
Varsity Scout Coach, Team 6989, Great Salt Lake Council, Boy Scouts of America

3F Banana Bread

Servings: 8–10 | Challenge Level: Moderate

"The '3F' stands for 'Fresh, Fun, and Fantastic'! If you have bananas that are a little too ripe or if they got squished in the backpack during your hiking trip, don't throw them away. A scout is thrifty, so he or she should know these will make a perfect ingredient for 3F Banana Bread!

This recipe won first prize at the Dutch oven cook-off during second summer session at Camp Oljato, California, in 2004."

Preparation at Camp:

1. Peel fresh bananas, removing any stringy veins. Cut bananas into flat round circles and set aside.

2. In a large-size bowl, tear the bread slices into small pieces less than 1 inch on a side. To the bowl, add sweetened condensed milk, melted butter, and milk or water.

3. With clean hands, thoroughly mix the bread pieces until they all stick together. Don't squish them or make them too mushy!

4. Grease Dutch oven with 1 tablespoon butter. Place one-third of bread mix into the oven and spread to cover the bottom. Place one-third of the banana slices on top of the bread mix, arranging slices side-by-side.

5. Repeat the layering pattern: one-third bread, one-third bananas, one-third bread, and, finally, one-third of the bananas.

6. Using 17 coals on the lid and 8 briquettes under the oven, bake for 20–30 minutes or until you notice the fantastic aroma of the cooked bananas and the top layer turning brown.

7. Remove oven from coals and let stand for at least 10 minutes. 3F Banana Bread can be served warm or cold.

6 ripe bananas

1 loaf of bread (your choice)

1 (14-ounce) can sweetened condensed milk

2 tablespoons butter, melted

½ cup milk or water

1 tablespoon butter to grease oven

Required Equipment:

12-inch Dutch oven
Large-size mixing bowl

Giao Quynh Bui-Le, Fremont, California
Committee Chair, Troop 654, Santa Clara County Council, Boy Scouts of America

Grandpa Yardley's Sourdough Pancakes

Servings: 4–6 | Challenge Level: Easy

"My kids call these 'Grandpa Yardley's Pancakes' because my Dad always makes them."

1 cup sourdough starter (see recipe for Prospector's Sourdough Starter)

2 cups all-purpose flour

2 cups milk

2 eggs

1 teaspoon baking soda

3 tablespoons sugar

1 teaspoon salt

2 teaspoons baking powder

1 teaspoon vanilla extract

1 teaspoon vegetable oil

Butter to taste

Maple syrup to taste

Preparation at Camp:

1. In a large bowl, mix together all ingredients except butter and maple syrup.

2. Grease skillet with butter over medium heat. Once butter melts, pour 1/2 cup of batter into skillet. When top of pancake begins to bubble, flip and brown the opposite side.

3. Repeat step 2 until all batter is used.

4. Serve with maple syrup.

Required Equipment:

Large-size frying pan
Large-size mixing bowl

Jamison Yardley, Centerville, Utah
Varsity Scout Coach, Team 6989, Great Salt Lake Council, Boy Scouts of America

Chief Okemos Flat Bread

Servings: 6 | Challenge Level: Easy

Preparation at Camp:

1. Allow dinner roll dough to thaw and rise.

2. Combine olive oil, garlic salt, rosemary, and black pepper in a small-size bowl.

3. Press two rolls together and flatten. Sprinkle both sides with seasoning oil. Repeat for remaining rolls, making a total of six individual pieces.

4. Place bread on a grill over medium heat for 1–2 minutes per side or until bread turns a light brown.

Required Equipment:

Small-size mixing bowl

12 premade frozen dinner rolls

½ cup olive oil

½ teaspoon garlic salt

1 teaspoon rosemary

1 teaspoon ground black pepper

Sally Logan, Leslie, Michigan
Committee Member, Troop 141, Chief Okemos Council, Boy Scouts of America

Bayou City Bread

Servings: 25 | Challenge Level: Easy

"I've been camp cooking since I was 13 years old and have always loved it. One of my favorite camping memories was of baking 48 1-pound loaves of yeast bread in 16 Dutch ovens for a camp-wide dinner."

3 cups old-fashioned oatmeal

4 cups whole wheat flour

2 teaspoons baking powder

½ cup powdered milk

1 tablespoon salt

1 cup light brown sugar

½ teaspoon powdered cinnamon

½ teaspoon nutmeg

2 cups diced mixed dried fruit (your choice)

2 cups diced nuts (your choice)

½ cup vegetable oil

¾ cup honey

⅛ cup molasses

2 cups water

Preparation at Home:

1. In a very large-size bowl, combine oatmeal, flour, baking powder, powdered milk, salt, brown sugar, cinnamon, nutmeg, diced fruits, and diced nuts. Mix thoroughly to ensure there are no clumps.

2. In a separate bowl, whisk together oil, honey, molasses, and water.

3. Fold all ingredients together in the very large-size bowl, adding water as needed to get thick, but still spreadable, dough.

4. Spread dough nearly to edges of a lightly greased 17¼x11 ½-inch cookie sheet.

5. Bake at 300 degrees for 60–70 minutes. Score bread into 2x2-inch squares.

6. For backpacking, reduce oven temperature to lowest setting and continue baking until bread becomes bone dry. Pieces can also be dried in a food dehydrator.

7. Store bread in ziplock bags for camp or trail.

Tip: I've kept dried Bayou City Bread for six months in ziplock bags with no problems. Don't know if it lasts longer than that because it's always been gone by then! It is very dense. But then again, that's the beauty of it.

Chris Counts, Clear Lake City, Texas
Assistant Scoutmaster, Troop 957, Sam Houston Area Council, Boy Scouts of America

Catalina Logan Bread

Servings: 18 | Challenge Level: Easy

"I adapted this recipe from one I found in *Backpacker* magazine in the early 1970s. It's nutritious, durable, filling, compact, and unbreakable! It's especially good for longer backpack trips. For long-term storage before a hike, the bread can be frozen or stored in cloth bags in a dry place."

Preparation at Home:

1. Mix together rye and wheat flour, wheat germ, brewer's yeast, powdered milk, and brown sugar.

2. Stir in nuts, raisins, and dried apricots. Add peanut oil, honey, molasses, maple syrup, and eggs. Mixture should be heavier than bread dough, quite thick but still somewhat sticky.

3. Press bread mix into greased 9x13-inch pan, forming a layer about 1-inch deep. Alternatively, standard bread pans can be used, filling approximately half-full with the dough.

4. Bake at 250 degrees F for about 2 hours, keeping in mind that Logan bread burns easily. When finished baking, the bread should have the appearance of fruitcake.

Tip: To reduce weight further, and produce more durability for longer duration storage, the bread can also be baked with the oven at its lowest heat setting, requiring 3–6 hours, depending on the characteristics of your oven.

2 cups rye flour

1 cup whole wheat flour

¾ cup wheat germ

¾ cup brewer's yeast

½ cup nonfat powdered milk

¼ cup brown sugar

½ cup chopped walnuts or pecans

½ cup raisins

1 cup chopped dried apricots

2 tablespoons peanut oil

½ cup honey

¼ cup molasses

¼ cup maple syrup

6 eggs

Option: Any other chopped dried fruit can be substituted for the raisins and apricots. Strawberries, dried in a home dehydrator, are wonderful. Others fruits that work well include blueberries, figs, and peaches.

Katie Salyer Cox, Tucson, Arizona
Leader and Trainer, USA Girl Scouts Overseas and Sahuaro Council, Girl Scouts of the USA

Journey Cakes

Servings: 3 / Multiply as Required | Challenge Level: Easy

"Versions of this cornbread recipe are known to date back over two hundred years. Frequently referred to as 'Johnny cakes', it is thought that the original name may have actually been 'journey cakes' as this was perfect bread for a long expedition. This recipe comes from our book *Lipsmackin' Vegetarian Backpackin'*."

2 cups corn meal

¼ cup all-purpose bleached wheat flour

3 tablespoons King Arthur dried whole egg powder

⅓ cup Nido whole milk powder

½ cup brown sugar

½ teaspoon salt

½ teaspoon ginger

1 tablespoon butter per serving, added on the trail

⅓ cup water per serving, added on the trail

Preparation at Home:

1. In a large-size bowl combine and thoroughly mix all dry ingredients.

2. Divide mixture evenly between three quart-size ziplock bags, about one heaping cupful each. Carry butter separately.

Preparation on Trail:

1. To prepare one serving add ⅓ cup of water to one bag of cake mix. (Add more water as needed.) Knead contents thoroughly.

2. Melt one tablespoon of butter in a pan. Cut a corner from the bottom of the bag and squeeze several dollops into the pan. Cook both sides as you would a pancake.

Required Equipment:

Small-size frying pan or cook pot lid

Christine Conners, Statesboro, Georgia
Former Girl Scout, Hawaii Council, Girl Scouts of the USA

Tim Conners, Statesboro, Georgia
Former Leader, Coastal Empire Council, Boy Scouts of America

World's Largest S'mores

Servings: 10–12 | Challenge Level: Easy

"Recently, when I told my scouts that anything could be cooked in a Dutch oven, they were incredulous and asked, 'What about s'mores?' I said, 'Sure!' and I created this recipe on the spot. It turned out fantastic, and we've enjoyed it on many campouts since."

Preparation at Camp:

1. Start 25 briquettes.

2. Over 8 coals, melt butter in Dutch oven. Crumble 10 of the graham crackers, and combine with the melted butter.

3. Cover butter-cracker mix with a layer of marshmallows, then several chocolate pieces, followed by a portion of the remaining graham crackers, broken into large pieces.

4. Repeat layering until all ingredients are used up. Finish by topping with marshmallows.

5. Using the 8 coals already under the oven, and placing 17 briquettes on the lid, bake for about 25 minutes until marshmallows turn golden brown.

Required Equipment:

12-inch Dutch oven

½ cup (1 standard stick) butter

20 graham crackers

1 (16-ounce) bag mini marshmallows

2 (2.6-ounce) bars milk chocolate, broken into pieces

John "The Scout Camp Chef" Jones, North Tonawanda, New York
Scoutmaster, Troop 184, Greater Niagara Frontier Council, Boy Scouts of America

Fake It 'Till You Bake It Cookie Cobbler

Servings: 6–8 | Challenge Level: Easy

"This recipe was an accident. I was in the middle of giving a big outdoor cooking presentation to scout leaders and trainers and assumed I brought refrigerated biscuits for my demonstration. But when I reached into my cooler, I pulled out cookie dough instead! Of course, I started to panic, but the rule of a good presenter is to never show weakness. So I pretended like I meant to bring cookie dough and proceeded to prepare the recipe as I had planned to do with the biscuits. The audience loved my cookie cobbler, and a fabulous new treat was born!"

1 (21-ounce) can pie filling (your choice)

2 (18-ounce) rolls refrigerated cookie dough (your choice)

Options: The possible combinations are virtually endless with this recipe. A favorite duo is cherry pie filling with chocolate chip cookie dough.

Preparation at Camp:

1. Pour pie filling into greased Dutch oven.

2. Break off pieces of cookie dough and lay evenly over the pie filling.

3. Using 17 coals on the lid and 8 briquettes under the oven, bake for 25–30 minutes until cookie dough rises to a golden brown.

Required Equipment:

12-inch Dutch oven

Connie Knie, Farmington Hills, Michigan
Assistant Scoutmaster, Troop 179, Clinton Valley Council, Boy Scouts of America

Black Forest Cream Cheese Pound Cake

Servings: 6–8 | Challenge Level: Easy

Preparation at Camp:

1. In a medium-size bowl, mix eggs, milk, and cream cheese until smooth.

2. Add cake mix and almond extract. Mix well.

3. Pour half of cake batter into a well-greased 10-inch tube cake pan.

4. Add cherry pie filling to form a layer on top of batter

5. Pour in remaining cake batter.

6. Place cake pan on trivet in Dutch oven.

7. Using 21 coals on the lid and 10 briquettes under the oven, bake for 40–50 minutes.

8. Remove from oven and set aside to cool. Serve with optional whipped cream.

Required Equipment:

Deep 14-inch Dutch oven with trivet
10-inch tube cake pan
Medium-size mixing bowl

4 eggs

½ cup milk

1 (8-ounce) package cream cheese, softened

1 (18¼-ounce) box Betty Crocker SuperMoist milk chocolate cake mix

1 teaspoon almond extract

¾ cup cherry pie filling

Whipped cream (optional)

Robert Dowdy, Great Falls, Montana
Scoutmaster, Troop 143, Montana Council, Boy Scouts of America

Oooey Gooey Extwa Toowy Bwownies

Servings: 10–12 | Challenge Level: Easy

"If you are having trouble pronouncing the name, take a big bite of this dessert. Just before you are about to swallow, say: 'Oooey Gooey Extra Chewy Brownies'. You will then say the name as it is meant to be pronounced! This recipe won third prize in the dessert competition at the 2003 Hardford District Spring Camporee."

2 (21-ounce) boxes Betty Crocker Hershey Supreme Ultimate Fudge brownie mix

¼ cup water

1 cup vegetable oil

4 eggs

1 (6-ounce) bag semisweet chocolate morsels

1½ cups chopped walnuts

1½ cups peanut butter, warmed and softened

Options: 1½ cups marshmallow creme or one (12-ounce) jar caramel topping can be substituted for the peanut butter. Butterscotch, white chocolate, or chocolate-vanilla swirl chips can be used in place of the chocolate morsels.

Preparation at Camp:

1. In a large-size bowl, combine brownie mix, water, vegetable oil, eggs, chocolate morsels, and walnuts.

2. Pour mixture into greased Dutch oven.

3. Add peanut butter to the top of mixture and swirl gently with a spoon.

4. Using 17 coals on the lid and 8 briquettes under the oven, bake for 45 minutes to 1 hour or until the brownie becomes oooey gooey extra chewy!

Required Equipment:

12-inch Dutch oven
Large-size mixing bowl

Kimra Simmons, Abingdon, Maryland
Webelos Den Leader, Pack 936, Baltimore Area Council, Boy Scouts of America

2 x 2 Cobbler

Servings: 12–14 | Challenge Level: Easy

"This recipe was passed down to me by my Scoutmaster, Gary Bolen. Gary is a very accomplished scouter who has spent many nights camping at just about every Council event. If there ever was anything I wanted to know about camping, I knew he would be able to help . . . except when it came to cooking. Everyone in our Troop knows to never let Gary in the kitchen unless he is making his cobbler!"

Preparation at Camp:

1. In large-size bowl, mix Bisquick, milk, sugar, and eggs.

2. Line Dutch oven with aluminum foil. Grease foil.

3. Pour batter into oven.

4. Pour pie filling directly into the middle of batter, not around the edges. (As it bakes, the batter will rise, covering the top of the filling.)

5. Break or cut the butter into pieces and place around the edges of batter. The butter will melt to give the top crust a golden brown color.

6. Using 18 coals on the lid and 9 briquettes under the oven, bake for 35 minutes. Serve warm.

Required Equipment:

12-inch Dutch oven
Large-size mixing bowl
Heavy-duty aluminum foil

2 cups Bisquick

2 cups milk

2 cups sugar

2 eggs

2 (21-ounce) cans pie filling (your choice)

1 cup (2 standard sticks) butter

Option: Our favorite fruit filling combo is blueberry and cherry.

Kevin Joiner, Columbus, Georgia
Treasurer, Troop 98, Chattahoochee Council, Boy Scouts of America

Yippee Cake

Servings: 2–4 | Challenge Level: Easy

"This cake is the dishwasher's dream-come-true, as it is both prepared and baked in the same pan. It is especially camp-friendly because it requires no eggs or dairy products. Yippee!"

¾ **cup all-purpose flour**

½ **cup sugar**

1½ **tablespoons cocoa powder**

½ **teaspoon baking soda**

¼ **teaspoon salt**

3 **tablespoons vegetable oil**

½ **teaspoon vanilla extract**

1 **tablespoon vinegar**

½ **cup cold water**

2 **tablespoons powdered sugar**

Options: To make a white cake, simply leave out the cocoa powder. Frosting can be used as a topping instead of powdered sugar.

Preparation at Camp:

1. Preheat Dutch oven using 16 coals on the lid and 7 briquettes under the oven.

2. In an 8-inch square ungreased pan, combine flour, sugar, cocoa powder, baking soda, and salt.

3. Make three holes in the flour mixture: a larger one in the center and two smaller ones on either side.

4. Pour vegetable oil into the center hole. In the first hole to the side, pour vanilla extract. In the final hole, add vinegar.

5. Pour cold water over all and thoroughly mix batter with fork.

6. Place pan on a trivet in preheated Dutch oven and bake for about 20–25 minutes.

7. Sprinkle with powdered sugar and serve.

Required Equipment:

12-inch Dutch oven with trivet

8-inch square baking pan

Tip: Yippee Cake can also be baked in a box oven at 325 degrees F for about 25 minutes.

Julia Whiteneck, Bedford, Massachusetts
Girl Scout Trainer, Patriots' Trail Council, Girl Scouts of the USA

Japeechen Apple Bars

Servings: 2–4 | Challenge Level: Easy

"This is a great recipe at home or at camp. Lots of compliments and crumbs!"

Preparation at Home:

1. Mix flour, baking soda, cinnamon, salt, and brown sugar and place into a gallon-size ziplock freezer bag.

Preparation at Camp:

1. Add to the ziplock bag of dry ingredients the applesauce, oil, egg, and diced apple.

2. Carefully seal bag and squish to mix contents.

3. Cut a corner from bottom of the bag and squeeze contents into a greased 8-inch square baking pan.

4. Place pan on a trivet inside Dutch oven. Using 17 coals on the lid and 8 briquettes under the oven, bake for 25–30 minutes or until a toothpick or fork inserted in middle comes out clean.

Required Equipment:

12-inch Dutch oven with trivet

8-inch square baking pan

Tip: Musselman's Homestyle Chunky applesauce works well in this recipe.

1 cup all-purpose flour

½ teaspoon baking soda

½ teaspoon powdered cinnamon

½ teaspoon salt

¾ cup packed brown sugar

¾ cup applesauce

¼ cup vegetable oil

1 egg

1 Granny Smith apple, peeled and diced

Page Davies, Glenshaw, Pennsylvania
Japeechen District Commissioner, Greater Pittsburgh Council, Boy Scouts of America

Mountain Dew Blackberry Cobbler

Servings: 8–10 | Challenge Level: Easy

2 (21-ounce) cans blackberry filling

1 (18¼-ounce) box yellow cake mix

1 (12-ounce) can Mountain Dew

Preparation at Camp:

1. Pour blackberry filling into bottom of greased Dutch oven, spreading evenly.

2. Sprinkle dry cake mix on top of blackberry filling. Do not stir!

3. Pour Mountain Dew over top of cake mix. Again, do not stir.

4. Bake for 35–45 minutes using 7 coals under the oven and 16 briquettes on the lid.

Required Equipment:

12-inch Dutch oven

Freddie Tuten, Guyton, Georgia
Committee Member, Troop 295, Coastal Empire Council, Boy Scouts of America

Michelle Tuten, Guyton, Georgia
Volunteer, Troop 295, Coastal Empire Council, Boy Scouts of America

Brownie Pudding

Servings: 5–6 | Challenge Level: Easy

"This recipe won second place in the 'dessert category' in *Scouting* magazine's 2005 'Camp Food Favorites' outdoor cooking contest. We previously entered this recipe at a District Camporee cook-off, where two requirements were: (1) boxed cake mixes could not be used, and (2) the recipe had to include fruit. (Did the cook-off organizers think this would make the food healthy? What were they thinking!) So we sliced up a banana, added it to the brownie mix, and joked about the requisite 'fruit molecules' being present. Apparently, it was enough, because we took third place!"

Preparation at Home:

1. In a quart-size ziplock freezer bag, combine flour, sugar, two tablespoons cocoa powder, baking powder, and salt. Label this bag "Brownie."

2. In a separate quart-size ziplock bag, combine the brown sugar and ¼ cup cocoa powder. Label this bag "Topping."

Preparation at Camp:

1. Pour milk, cooking oil, and vanilla extract into the Brownie bag and knead by hand.

2. Cut a small corner from the bottom of the bag and squirt batter into foil-lined Dutch oven.

3. Sprinkle contents of the Topping bag over brownie batter.

4. Pour 1¾ cups hot water over the top of everything.

5. Bake for 45 minutes using 17 coals on the lid and 8 briquettes under the oven. Refresh coals as necessary.

6. Allow brownie pudding to cool for 15 minutes before serving.

Required Equipment:

12-inch Dutch oven
Heavy-duty aluminum foil

1 cup all-purpose flour

¾ cup sugar

2 tablespoons unsweetened cocoa powder

2 teaspoons baking powder

½ teaspoon salt

¾ cup brown sugar

¼ cup unsweetened cocoa powder

½ cup milk

2 tablespoons cooking oil

1 teaspoon vanilla extract

1¾ cup hot water

Option: Yes, a few banana "molecules" can be added to the batter if the cooking contest requires the recipe to contain fruit!

Erich Wolz, Houston, Texas
Assistant Scoutmaster, Troop 505, Sam Houston Area Council, Boy Scouts of America

The Clos Family's Secret Award-Winning Chocolate Fondue Recipe

Servings: 8–10 | Challenge Level: Easy

"We prepared this recipe when I had to find something to make for dessert at a Cub Scout campout. I knew everyone would love it, it was foolproof, and it was a dish that the scouts could assemble themselves. This recipe has since won two cook-out competitions: Cub Scout Whoop-O-Ree 2003 and Boy Scout Introduction to Outdoor Leader Skills Training 2004."

Fondue:

1 (12-ounce) package semi-sweet chocolate chips

⅔ cup sour cream

½ cup evaporated milk or cream

Dipper Suggestions:

Bananas

Strawberries

Pineapple

Pound cake

Angel food cake

Caramels

Macaroons

Twinkies

Marshmallows

Option: For Crackers-On-My-Pillow S'mores, dunk your marshmallow in fondue then roll it in graham cracker crumbs!

Preparation at Camp:

1. In Dutch oven warmed over 8 coals, melt chocolate chips.

2. Add sour cream and stir until smooth.

3. Thin mixture with evaporated milk or cream as necessary.

4. Keep warm over low heat, removing or adding coals as required.

5. Serve with your favorite dippers.

Required Equipment:

12-inch Dutch oven

The Clos Family
George Sr./Scoutmaster, Della/Committee Member, George Jr./First Class Scout,
Andrew/First Class Scout, Jamie/Second Class Scout, Palatine, Illinois
Troop 335, Northwest Suburban Council, Boy Scouts of America

Polar Bear Bread Pudding

Servings: 12–14 | Challenge Level: Easy

"I first prepared this recipe at a campout when the weather was freezing cold. My son and I were helping to launch a new troop one early November, and the temperature never rose above 32 degrees F the entire trip. This was a little rough on the very inexperienced scouts as no one was prepared for temperatures that low so early in the season. Fortunately, Polar Bear Bread Pudding helped keep the boys a little warmer that weekend!"

Preparation at Camp:

1. Mix all ingredients, except for the condensed milk, in a large-size bowl.

2. Pour mixture into greased Dutch oven.

3. Bake for 1 hour using 6 coals under the oven and 15 briquettes on the lid. Refresh coals as needed.

4. Add condensed milk and stir.

5. Remove coals from under the oven and continue cooking for 15 more minutes, using only the briquettes on the lid. Serve.

Required Equipment:

12-inch Dutch oven
Large-size mixing bowl

1½ (1-pound) loaves white bread, cubed

1 quart milk (2 percent or whole)

2 cups sugar

3 eggs

2 apples, diced with skins

2 tablespoons vanilla extract

¼ cup (½ standard stick) butter

2 teaspoons powdered cinnamon

1 (14-ounce) can sweetened condensed milk

Sally Logan, Leslie, Michigan
Committee Member, Troop 141, Chief Okemos Council, Boy Scouts of America

Denny's Dutch Oven Pineapple Cake

Servings: 8–10 | Challenge Level: Easy

1 (18½-ounce) package Duncan Hines yellow cake mix

⅓ cup vegetable oil

3 eggs

1 (20-ounce) can crushed pineapple

½ cup (1 standard stick) butter

1 cup brown sugar

1 (20-ounce) can sliced pineapple

Preparation at Camp:

1. Pour cake mix, vegetable oil, eggs, and crushed pineapple, with its juice, into a gallon-size ziplock bag. Knead to break egg yokes and to thoroughly mix batter together. If a little more liquid is required, use some of the juice from the can of pineapple slices.

2. Prepare 23 coals. Arrange 7 of the briquettes under the Dutch oven.

3. Melt butter in the oven and stir in brown sugar, making sure that the bottom is covered.

4. Arrange pineapple slices over the buttered sugar.

5. Pour cake batter over the slices.

6. Place 16 briquettes on the lid. Bake for 35–45 minutes until cake is lightly browned on top, and a toothpick or fork inserted pulls out clean of dough.

Required Equipment:

12-inch Dutch oven
Gallon-size ziplock bag

Dennis L. Elliott, Dublin, Ohio
Committee Member, Troop 200, Simon Kenton Council, Boy Scouts of America

North Carolina Rhubarb Crunch

Servings: 6–8 | Challenge Level: Easy

"Mark Cusick, of the Barracuda Patrol, was the source for this recipe. Rhubarb Crunch won the Dessert Award on our first X-Cap campout."

Preparation at Camp:

1. Combine all batter ingredients in a large-size bowl. Spoon into bottom of greased Dutch oven.

2. Mix topping ingredients in a bowl. Sprinkle over rhubarb mix and pat down evenly.

3. Bake for 35–45 minutes using 17 coals on the lid and 8 briquettes under the oven.

4. Serve warm with optional whipped cream.

Required Equipment:

12-inch Dutch oven
Large-size mixing bowl

Batter:

1½ pounds rhubarb stalks, sliced into 1-inch pieces

¾ cup granulated sugar

2 tablespoons all-purpose flour

1 teaspoon powdered cinnamon

⅛ teaspoon salt

Topping:

¾ cup quick oatmeal

¾ cup brown sugar

¼ cup butter, melted

Whipped cream (optional)

Ed Bedford, Chapel Hill, North Carolina
Scoutmaster, Troop 820, Occoneechee Council, Boy Scouts of America

Cinnamonboy's Apple Crisp

Servings: 10–12 | Challenge Level: Easy

Fruit Mix:

10 medium apples, peeled and sliced

1 cup berry fruit (blueberries, strawberries, raspberries, blackberries, or cranberries)

1 cup granulated sugar

2 tablespoons powdered cinnamon (or more to taste)

Topping:

¾ cup packed brown sugar

½ cup all-purpose flour

½ cup old-fashioned oats

½ cup chopped nuts (your choice, but see tip below for suggestions)

1 teaspoon powdered cinnamon

¾ teaspoon ground cloves

⅓ cup butter

Whipped cream (optional)

Preparation at Camp:

1. To prepare fruit mix, place sliced apples in a large gallon-size ziplock freezer bag.

2. Add berry fruit, granulated sugar, and powdered cinnamon. Shake well.

3. Pour fruit mix into a well-greased Dutch oven.

4. Mix all topping ingredients in a medium-size bowl. Sprinkle topping over fruit in oven.

5. Using 12 coals under the oven and 8 briquettes on the lid, cook for 15 minutes. Check crisp. If top is becoming dark brown, remove some of the coals from the lid. If crisp has not begun to develop a light brown hue, add a few coals under the oven.

6. Continue cooking for an additional 15 minutes.

7. Top with optional whipped cream then serve.

Required Equipment:

12-inch Dutch oven
Medium-size mixing bowl
Gallon-size ziplock freezer bag

Tip: Wild nuts, such as beechnuts, butternuts, or hickory nuts, work well in this recipe. Scouts can work out some of their excess energy by foraging for them!

Jim "Cinnamonboy" Rausch, Ellsworth, Maine
Scoutmaster, Troop 86, Katahdin Area Council, Boy Scouts of America

Buffalo Patrol Cobbler

Servings: 8–10 | Challenge Level: Easy

"This recipe comes to you from the Buffalo Patrol. It began as a mistake when, on our shopping trip for ingredients, we accidentally bought corn muffin mix instead of cake mix. The cobbler was for our closing feast, and I was responsible for preparing it. When I discovered our mistake, there was nothing to do but improvise! The modified cobbler was a huge hit, and there wasn't a crumb left. I received a lot of comments about my 'unique' cobbler. You too will find the corn muffin topping gives this recipe a special flavor that will have your scouts begging for more!"

Preparation at Camp:

1. Pour apple and cherry pie fillings into a seasoned Dutch oven.

2. Sprinkle dry corn muffin mix over top of filling.

3. Lay pats of butter evenly over corn muffin mix.

4. Sprinkle all with brown sugar and cinnamon.

5. Using 12 coals on the lid and 13 briquettes under the oven, bake for 30 minutes.

Required Equipment:

12-inch Dutch oven

1 (21-ounce) can apple pie filling

1 (21-ounce) can cherry pie filling

2 (8½-ounce) packages Jiffy corn muffin mix

½ cup (1 standard stick) butter, sliced into pats

1 cup brown sugar

3 tablespoons ground cinnamon

Dave Shultz, Custar, Ohio
Scoutmaster, Troop 357, Erie Shores Council, Boy Scouts of America

SMACOs

Servings: 1 / Multiply as Required | Challenge Level: Easy

"SMACOs were the result of a disaster. In 1995, I was a Webelos leader for my son's den. We were attending summer camp at Camp Clark, nestled on the shore of the Pacific Ocean. One evening, we were attempting to make 'Fried Chocolate,' which entailed deep-frying a rolled flour tortilla filled with chocolate morsels in a Dutch oven. It just wasn't coming out as expected. I was close to the oven, kneeling and using tongs to hold the tortillas down in the hot oil, when the boys came rushing through the campsite, playing a game of predator-and-prey. The Dutch oven was knocked over, and cooking grease splashed onto my scout pants. I can safely say that the boys have never seen a sight like me quickly ripping my pants off to get the hot oil off my body! Fortunately, I only incurred minor burns and they healed without evidence.

Needless to say, my fellow leader, John, and I were not happy about the situation, and we sent the boys off to their tents. About midnight, with the scouts in bed, I was sitting around the campfire with John discussing what we could do to remedy the situation. We now had a lot of chocolate and tortillas left over, but not enough oil to fry. We were planning to have s'mores the next evening, so I asked, 'What do you think it would taste like if we substitute tortillas for graham crackers?' Being the adventurous leaders we were, we pulled out the supplies and tried it—yuck. Cold tortillas with roasted marshmallows and cold chocolate just didn't work! 'But what if we roasted them all together?' So then, in the middle of the night, we grabbed our Dutch oven, placed it on the fire, and SMACOs were born, a combination of s'mores and tacos. We kid-tested our recipe the next evening, and it was an instant success.

Since then, I have shared SMACOs at Wood Badge, Commissioner College, Outdoor Basic Leader Training, and with Boy Scout units across the Pacific Northwest, in Cascade Pacific Council, Mount Baker Council, Chief Seattle Council, Oregon Trail Council, and others. My son, who is now an Eagle Scout, took the recipe to National Jamboree several years ago, where he shared it with fellow scouts from other states. I know of at least two overseas units, from Japan and Australia, that have been taught the recipe. On many occasions, I've been to a unit with which I have no connection and am 'introduced' to SMACOs. They don't know where the recipe came from, but they love it, and I smile."

Preparation at Camp:

1. Dip fingers into water and dampen one side of tortilla.

2. Place tortilla, damp-side down, into a Dutch oven or frying pan over medium heat.

3. Sprinkle chocolate morsels over half of tortilla. Add mini marshmallows to top of chocolate.

4. With tongs, fold tortilla over the top of chocolate and marshmallows.

5. Place lid on Dutch oven or frying pan and wait about 30 seconds.

6. Remove lid and flip tortilla. Replace lid and continue warming tortilla for another 30 seconds.

7. Remove SMACO, slice with a pizza cutter, and enjoy.

Required Equipment:

Dutch oven or frying pan with lid
Tongs
Pizza cutter

Small cup of water

1 small flour tortilla, taco size

⅛ cup semisweet chocolate chips

⅛ cup mini marsh-mallows

Peter Van Houten, Beaverton, Oregon
Former Scoutmaster / District Commissioner, Cascade Pacific Council, Boy Scouts of America

Gator Cheesecake

Servings: 10–12 | Challenge Level: Easy

"My cheesecake recipe began as a challenge. I used to brag that I could cook anything in a camp Dutch oven that could be prepared in the kitchen. A fellow scouter bet me a steak dinner that I couldn't make a good cheesecake. He had tried for years and wasn't able to do it. Well, don't tell this guy that something can't be done. After about fifteen failed attempts, I created Gator Cheesecake, and it has worked for me since."

Crust:

1 (14.4-ounce) package graham crackers, finely crumbled

½ cup (1 standard stick) butter, melted

1 cup sugar

Filling:

3 (8-ounce) packages cream cheese

2 eggs

1 cup sugar

1 tablespoon lemon or lime juice

1 cup all-purpose flour

½ tablespoon vanilla

1 (14-ounce) can sweetened condensed milk

Topping:

Pie filling, ice cream, or sliced fruit (your choice)

Options: You can substitute the graham crackers with vanilla wafers, Oreos, gingerbread cookies, or just about any snack cookie. You will need three cups of crumbs.

Preparation at Camp:

1. To prepare the crust, mix graham cracker crumbs, melted butter, and 1 cup of sugar together in a medium-size bowl.

2. Press crumb mixture into well-greased Dutch oven.

3. Place all filling ingredients together in medium-size bowl and mix well.

4. Pour filling over crumb crust in Dutch oven.

5. Arrange 12 coals around the outside edge on the lid and an additional 4 coals in the middle of the lid. Use 6 coals under the oven.

6. Bake for 45 minutes or until top is golden brown.

7. Remove oven from coals and set aside to cool. Serve with your favorite topping.

Required Equipment:

12-inch Dutch oven
Medium-size mixing bowl

Mark Case Sr., Barberville, Florida
Cubmaster and Chaplain, Pack 199, Central Florida Council, Boy Scouts of America

Ruth and Phil's Monkey Bread

Servings: 8–10 | Challenge Level: Easy

"Grandma Ruth and Grandpa Phil taught us this recipe. We often make Monkey Bread on camping trips. It's a lot of fun rolling the dough and tossing the balls. And there are never any crumbs left when we're done!"

Preparation at Camp:

1. Cut each biscuit in half and roll into balls.

2. Place sugar and cinnamon into a double-lined paper lunch bag and shake to mix.

3. Roll dough balls in melted butter and drop, 4 or 5 at a time, into the bag containing sugar and cinnamon. Shake gently until the balls are covered with the mix.

4. Place dough balls in a foil-lined Dutch oven.

5. Using 17 coals on the lid and 8 briquettes under the oven, bake for 25–30 minutes until the bread rises to a golden brown.

Required Equipment:

12-inch Dutch oven

2 paper lunch bags

Heavy-duty aluminum foil

2 (12-ounce, 10-count) containers refrigerated buttermilk biscuit dough (such as Pillsbury)

1 cup sugar

1 teaspoon ground cinnamon

½ cup (1 standard stick) butter, melted

Options: Garlic bread can be made using the same method by substituting the sugar-cinnamon mix with a garlic-salt-Italian seasoning blend. A fun variation is to roll the dough into "snakes" instead of balls. Lay the dough snakes side-by-side in Dutch oven. Spread melted butter on top, then sprinkle with cinnamon-sugar or garlic-salt-seasoning mix. Bake for 25–30 minutes if snakes are fat, less if they are skinny.

Keith and Kyle Price, Milltown, New Jersey
Eagle Scouts, Troop 33, Central New Jersey Council, Boy Scouts of America

Troop 400 Peach Cobbler

Servings: 8–10 | Challenge Level: Moderate

"Each October, a large number of folks attending the popular Great Ogeechee Seafood Festival in Richmond Hill, Georgia, make it a point to visit the cobbler booth run by Boy Scout Troop 400. The booth features a huge cooking table, with up to 18 Dutch ovens simultaneously baking cobbler using fresh peaches. When we first began, the cobbler immediately became a community favorite, the perfect dessert after sampling the other main-course selections at the festival. Our first year of operation, the cobbler received no awards, but then, no 'non-seafood' awards were available! The next year, the festival created a best 'non-seafood' category. In the years since, the troop has always won either the 'best non-seafood dish' award or 'best overall dish.'

The members of Troop 400 have always been avid Dutch oven cooks. The troop even offers 'Dutch Oven Cooking' patches to any patrol that leaves their camp stoves at home on an outing, cooking all their meals in a Dutch oven. It is this obvious enthusiasm for Dutch oven cooking that shows through at the festival, and makes the Troop 400 Peach Cobbler all the more popular!"

8 cups sliced peaches (preferably fresh)

1 tablespoon ground cinnamon

1 tablespoon cornstarch

1 teaspoon nutmeg

1 tablespoon vanilla extract

Brown sugar to taste (optional)

¼ cup (½ standard stick) butter

2 frozen preformed pie crusts, thawed

Vanilla ice cream (optional, but strongly suggested!)

Preparation at Camp:

1. Thaw peaches if frozen.

2. Mix peaches, cinnamon, cornstarch, nutmeg, and vanilla extract in a large bowl. If you've made the mistake of not using sweet Georgia peaches, you'll want to add brown sugar to taste.

3. Preheat Dutch oven using 17 coals on the lid and 8 briquettes under the oven.

4. Melt butter in the oven.

5. Pour half of the peach mixture into oven and cover with one pie crust.

6. Cover and bake 20–25 minutes or until crust is golden brown.

7. Open oven and chop baked crust into pieces, mixing into the peaches.

8. Add remaining peach mixture and cover with second pie crust.

9. Cover and bake an additional 20–25 minutes or until crust is golden brown.

10. Serve alone or a la mode.

Options: This recipe is suitable for using all sorts of different fruits. Try apples, blueberries, raspberries, and an apple-raspberry combination.

Required Equipment:

12-inch Dutch oven

Large-size mixing bowl

Brad Thompson, Richmond Hill, Georgia
Scoutmaster, Troop 400, Coastal Empire Council, Boy Scouts of America

Raven Knob Pumpkin Enchantment

Servings: 8–10 | Challenge Level: Moderate

"We had started a Troop 934 tradition of having an annual spring Dutch oven cook-off. We thought we had prepared some pretty decent meals, but then along came Alex Eaton, an Eagle Scout of mine who was a real chef-of-the-woods. Instead of our normal fare of pizza, stews, and cobblers, he was soon producing meals of mussels, crab imperial on portabella mushrooms, Dutch oven breads, casseroles, and more in his backcountry kitchen. This recipe was one from his repertoire, which we first prepared on a cold February weekend at Raven Knob, the official camp of the Old Hickory Council in North Carolina."

Crust:

1 (18½-ounce) package yellow cake mix, with 1 cup reserved for topping

1 egg, beaten

½ cup (1 standard stick) butter, melted

Filling:

3 eggs, beaten

3 teaspoons pumpkin pie spice

1 cup milk

¾ cup brown sugar

1 (29-ounce) can pumpkin

Topping:

1 cup of previously reserved yellow cake mix

¼ cup sugar

1 teaspoon ground cinnamon

3 tablespoons cold butter

Preparation at Camp:

1. To prepare crust, blend together cake mix (minus 1 cup of mix set aside for topping), egg, and melted butter in a medium-size bowl.

2. Press crust mix into bottom and 1½ inches up the sides of well-greased Dutch oven.

3. To prepare filling, combine all filling ingredients in a medium-size bowl and mix well.

4. Pour filling into oven to fill crust.

5. To prepare topping, combine cup of reserved cake mix, sugar, and cinnamon. Cut in butter until coarse crumbs are formed.

6. Sprinkle topping over pumpkin filling.

7. Bake using 17 coals on the lid and 8 briquettes under the oven for 1 hour or until an inserted toothpick or fork comes out clean. Refresh coals as required while baking.

Required Equipment:

12-inch Dutch oven
Medium-size mixing bowl

Keith Huffstetler, Winston-Salem, North Carolina
Former Scoutmaster, Troop 934, Old Hickory Council, Boy Scouts of America

Hideout Canyon Caramel Cake

Servings: 10–12 | Challenge Level: Moderate

"This dish is named for Hideout Canyon, the historic locale where Butch Cassidy and his gang disappeared from the law. There is now a campground in Hideout Canyon. And it was also here that this recipe won first place in a cook-off sponsored by Helaman Boy Scout Camp. Be careful. This dessert disappears fast!"

Preparation at Camp:

1. To prepare caramel topping, combine water, brown sugar, and ¼ cup butter in a medium-size saucepan. Bring to a boil then set aside.

2. To prepare batter, cream together ¼ cup softened butter and 1 cup sugar in a large-size mixing bowl. Add chopped apple.

3. In a separate, medium-size bowl, combine flour, nutmeg, cinnamon, baking powder, salt, and baking soda.

4. Add contents of medium-size bowl to the apple mix along with milk. Next, stir in vanilla, raisins, and nuts.

5. Spread batter mix into a greased Dutch oven, and pour topping over all.

6. Using 9 coals under the oven and 18 briquettes on the lid, bake for 45–55 minutes. Refresh coals as needed.

7. Serve in bowls, pouring caramel mixture from the bottom of the Dutch oven over the dished up cake. Top with optional ice cream or whipped cream.

Required Equipment:

12-inch Dutch oven
Medium-size saucepan
Large-size mixing bowl
Medium-size mixing bowl

Topping:

4 cups water

2 cups brown sugar

¼ cup (½ standard stick) butter

Batter:

¼ cup (½ standard stick) butter, softened

1 cup sugar

1 apple, peeled and chopped

2 cups all-purpose flour

1 teaspoon nutmeg

1 teaspoon cinnamon

2½ teaspoons baking powder

½ teaspoon salt

1½ teaspoons baking soda

1 cup milk

1 teaspoon vanilla

1 cup raisins

½ cup chopped nuts (pecans or walnuts)

Darren Landon, American Fork, Utah
Venture Advisor / District Committee Member, Troop 1184, Utah National Parks Council, Boy Scouts of America

Ding Dong Cobbler

Servings: 12 | Challenge Level: Moderate

"Out troop's cooking philosophy: No matter what the recipe is, if you don't have fun preparing it, it's not worth the effort!"

2 (18¼-ounce) boxes Betty Crocker yellow cake mix

6 eggs

⅔ cup vegetable oil

2½ cups water

1 (21-ounce) can cherry pie filling

12 Ding Dongs

1 single-serving packet instant hot chocolate mix

20 large marshmallows

3 tablespoons butter

Options: Substitute chocolate cake mixes for the yellow, Twinkies for the Ding Dongs, and apples or peaches for the cherries.

Preparation at Camp:

1. Pour both packages of cake mix into a large bowl. Combine with eggs, vegetable oil, and water.

2. Open can of cherry pie filling and unwrap Ding Dongs to save necessary time in a later step.

3. Pour can of cherry filling into bottom of oven. Next, pour half of cake batter over cherries.

4. Place 6 Ding Dongs on cake batter, spacing them evenly. Sprinkle half of the hot chocolate mix over Ding Dongs.

5. Pour other half of cake batter into oven. Place remaining 6 Ding Dongs on cake batter.

6. Set marshmallow pieces on top of batter and Ding Dongs. Sprinkle remaining hot chocolate mix over Ding Dongs.

7. Cover all with small pieces of butter to aid in browning.

8. Bake using 8 coals arranged in a ring under the oven and 17 briquettes on the lid. Cake will be ready to serve when browned on top and a toothpick or fork comes out clean, about 45 minutes.

Required Equipment:

12-inch Dutch oven
Large-size mixing bowl

Curt "The Titanium Chef" White, Forks, Washington
Scoutmaster, Troop1467, Chief Seattle Council, Boy Scouts of America

Gorp Pie

Servings: 8–10 | Challenge Level: Moderate

Preparation at Camp:

1. In large bowl, prepare crust dough by combining flour with ⅓ cup brown sugar.

2. Cut butter into the flour-sugar until the mixture resembles coarse crumbs.

3. Line Dutch oven with lightly greased heavy-duty aluminum foil. Press the crumbed dough into oven.

4. Using 17 coals on the lid and 8 briquettes under the oven, bake for about 15–20 minutes until the edges become golden brown.

5. While the crust is baking, prepare filling by combining egg, salt, vanilla, and ⅓ cup brown sugar in a large bowl. Add nuts, fruit, and chocolate chips.

6. Spoon filling over crust once crust is finished baking. Refresh coals, if required, and cook for an additional 15–20 minutes until top is set.

7. Allow Gorp Pie to cool completely before slicing and serving.

Required Equipment:

12-inch Dutch oven

Large-size mixing bowl

Heavy-duty aluminum foil

Crust:

1¼ cups all-purpose flour

⅓ cup packed brown sugar

¾ cup (1½ standard sticks) cold butter

Filling:

1 egg

¼ teaspoon salt

1 teaspoon vanilla

⅓ cup packed brown sugar

1½ cups roasted and salted mixed nuts

2 cups mixed dried fruit

1 cup raisins or dried cranberries

1 cup chocolate chips

Linda Pfaff, Ogden, Utah

Commissioner, Troop 285, Trapper Trails Council, Boy Scouts of America

Rick's Tubed and Groovy Apple Pie

Servings: 6–8 | Challenge Level: Moderate

"I was going to enter my Tubed and Groovy Apple Pie recipe in a cooking contest at a Boy Scout Klondike Derby. I built the pie, got it into the Dutch oven, and set the oven over some coals by the edge of the campfire. Then I went back to the kitchen area to work on dinner. Big mistake. It was pretty cold, and some of the younger scouts decided to stoke up the fire. Thirty minutes later, I looked over and saw my Dutch oven in the middle of an inferno. My guess is that the interior of the oven hit somewhere close to 500 degrees. The crust was black and hard. But, you know, we ate it anyway, and it was still pretty good."

1 (15-ounce) package of 2 refrigerated "tube" pie crusts (such as Pillsbury Unroll and Bake)

½ cup sugar

2 tablespoons ground cinnamon

½ teaspoon allspice

7 apples (Gala or Granny Smith preferred)

2 tablespoons milk

Preparation at Camp:

1. Unroll the first crust into an ungreased 9-inch pie tin and form it to the shape of the pan. The dough should slightly overlap the rim all the way around.

2. In a small ziplock bag, combine the sugar, cinnamon, and allspice.

3. Peel, core, and thinly slice the apples.

4. Lay about one quarter of the apple slices flat onto the crust, overlapping them as needed to make the first layer. Sprinkle the apple slices with about one quarter of the sugar mix. Repeat this pattern with the remaining apples and sugar mix.

5. Lay the second crust over the pie. Seal the edges using the tines of a fork. Do this by wetting the fork tines and pressing the tines into the dough in a radial pattern around the entire rim of the pie tin. Rewet the fork as required.

6. Trim off any excess crust with a knife. (The excess can be re-rolled, squished with some extra cinnamon and sugar, and baked with the pie as "the cook's treat.")

7. Use the knife to cut small slots in the top crust to permit steam to escape while baking. Be artistic, and make decorative slot patterns!

8. Brush top of pie dough with milk.

9. Place pie tin on a trivet inside Dutch oven.

10. Using 16 coals on the lid and 7 briquettes under the oven, cook for 45–60 minutes until the top becomes golden brown. Refresh coals as needed.

11. Cut pie and serve hot.

Required Equipment:

12-inch Dutch oven with trivet

9-inch pie tin

Small-size ziplock bag

Tip: When preparing crusts from a box or from scratch, try this groovy technique for tubing pie dough: Lay out a sheet of aluminum foil about 15 inches long. Dust foil with flour and lay one crust on it (make sure crusts are about 11 inches in diameter to fully cover a 9 inch pie tin). Dust the pie crust and lay a second sheet of aluminum foil over the first crust. Sprinkle second sheet of foil with flour and lay the second crust on it. Dust the second crust and lay one more sheet of foil on top. Gently roll the sheets together around a paper towel tube. Pinch the ends of the foil to seal. Store and keep cool until it's time to make pie.

Options: A variety of pies can be made using a 21-ounce can of your favorite premade pie fillings instead of sliced apples. In addition, a chicken pot pie is a breeze when the pie crust is filled with an 18.8-ounce can of Campbell's Chunky Herb Roasted Chicken with Potatoes and Garlic soup.

Rick LaCourse, Laurel, Maryland
Assistant Scoutmaster, Troop 259, National Capital Area Council, Boy Scouts of America

Blue Ridge Mountain Sweet Potato Cobbler

Servings: 10–12 | Challenge Level: Moderate

"This dish is based on an old Southern recipe my grandmother used to make. My mom and her sisters never learned my grandmother's secrets to this great dessert, so I had to work it out by trial and error. The scouts in our troop love it, even the ones who say they don't like sweet potatoes!"

2 cups sugar

½ cup (1 standard stick) butter

2 cups water

1½ tablespoons vanilla extract

Nonstick vegetable spray (such as PAM)

1 (16.3-ounce/8-count) container refrigerated Pillsbury "Grands!" Flakey Biscuits

3 medium sweet potatoes, peeled and thinly sliced

Pumpkin pie spice to taste

1 premade refrigerated pie crust

Preparation at Camp:

1. Mix sugar, butter, water, and vanilla in a sauce pan. Heat until melted and blended, but do not boil. Set aside.

2. Line Dutch oven with heavy-duty aluminum foil. Spray foil with vegetable spray.

3. Separate each biscuit into two equal parts by dividing between layers, leaving 16 round pieces. Line bottom of oven with 8 of the biscuit halves.

4. Place half of the sliced sweet potatoes over the biscuits and thoroughly cover with pumpkin pie spice.

5. Create a second layer using remaining biscuits and sweet potatoes.

6. Pour sugar-butter mixture on top of sweet potatoes and biscuits. Over it all, add a healthy coating of pumpkin pie spice.

7. Cut pie crust into strips and form a lattice on top of the potatoes, using half of the strips in one direction and half in a pattern crossways to the first. Spray crust lightly with vegetable spray.

8. Place 20 coals on the lid and 5 briquettes under the oven, arranging the coals on the lid in a circle around the outer edge, leaving two coals in the middle of the lid.

9. Bake for approximately 40 minutes or until potatoes are fork tender and crust is golden brown.

Required Equipment:

12-inch Dutch oven
Medium-size sauce pan
Heavy-duty aluminum foil

Tip: The key to making this dish a success is to be sure that the liquid sugar-butter mixture rises to the second layer of potatoes when it is poured into the oven. If it doesn't reach the second layer, add extra water as required.

Dean Perry, Rutherfordton, North Carolina
Scoutmaster, Troop 132, Piedmont Council, Boy Scouts of America

Ray's World Famous Dutch Oven Pound Cake

Servings: 10–12 | Challenge Level: Moderate

"One November, the troop decided to prepare an old-fashioned Thanksgiving dinner for their parents at our scout cabin in Fort Wayne. The boys wanted to add a Dutch oven dessert contest to the festivities. They invited the adult leaders to enter into competition with them. We accepted the challenge.

About a dozen desserts were made that day for the contest. Most were cakes. The boys asked who would serve as judges. I suggested that we let the parents and guests decide without telling them that a contest was underway. 'How?' the boys asked. I said we should put the desserts on the serving table in the kitchen and go back afterward to see how much of each dessert remained. The dessert with the least left over would be the winner.

I purposely did not eat any of the cake I made so the boys would have a better chance of winning. But, alas, Ray's World Famous pound cake was completely gone, with only a few crumbs left on the plate!"

Dry Ingredients:

3 cups sugar

3 cups flour

¼ teaspoon salt

Wet Ingredients:

2 cups (4 standard sticks) butter, softened

1 cup milk

6 eggs, well beaten

3 teaspoons "vanilla, butter, and nut" flavoring

Preparation at Camp:

1. Mix dry ingredients together in a large-size bowl. Reserve a small amount of flour for dusting the cake pan.

2. Mix wet ingredients together in a separate, medium-size bowl.

3. Combine dry and wet ingredients together in the large-size bowl and beat well.

4. Using 20 coals on the lid and 10 briquettes underneath, preheat Dutch oven.

5. Meanwhile, grease and flour angel food cake pan. Pour batter into the pan, shaking to settle the batter down.

6. Place cake pan on a trivet inside preheated oven and replace lid. Bake for 45 minutes, then refresh coals. Do not lift the lid!

7. Continue baking for an additional 45 minutes or until top of cake is a light brown.

8. Remove pound cake and allow to cool completely. Place a dinner plate over the pan and invert. The cake should slip onto the plate.

Option: Top cake with your favorite icing.

Required Equipment:

Deep 14-inch Dutch oven with trivet

10-inch angel food cake pan

Large-size mixing bowl

Medium-size mixing bowl

Tip: "Vanilla, butter, and nut" flavoring is a blend normally found near the vanilla extract at your grocer.

Ray McCune, Fort Wayne, Indiana
Feature Editor of *MidWest Outdoor Magazine*'s Kampfire Kookin' Column
Assistant Scoutmaster and Founder of Troop 38, Anthony Wayne Area Council, Boy Scouts of America

Chattahoochee Cheesecake

Servings: 6–8 | Challenge Level: Moderate

2 (8-ounce, 8-count) containers Pillsbury refrigerated crescent roll dough

2 (8-ounce) packages cream cheese, softened

1 cup sugar

1 teaspoon vanilla extract

½ cup (1 standard stick) butter, melted

¼ cup sugar

1 teaspoon ground cinnamon

Preparation at Camp:

1. Using dough from one container of crescent rolls, line bottom of greased Dutch oven. Pinch the rolls together, forming a single flat dough round. This will become your bottom crust.

2. In a medium-size bowl, mix together cream cheese, sugar, and vanilla.

3. Spread cream cheese mixture over the crescent dough at bottom of oven.

4. Using second container of crescent rolls, flatten dough over the top of the cream cheese mixture, pinching together the dough in the same manner as was done for the bottom. This will become your top crust.

5. Pour melted butter on the crust, then sprinkle sugar and cinnamon over the top.

6. Using 17 coals on the lid and 8 briquettes under the oven, bake for about 30 minutes.

7. Let oven completely cool. Cut cheesecake into slices and chill, if possible, before serving.

Required Equipment:

12-inch Dutch oven
Medium-size mixing bowl

Vikki Voorhees Condrey, Columbus, Georgia
Assistant Scoutmaster, Troop 98, Chattahoochee Council, Boy Scouts of America

Camp Webster Cheesecake

Servings: 10–12 | Challenge Level: Moderate

"This recipe is named for June Norcross Webster Scout Reservation here in the town of Ashford, where we do most of our scouting. The cheesecake is unique in that it bakes its own light crust into the bottom. It's been pleasing the palates of its partakers for some time now!"

Preparation at Camp:

1. In a large-size bowl, mix ricotta and cream cheese thoroughly.

2. Add sugar, lemon juice, eggs, flour, arrowroot powder, butter, vanilla, and sour cream. Mix well.

3. Pour cheesecake batter into greased springform pan.

4. Place pan in Dutch oven on a trivet, raising it about ¾-inch above bottom of oven.

5. Add 1 cup water to bottom of oven to provide moisture during the baking period. Ensure that the base of the pan sits above the surface of the water.

6. Bake for 1 hour using 15 coals on the lid and 15 briquettes under the oven. Refresh coals as required.

7. Remove Dutch oven from coals and let sit for at least 1 hour. Do not open the oven during this period!

8. Top with your favorite fruit filling, slice into 10 to 12 wedges, and serve.

Required Equipment:

Deep 14-inch Dutch oven with trivet
10-inch round by 3-inch deep springform cake pan
Large-size mixing bowl

1 (15-ounce) container ricotta cheese

2 (8-ounce) packages cream cheese

1 cup sugar

2 tablespoons lemon juice

4 eggs

3 tablespoons all-purpose flour

3 tablespoons arrowroot powder

½ cup (1 standard stick) butter, softened

1½ teaspoons vanilla extract

2 cups sour cream

1 cup water

2 (21-ounce) cans fruit topping (cherry, blueberry, peach, or apple)

Tom Wohlhueter, Ashford, Connecticut
Assistant Scoutmaster / District Scouter, Troop 92, Connecticut Rivers Council, Boy Scouts of America

Not a Trace Coconut Cake

Servings: 10–12 | Challenge Level: Moderate

"This recipe has taken several first-place awards during Scoutmaster cook-offs at Camp Bud Schiele summer camp. In fact, it has won every time it has been entered! Cleaning is easy because the guys always scrape the oven clean. They 'leave no trace'!"

Nonstick vegetable spray (such as PAM)

1 (16-ounce) container vanilla frosting

1 (14-ounce) bag shredded coconut

1 (18¼-ounce) box white cake mix (plus eggs, oil, and water per cake mix directions)

1 (12-ounce) can Coco Lopez Cream of Coconut

1 (16-ounce) container sour cream

1 (16-ounce) container whipped topping (such as Cool Whip)

Preparation at Camp:

1. Line Dutch oven with heavy-duty aluminum foil. Spray foil with vegetable spray.

2. Melt frosting by placing container in warm water. Once melted, pour frosting into Dutch oven, spreading evenly over the bottom.

3. Thinly cover frosting with some, not all, of the shredded coconut.

4. Follow directions on the cake mix to prepare the batter (this can be done using a bowl or in a ziplock bag: eggs first, with oil and water, followed by the dry mix).

5. Pour cake batter over frosting and coconut.

6. Bake using 5 coals under the oven, lining the rim of the lid with 18 coals with another 2 in the middle of the lid.

7. Check cake after 30 minutes, but continue cooking if necessary until a toothpick inserted in the middle of cake comes out clean of dough mix. Note that the batter will bake, but the frosting and coconut in the bottom should remain liquefied.

8. When cake is finished baking, use a fork to make holes across top. Pour Coco Lopez over cake.

9. Return oven to coals but with briquettes removed from lid. Allow Coco Lopez to sink in and dry on top, being careful not to burn the cake.

10. In medium bowl, mix whipped topping and sour cream together with most of the remaining coconut.

11. Cover cake with whipped topping mixture and sprinkle remainder of coconut over the top. Serve warm.

Required Equipment:

12-inch Dutch oven
Medium-size mixing bowl
Heavy-duty aluminum foil

Tip: Coco Lopez Cream of Coconut can be found near piña colada drink mixes at the grocer.

Dean Perry, Rutherfordton, North Carolina
Scoutmaster, Troop 132, Piedmont Council, Boy Scouts of America

Balooberry Coffee Cake

Servings: 8–10 | Challenge Level: Moderate

"I was given this recipe by a coworker and converted the cooking instructions to make it Dutch oven–friendly. Anything cooked in an electric oven can be cooked outdoors in a Dutch oven!"

2 cups all-purpose flour

1 teaspoon salt

1 teaspoon baking soda

½ cup (1 standard stick) butter, softened

1 cup sugar

3 eggs

1 teaspoon vanilla extract

1 tablespoon lemon juice

1 cup sour cream

2 cups blueberries

¾ cup brown sugar

½ cup pecans

½ teaspoon ground cinnamon

Preparation at Camp:

1. Mix flour, salt, and baking soda in a medium-size bowl and set aside.

2. Cream softened butter and sugar in a separate, large-size bowl. Add eggs, vanilla extract, and lemon juice. Mix well.

3. Add the flour mixture to the butter mixture followed by the sour cream. Blend together.

4. Pour half of the batter into Dutch oven.

5. Spread 1 cup of blueberries over batter and gently press in.

6. Mix brown sugar, pecans, and cinnamon in medium-size bowl. Spread evenly over batter in oven.

7. Pour remaining batter into oven.

8. Spread remaining cup of blueberries over batter and gently press in.

9. Using 18 coals on the lid and 8 briquettes under the oven, bake for 45 minutes, refreshing coals as required.

Required Equipment:

12-inch Dutch oven
Medium-size mixing bowl
Large-size mixing bowl

Paul Vanover, Morganton, North Carolina
Scoutmaster, Troop 899, Piedmont Council, Boy Scouts of America

Hessel's Pineapple Mandarin Upside-Down Cake

Servings: 12–14 | Challenge Level: Moderate

"This recipe took first place in the 18th annual Scout Rally in Hessel, Michigan."

Preparation at Camp:

1. Pour juice from the cans of pineapples into a large-size bowl. Reserve the actual pineapple slices for a later step.

2. Add cake mixes, vegetable oil, and eggs to the pineapple juice. Mix until smooth. Add a little water if necessary.

3. Line Dutch oven with greased heavy-duty aluminum foil.

4. Place pineapple slices around the bottom of the Dutch oven with cherries set in the middle of the pineapple slices.

5. In the spaces between pineapples, add mandarin oranges so that the entire bottom is covered with fruit. There will be some fruit left over.

6. Pour cake batter over the top of the fruit in Dutch oven.

7. Bake for 45 minutes using 7 coals under the oven and 16 briquettes on the lid.

8. Remove coals from under the oven, and continue baking until a toothpick or fork inserted in the middle of the cake comes out clean.

9. When the cake is done baking, flip upside down onto bottom of the Dutch oven lid and remove aluminum foil. Pour maple syrup over the cake and serve.

Required Equipment:

12-inch Dutch oven

Large-size mixing bowl

Heavy-duty aluminum foil

Tip: Be careful to avoid too much heat under the oven, or the fruit will burn.

Terry Vanalstine, Bellaire, Michigan
Scoutmaster, Troop 76, Scenic Trails Council, Boy Scouts of America

---

2 (20-ounce) cans sliced pineapple

2 (18¼-ounce) boxes Duncan Hines Pineapple Supreme cake mix

⅔ cup vegetable oil

6 eggs

1 (10-ounce) jar maraschino cherries

2 (11-ounce) cans mandarin oranges

½ cup pure maple syrup

Three Rivers Muddy Pudding

Servings: 6–8 | Challenge Level: Moderate

Cake Batter:

1 (9-ounce) box Jiffy devil's food cake mix

1 egg

½ cup cold water

Mud Ingredients:

¼ cup unsweetened cocoa powder

1 cup brown sugar

2 cups hot water

1 teaspoon vanilla extract

1 teaspoon coconut extract

Topping:

1 cup chocolate chips

1 cup coconut flakes

1 (8-ounce) container whipped topping (such as Cool Whip)

1 (10-ounce) jar maraschino cherries

Preparation at Camp:

1. Preheat Dutch oven with 8 coals under the oven and 12 briquettes on the lid.

2. Prepare cake batter in a medium-size bowl by combining cake mix, egg, and cold water.

3. Pour cake batter into greased 9-inch round cake pan.

4. Prepare mud ingredients in medium-size bowl by combining cocoa powder, brown sugar, hot water, vanilla extract, and coconut extract.

5. Pour mud over batter. The mud might look very runny, but this is normal.

6. Place pan on trivet in Dutch oven.

7. Bake for 25–35 minutes.

8. Sprinkle top of cake with chocolate chips. Replace lid and wait 3 minutes for chips to melt.

9. Spread melted chocolate chips evenly over the cake and cover with coconut flakes.

10. Serve warm with a dollop of whipped topping and cherries on top.

Required Equipment:

14-inch Dutch oven with trivet

9-inch round cake pan

Medium-size mixing bowl

Tips: This recipe can also be cooked directly in a smaller Dutch oven without need for a cake pan. Or it can be prepared using a cake pan in a box oven.

David "Juan Barbearo" Barber, Shasta Lake, California
Assistant Scoutmaster, Troop 122, Golden Eagle Council, Boy Scouts of America

Raccoon Stealin' Apple Strudel

Servings: 8–10 | Challenge Level: Moderate

"While cooking this recipe in the dark, a raccoon came along and began taking the red hot coals off the Dutch oven lid with his front paws. We couldn't believe he didn't burn himself! The aroma was wonderful. He wanted what was inside!"

Preparation at Camp:

1. To prepare filling, mix 1 cup sugar, 1 tablespoon cinnamon, and 3 tablespoons flour in a medium-size bowl and set aside.

2. Peel, core, and slice apples. Layer apples at the bottom of greased Dutch oven, sprinkling a little of the sugar-cinnamon-flour mixture over each layer as you go.

3. To make crumble topping, combine 1½ cups flour, 1 cup sugar, and 2 teaspoons cinnamon in medium-size bowl.

4. Cut butter into pieces and add to dry topping ingredients. Continue cutting and mixing butter into the dry mixture until it becomes crumbly.

5. Pour crumble topping evenly over the apples.

6. Using 17 coals on the lid and 8 briquettes under the oven, bake for 45 minutes.

7. Set lid ajar to permit steam to escape and continue baking for an additional 45 minutes. This step helps to ensure a crunchy topping. Refresh coals as necessary.

8. Strudel is ready to serve once the apples begin to bubble on the top outer edges.

Required Equipment:

12-inch Dutch oven
Medium-size mixing bowl

Filling:

1 cup sugar

1 tablespoon ground cinnamon

3 tablespoons all-purpose flour

4 pounds apples (Jonathans work well)

Crumble Topping:

1½ cups all-purpose flour

1 cup sugar

2 teaspoons ground cinnamon

¾ cup (1½ standard sticks) butter

Tip: Cleanup is easier if the Dutch oven is first lined with heavy-duty aluminum foil coated with non-stick spray.

Daniel Czarnecki, Grand Haven, Michigan
Advancement Chairperson, Troop 165, Gerald R. Ford Council, Boy Scouts of America

Linda Czarnecki, Grand Haven, Michigan
Committee Member, Troop 165 / Venture Crew 2165, Gerald R. Ford Council, Boy Scouts of America

Ray's World Famous Bread Puddin'

Servings: 8–10 | Challenge Level: Moderate

"This recipe won first place in *Scouting* magazine's 2001 'Great Tastes in Camp Cooking' recipe contest."

4 eggs

2 cups milk

8 slices white bread

Butter, enough to spread on 1 side of each of 8 slices of bread

2 cups applesauce

Ground cinnamon to taste

2 cups brown sugar

2 cups raisins

Whipped cream or ice cream (optional)

Preparation at Camp:

1. In medium-size bowl, beat eggs and milk and set aside.

2. Butter 4 slices of bread on one side and lay in a single layer, butter-side down, in bottom of foil-lined Dutch oven.

3. Spread half of the applesauce over the bread layer. Sprinkle generously with cinnamon. Put about half of the brown sugar over the cinnamon and applesauce. Scatter all the raisins over the brown sugar.

4. Cut the other 4 slices of bread diagonally and butter them. Set butter-side down over raisins.

5. Spread the remainder of the applesauce over the bread. Put the rest of the brown sugar over the applesauce and sprinkle generously with cinnamon.

6. Pour the egg-and-milk mixture over and between the slices of bread.

7. Put lid on Dutch oven and let the bread soak in the egg-and-milk mixture for 30 minutes.

8. Bake for 45 minutes using 7 coals under the oven and 16 briquettes on the lid.

9. Cool and serve with optional whipped cream or ice cream.

Required Equipment:

12-inch Dutch oven

Medium-size bowl

Heavy-duty aluminum foil

Ray McCune, Fort Wayne, Indiana
Feature Editor of *MidWest Outdoor Magazine*'s Kampfire Kookin' Column
Assistant Scoutmaster and Founder of Troop 38, Anthony Wayne Area Council, Boy Scouts of America

Grandpa's Golden Apple Caramel Cake

Servings: 10–12 | Challenge Level: Moderate

"Grandpa's Golden Apple Caramel Cake won first place in the dessert category at our local Fourth of July 'Cherry Days Cook-Off.' This dish goes great with ice cream."

Preparation at Camp:

1. In large bowl, mix apple slices and sugar.

2. Add flour, baking soda, cinnamon, nutmeg, and salt. Stir well.

3. In a separate bowl, beat eggs, vegetable oil, and vanilla together.

4. Stir the egg mixture into the apple mixture, blending until apples are thoroughly moistened. The mixture will be thick.

5. Stir in chopped walnuts and pecans.

6. Pour cake batter into Dutch oven.

7. Bake for 45 minutes using 17 coals on the lid and 8 briquettes under the oven.

8. Prepare the caramel topping while the cake bakes by mixing all topping ingredients in a saucepan.

9. Bring to a low boil over medium heat and cook for 3 minutes.

10. Once the cake has finished baking, pour the caramel topping over the cake and serve.

Required Equipment:

12-inch Dutch oven
Medium-size saucepan
Large-size mixing bowl
Medium-size mixing bowl

Cake:

3 large Golden Delicious apples, sliced

2 cups sugar

2 cups all-purpose flour

1½ teaspoons baking soda

1 teaspoon cinnamon

1 teaspoon nutmeg

1 teaspoon salt

2 large eggs

¾ cup vegetable oil

2 teaspoons vanilla extract

½ cup chopped walnuts

½ cup chopped pecans

Caramel Topping:

1 cup brown sugar

¾ cup butter

1 cup heavy whipping cream

2 teaspoons vanilla

Mark Brown, Ogden, Utah
Committee Member, Troop 236, Trapper Trails Council, Boy Scouts of America

Kathy Jurgen's Chocoholic Cake

Servings: 8–10 | Challenge Level: Moderate

2 cups cake flour

2 cups sugar

½ cup (1 standard stick) butter

½ cup shortening (such as Crisco)

2½ squares semi-sweet solid chocolate (such as Baker's)

1 cup water

½ cup buttermilk

2 eggs

1 teaspoon baking soda

1 teaspoon vanilla extract

1 (16-ounce) container chocolate frosting

Option: Powdered sugar may be substituted for the frosting.

Preparation at Camp:

1. In a medium-size bowl, mix flour and sugar. Set aside.

2. In a small saucepan, combine butter, shortening, solid chocolate, and water. Bring to a boil.

3. Add melted butter mixture to flour and sugar in the bowl. Stir well, and allow to cool slightly.

4. To the flour-butter mixture, add buttermilk, eggs, baking soda, and vanilla extract. Mix well.

5. Pour cake mixture into greased cake pan.

6. Place cake pan on trivet in Dutch oven.

7. Using 16 coals under the oven and 10 briquettes on the lid, bake for 20 minutes.

8. Insert fork into cake. If tines come out clean and top is beginning to brown, the cake is ready.

9. If cake is not ready, continue baking for an additional 10 minutes or until top of cake browns.

10. Set cake aside to cool. Spread frosting over top, then serve.

Required Equipment:

12-inch Dutch oven with trivet

Small-size saucepan

9-inch round cake pan (approximately 3 inches deep)

Medium-size mixing bowl

Dr. Pamela Jurgens-Toepke, New Lenox, Illinois
Committee Member, Troop 40, Tomahawk Council, Boy Scouts of America

Abraham Lincoln Strawberry-Peach Cobbler

Servings: 8–10 | Challenge Level: Moderate

"I first prepared this cobbler several years ago at Illinek, our local Scout Camp near Springfield, Illinois. Our troop was camping there on a weekend late summer. It began to drizzle as evening approached. I was concerned that the rain might extinguish the coals on top of the Dutch ovens as they were uncovered in the fire ring, not under the dining shelter. One of the other assistant scoutmasters simply pulled off a couple of sheets of aluminum foil just large enough to loosely cover the coals on each of the lids. The foil kept off the rain but allowed the ovens to continue to heat. The cobbler, along with the rest of the meal, was awesome!"

Preparation at Camp:

1. In a medium-size bowl, combine brown sugar, flour, oatmeal, and cinnamon. Cut in the butter with a fork. Set aside.

2. Drain the sliced peaches and reserve the juice.

3. In a large bowl, slice peaches into 1-inch pieces. Cut partially thawed strawberries in halves or quarters, depending on size of strawberries. Mix the peaches, strawberries, and ¼ cup of the reserved peach juice.

4. Pour peaches and strawberries into Dutch oven.

5. Sprinkle sugar-flour-oatmeal topping evenly over top of the fruit mixture.

6. Using 21 coals on the lid and 10 briquettes under the oven, bake for about 30 minutes or until the cobbler is heated through and topping is slightly browned.

7. Spoon the warm cobbler into bowls. Top with optional vanilla pudding.

Required Equipment:

12-inch Dutch oven
Medium-size mixing bowl
Large-size mixing bowl

½ cup firmly packed brown sugar

¼ cup whole wheat flour

½ cup quick oatmeal

1 teaspoon ground cinnamon

¼ cup (½ standard stick) butter

2 (29-ounce) cans sliced peaches

1 (16-ounce) bag whole frozen strawberries, partly thawed

Vanilla pudding (optional)

Larry Boehme, New Berlin, Illinois
Assistant Scoutmaster, Troop 27, Abraham Lincoln Council, Boy Scouts of America

Teenage Sugar Addict Orange Rolls

Servings: 8–10 | Challenge Level: Difficult

"My teenagers, sugar addicts that they are, can only eat two of these at breakfast. Even they admit this is an incredibly rich recipe."

Dough:

1½ tablespoons active dry yeast

1 teaspoon sugar

½ cup warm water (100–110 degrees F)

1 cup warm milk

½ cup sugar

½ cup (1 standard stick) butter, melted

2 eggs, beaten

1 teaspoon salt

5 cups all-purpose flour

Extra flour to work dough

Filling:

1 orange rind, grated

¼ cup (½ standard stick) butter, melted

½ cup sugar

Glaze:

¼ cup (½ standard stick) butter, melted

1 cup powdered sugar

Juice from 1 orange

Preparation at Camp:

1. In a large bowl, prepare the dough by combining yeast, 1 teaspoon sugar, and ½ cup warm water. Allow mixture to sit for 5–10 minutes. If the yeast is active, it should swell and bubble.

2. Blend in milk, ½ cup sugar, ½ cup melted butter, and eggs. Add the salt and flour.

3. Powder your hands with the extra flour, and knead the dough for approximately 10 minutes.

4. Cover the bowl with a moist towel and set aside in a warm area to rise until it doubles in volume. This should take about 45 minutes.

5. While the dough rises, prepare the filling in a small bowl by combining orange rind, ¼ cup melted butter, and ½ cup sugar.

6. Roll the risen dough flat into a rectangle approximately 9x13 inches on its sides.

7. Spread the filling mixture evenly over the dough, stopping just shy of the edges.

8. From the longer edge, roll the dough into a cylinder. Pinch edges of dough to seal.

9. Cut the roll into 1-inch thick round slices.

10. Place rolls in a Dutch oven lined with greased foil.

11. Using 22 coals on the lid and 10 briquettes under the oven, bake for 40–45 minutes or until rolls become a light golden brown. Check periodically to ensure rolls aren't burning.

12. While rolls bake, mix glaze in small-size bowl using ¼ cup melted butter, powdered sugar, and orange juice.

13. Pour glaze over the rolls when they are finished baking. Serve warm.

Required Equipment:

14-inch Dutch oven
Large-size mixing bowl
Small-size mixing bowl
Heavy-duty aluminum foil

Connie Knie, Farmington Hills, Michigan
Assistant Scoutmaster, Troop 179, Clinton Valley Council, Boy Scouts of America

Coca-Cola Cake

Servings: 10–12 | Challenge Level: Moderate

Cake:

2 cups all-purpose flour

2 cups granulated sugar

1 cup (2 standard sticks) butter

3 tablespoons cocoa powder

1 cup Coca-Cola

1 cup buttermilk

2 eggs

1 teaspoon baking soda

1 teaspoon vanilla extract

1½ cups mini marshmallows

Icing:

½ cup (1 standard stick) butter

3 tablespoons cocoa powder

½ cup Coca-Cola

1 pound confectioners' sugar

1 cup chopped pecans

Preparation at Camp:

1. To prepare cake batter, combine flour and granulated sugar in a large bowl, reserving a small amount of flour for dusting the cake pan.

2. In a saucepan, bring 1 cup butter, 3 tablespoons cocoa powder, and 1 cup Coca-Cola to a boil. Pour liquid over flour and sugar in bowl. Mix well.

3. Add buttermilk, eggs, baking soda, vanilla extract, and marshmallows, and mix well. Pour batter into greased and floured springform cake pan.

4. Place cake pan on trivet in Dutch oven.

5. Using 10 coals under the oven and 20 briquettes on the lid, bake for about 45 minutes, occasionally rotating the oven base and lid to prevent hot spots on the cake. Cake is ready when inserted toothpick comes out clean.

6. While cake is baking, prepare icing by combining ½ cup butter, 3 tablespoons cocoa powder, and ½ cup Coca-Cola in saucepan. Heat to boiling.

7. Remove pan from heat and add confectioners' sugar and pecans. Mix well.

8. Once cake is ready, pour hot icing over warm cake. Serve.

Required Equipment:

Deep 14-inch Dutch oven with trivet

10-inch round by 3-inch deep springform cake pan

Medium-size saucepan

Large-size mixing bowl

Michael Darnell, Okemos, Michigan
Assistant Scoutmaster, Troop 109, Chief Okemos Council, Boy Scouts of America

Moose Drops

Servings: 6–8 | Challenge Level: Easy

"My scouts usually placed a piece of waxed paper on a camp table and laid out the 'drops' in the cool evening air. This was a fun after-dinner activity, preparing the dessert while it was growing dark, enjoying the campfire, then topping off the evening with Moose Drops."

Preparation at Camp:

1. In a large saucepan over medium heat, blend the sugar, butter, milk, and cocoa powder.

2. Increase heat and boil for 3 minutes, stirring constantly.

3. Remove from heat. Add oatmeal and vanilla then stir.

4. Drop mixture by the teaspoon onto waxed paper.

5. Chill and serve.

Required Equipment:

Large-size sauce pan

Waxed paper

2 cups sugar

½ cup (1 standard stick) butter

½ cup milk

½ cup unsweetened cocoa powder

3 cups regular oatmeal (do not use quick or instant)

1 tablespoon vanilla extract

George Brown, Los Osos, California
Former Scoutmaster, Troop 216, Los Padres Council, Boy Scouts of America

Icky Sticky Chocolate Rolls

Servings: 8–10 | Challenge Level: Easy

"I prepared this with my girls for a Try-It event. The candies taste and look like Tootsie Rolls. Caution! A little goes a long way: Icky Sticky Chocolate Rolls are very sweet!"

2 tablespoons butter

2 squares unsweetened baking chocolate

½ cup corn syrup (such as Karo)

1 teaspoon vanilla extract

3 cups powdered sugar

¾ cup nonfat powdered milk

Preparation at Camp:

1. Let butter soften in a gallon-size ziplock freezer bag.

2. Melt chocolate in a small pot, and allow to cool slightly.

3. Add chocolate and the remainder of ingredients to the butter in the ziplock bag.

4. Carefully seal bag. Let the kids mush the contents thoroughly while passing the bag around, taking turns.

5. Form candy into balls, rolls, or one giant roll!

Required Equipment:

Small-size cook pot
Gallon-size ziplock freezer bag

Nadine Peacock, Orlando, Florida
Leader, Citrus Council, Girl Scouts of the USA

Alpine Peaches and Pears

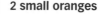

Servings: 4–6 | Challenge Level: Easy

"This recipe can be served as a hot dessert to warm up the troop on a winter campout, or served cool on a hot day by chilling the pot in a cold stream."

Preparation at Camp:

1. Peel oranges using a knife. Cut oranges in half crossways and break each half into four segments. Using a knife to peel the oranges permits more flavor to seep from the cut edges.

2. In a medium-size pot, combine all ingredients.

3. Bring to a boil, then lower heat. Simmer for 5 minutes while carefully stirring.

4. Remove from heat and allow to rest, lid on, for at least 2 hours.

5. When ready to serve, reheat on low until steaming but not boiling.

Required Equipment:

Medium-size cook pot

2 small oranges

¼ cup honey

2 tablespoons lemon juice

1 (15-ounce) can peach halves in heavy syrup

1 (15-ounce) can pear halves in light syrup

5 whole cloves

2 whole cinnamon sticks

Option: One (15-ounce) can of mandarin oranges may be substituted for the fresh oranges, but the recipe will lose a bit of its tanginess.

Helen Greymorning, Missoula, Montana
Committee Member, Troop 1911, Montana Council, Boy Scouts of America

Chinese Chopsticks

Servings: 3–4 | Challenge Level: Easy

⅔ cup peanut butter

1 cup butterscotch morsels

1 (3-ounce) can chow mein noodles

Preparation at Camp:

1. Melt peanut butter and morsels together in a sauce-pan over medium heat.

2. Once sauce is smooth, stir in the noodles.

3. Drop mixture by the teaspoonful onto waxed paper.

4. Chill in a cooler or the evening air.

Required Equipment:

Medium-size sauce pan

Waxed paper

George Brown, Los Osos, California
Former Scoutmaster, Troop 216, Los Padres Council, Boy Scouts of America

Hansel and Gretel's Gingerbread Delight

Servings: 8–10 | Challenge Level: Easy

Preparation at Camp:

1. Prepare gingerbread mix in a medium-size bowl with water and egg.

2. In a medium-size pot, bring applesauce to a boil.

3. Drop gingerbread dough by the spoonful on top of boiling applesauce. Reduce flame.

4. Cover pot tightly. Heat for 20–30 minutes over very low heat or until gingerbread dumplings are cooked through.

5. Serve with whipped topping.

Required Equipment:

Medium-size cook pot with lid
Medium-size mixing bowl

1 (14½-ounce) box Betty Crocker ginger-bread mix

1¼ cups lukewarm water

1 egg

1 (24-ounce) jar applesauce

1 (16-ounce) container whipped topping (such as Cool Whip)

Julie Terranera, Port Orange, Florida
National Operational Volunteer / Instructor of Trainers / Lifetime Member, Citrus Council, Girl Scouts of the USA

Canoe Country Rice Pudding

Servings: 6–8 | Challenge Level: Moderate

"I made this pudding for the first time on a wood stove at my son's log home for Christmas dinner. You will find this to be a great treat after a day's paddle. This pudding has won first prize at our District's Roundtable Cook-Off."

1 cup water

½ teaspoon salt

½ cup long-grain rice (do not use instant)

1 quart milk

¼ cup (½ standard stick) butter

3 eggs, beaten

½ cup sugar

1 cup raisins (or dried currents or cranberries)

1 teaspoon vanilla extract

Ground cinnamon to taste

Preparation at Camp:

1. In a medium-size pot, bring water and salt to a boil.

2. Add rice and cook for 7 minutes or until water has evaporated.

3. Add milk and butter then stir. Cook over low heat for 1 hour 15 minutes, stirring occasionally.

4. Combine eggs, sugar, raisins, and vanilla in a medium-size mixing bowl.

5. Pour mixture into rice and stir slowly until pudding begins to thicken.

6. Add cinnamon to taste and serve.

Required Equipment:

Medium-size cook pot

Medium-size mixing bowl

Dennis Hebrink, Wyoming, Minnesota
Sunrise River District Chair, Northern Star Council, Boy Scouts of America

Bunco Banana Pie

Servings: 6–8 | Challenge Level: Moderate

"I first tested this on my Bunco group, and it was a big hit. The recipe uses those pervasive shortbread cookies, of which every Girl Scout troop has plenty leftover in the Spring."

Preparation at Camp:

1. Place open can of condensed milk, uncovered and up-right, into a shallow pot of simmering water. Make sure the can is opened to allow steam to escape, and don't allow water to get into the milk!

2. Simmer condensed milk in this manner until milk cara-melizes into a light brown toffee-like consistency, about 90 minutes.

3. While milk simmers, gently crush Trefoils in gallon-size ziplock freezer bag. Add melted butter to crushed cook-ies and mix thoroughly, first allowing melted butter to cool to a safe temperature before adding to the ziplock bag.

4. Spread cookie crust mixture into a 9x13-inch baking pan.

5. Pour caramelized condensed milk over shortbread crust.

6. Slice bananas into rounds and lay over the milk.

7. In a second gallon-size ziplock freezer bag, combine whipping cream, coffee, and powdered sugar. Carefully seal bag and shake vigorously until cream mix becomes thick and smooth.

8. Cut a corner from the bottom of the bag and squirt the whipped cream over the entire pie. Serve immediately.

Required Equipment:

Small-size cook pot
9x13-inch baking pan
2 one-gallon-size ziplock freezer bags

Julia Whiteneck, Bedford, Massachusetts
Girl Scout Trainer, Patriots' Trail Council, Girl Scouts of the USA

Ingredients

1 (14-ounce) can sweetened condensed milk

1 (10-ounce) box Trefoils (short-bread) Girl Scout Cookies

¼ cup (½ standard stick) butter, melted

3 firm bananas

1 pint whipping cream, chilled

½ teaspoon instant decaffein-ated coffee

2 tablespoons powdered sugar

Patriot's Path Dessert

Servings: 5 | Challenge Level: Easy

1 (1-pound) loaf nut bread (banana, cranberry, orange, or cinnamon)

1 (8-ounce) package cream cheese

2 bananas

2 tablespoons butter

⅓ cup powdered sugar

Preparation at Camp:

1. Cut nut bread into 10 slices.

2. Slice cream cheese into ½-inch pieces and distribute evenly on five nut bread slices.

3. Slice bananas into rounds and place on top of cream cheese. Cover each with a remaining slice of nut bread, making a total of five sandwiches.

4. Melt butter in skillet. Fry sandwiches over medium-low heat until golden brown on both sides. Be careful as butter browns quickly.

5. Sprinkle both sides of each sandwich with powdered sugar, then serve.

Required Equipment:

Large-size frying pan

Brigitta M. Pereillo, Landing, New Jersey
Webelos Leader, Pack 188, Patriots' Path Council, Boy Scouts of America

Flop Jacks

Servings: 4 | Challenge Level: Easy

"I found this recipe in my dad's copy of the Charles Sommers wilderness cooking pamphlet, filled with cooking ideas passed down and modified by the canoe guides at the Charles Sommers Canoe Base in Ely, Minnesota. In my years as a Scoutmaster, I've made modifications to this recipe, such as taking advantage of newer ingredients like premade pie dough.

Wilderness canoe routes were often long, so some of the preparation work for cooking actually took place in the canoes while still on the water. My dad used to prepare flop jacks while in the canoe, rolling the dough either on the bow deck or on a paddle blade. When they hit shore, he would have the day's cook fry them while he and the others set up camp. Needless to say, my dad was popular with hungry scouts. And I can still recall the taste of the flop jacks he made with fresh berries on my first canoe trip over 30 years ago."

Preparation at Camp:

1. Unroll pie crusts on a flat surface. Cut each crust in half to make 4 halves total.

2. Brush tops of each half with melted butter.

3. Scoop pie filing onto each half and fold the crust over, forming a triangle. Seal the edges by pinching them between your fingers.

4. Brush the outside of all flop jacks with butter. With a fork, pierce small vent holes in each, then sprinkle with sugar.

5. In a greased pan, fry flop jacks slowly on medium-low heat. Flip. Serve once the crusts are golden brown.

1 (15-ounce) package of 2 refrigerated pie crusts (such as Pillsbury)

3 tablespoons butter, melted

1 (21-ounce) can pie filling (your choice)

2 tablespoons sugar

Required Equipment:

Large-size frying pan

Curt "The Titanium Chef" White, Forks, Washington
Scoutmaster, Troop 1467, Chief Seattle Council, Boy Scouts of America

Cinnamon Banana Bake

Servings: 3 / Multiply as Required | Challenge Level: Easy

3 firm bananas

⅓ cup sugar

1 teaspoon ground cinnamon

Preparation at Camp:

1. Place unpeeled bananas over medium heat. Grill for 10–15 minutes, turning once. The skin will turn almost completely black.

2. Carefully remove bananas from grill. Peel and gently roll in cinnamon-sugar mixture. Serve while warm.

Susan Jorstad, East Stroudsburg, Pennsylvania
Den Leader, Pack 92, Minsi Trails Council, Boy Scouts of America

Dream S'mores

Servings: 1 / Multiply as Required | Challenge Level: Easy

"Early one morning, Lois Sanchez was suddenly awakened by a startling dream. This was no ordinary event, for in her dream she had a vision. To the casual observer, the vision would have been subtle and easy to forget. But not for Lois. As a result, the course of s'mores history was changed forever.

In her dream, Lois was camping. And while she was camping, she saw herself busily applying peanut butter to an otherwise ordinary s'mores. With that, her dream ended. The impact on Lois was tremendous. She shook her husband Michael from his slumber and breathlessly relayed what she saw. Like Lois, Michael is a s'mores enthusiast. He naturally shared her excitement.

They couldn't wait! That very day, they tested Dream S'mores on Pack 507. History tells us that their den loved the amended recipe so much, they always insist that their s'mores include peanut butter even when it means a trip back to the grocery for the forgotten jar.

As with many tales of the miraculous, there is an ironic epilogue to this remarkable story. Although Lois was chosen to be the messenger of an amazing recipe, she actually prefers her s'mores the old-fashioned way...without peanut butter!"

Preparation at Camp:

1. Spread peanut butter on one side of a graham cracker.

2. Place piece of chocolate onto the peanut butter.

3. Roast marshmallow on a stick until gooey.

4. Carefully place gooey marshmallow between plain graham cracker and the graham cracker with peanut butter and chocolate.

Required Equipment:

Roasting stick

1 teaspoon peanut butter

1 piece Hersey's milk chocolate

1 large marshmallow

2 graham crackers

Option: This recipe also tastes great with Reese's Peanut Butter Cups.

Lois Sanchez, Orange, California
Den Assistant Leader, Pack 507, El Capitan Council, Boy Scouts of America

Shudderuppers

Servings: 1 / Multiply as Required | Challenge Level: Easy

"This recipe is from Girl Scouts Peacepipe Council, which serves Southwestern Minnesota."

1 caramel candy cube

1 marshmallow

Hershey chocolate bar and graham crackers (optional)

Preparation at Camp:

1. Thread marshmallow onto a stick followed by a cube of caramel, and roast over a bed of coals, not a flaming fire.

2. When marshmallow is golden, not burned, pull it up over the caramel so that the caramel is inside the marshmallow. Be careful: the caramel will be hot!

3. Let cool. Eat as is or sandwich between chocolate bar and graham crackers to make a Shudderupper S'mores!

Required Equipment:

Roasting stick

Jeanie Haas, Redwood Falls, Minnesota
Membership and Marketing Specialist, Peacepipe Council, Girl Scouts of the USA

Fairy Fruit Rings

Serves: 1 / Multiply as Required | Challenge Level: Easy

Preparation at Camp:

1. Place doughnut on small sheet of heavy-duty aluminum foil.

2. Top donut with fruit filling.

3. Fold foil securely over donut and place on coals until donut warms, about 1 or 2 minutes.

Required Equipment:

Heavy-duty aluminum foil

1 sourdough or plain donut

¼ cup pie filling (cherry, apple, blackberry, blueberry, or peach)

Millie Hutchison, Pittsburgh, Pennsylvania
Girl Scout Trainer, Trillium Council, Girl Scouts of the USA

Heavenly Hobo Cherry Pie

Servings: 1 / Multiply as Required | Challenge Level: Easy

Butter to grease pie iron

2 (¾-inch) slices angel food cake or pound cake

2 tablespoons cherry pie filling

Whipped cream to taste

Preparation at Camp:

1. Butter each side of the pie iron cooking surface.

2. Place one slice of cake into each side of pie iron.

3. Spread cherry pie filling on one of the slices of cake.

4. Close pie iron and place on the coals of your fire.

5. Once the slice facing the coals becomes golden brown, flip and repeat on the opposite side. Cooking time will vary based on the heat of the coals, the type of material the pie iron is made from, and whether the pie iron has been preheated.

6. Remove from heat. Serve with whipped cream.

Required Equipment:

Pie iron

Tip: This recipe can also be prepared by wrapping the cake in heavy-duty aluminum foil instead of using the pie iron.

Margaret Bushman, Waterford, Michigan
Assistant Cubmaster, Pack 51, Clinton Valley Council, Boy Scouts of America

Casey's Pineapple Upside-Down Cake

Servings: 1 / Multiply as Required | Challenge Level: Easy

"My granddaughter, Casey, joined me at Tanglewood Camp every summer from the time she was two years old. Sadly, she didn't live long past her 18th birthday. Her cousin, Ashley, who came to Tanglewood with Casey, now teaches other girls at camp how to prepare Casey's best-loved cake: pineapple upside-down."

1 teaspoon butter

1 tablespoon brown sugar

1 pineapple ring

1 cake donut

Preparation at Camp:

1. Place butter at bottom of tuna can.

2. Add brown sugar followed by the pineapple ring.

3. Cut the donut in half as you would a bagel and place one of the halves on top of the pineapple ring.

4. Heat on a grill grate over campfire coals until the butter bubbles.

5. Carefully remove can, flip over onto a plate, and serve.

Required Equipment:

1 (6-ounce) clean tuna can, label removed

Donna Pettigrew, Anderson, Indiana
Tanglewood Day Camp Director and Master Trainer, Central Indiana Girl Scout Council, Girl Scouts of the USA

Camp Oest Apple Pie

Servings: 4 | Challenge Level: Easy

"I first prepared this recipe at Broad Creek Memorial Scout Reservation, where my family and I camped alone one night on Flint Ridge in the freezing cold watching a lunar eclipse while we ate our dessert. The recipe is named for our favorite Cub camp at Broad Creek, Camp Oest, where we often volunteer. Broad Creek is known for its green serpentine mine and a beautiful grove of hemlocks. My family absolutely loves that place. Whenever we arrive, we sing the camp hymn at the top of our lungs!"

1 (15-ounce) package of 2 refrigerated pie crusts (such as Pillsbury)

1 (21-ounce) can apple pie filling

1 cup brown sugar

½ cup granulated sugar

¼ cup (½ standard stick) butter

Preparation at Camp:

1. Cut each pie crust in half to make a total of four pieces.

2. Place each piece of crust on a separate sheet of heavy-duty aluminum foil that is at least twice the size of the pastry once it is folded in half.

3. Divide the apple pie filling among the four crusts.

4. Divide brown and granulated sugars among the four pies, leaving enough for sprinkling the outsides of the pies in a later step.

5. Fold each pie crust over. Close by pinching edges shut. If crust is reluctant to adhere, wet inside edges with water and pinch again.

6. Place a pat of butter on each side of pastry packet and sprinkle each side with sugar to taste.

7. Fold foil in half, centering the pastry in the pocket. Tightly seal by folding edges three times over. Leave a little room within the foil around the pastry itself.

8. Place foil packet directly onto coals and cook for 10–15 minutes per side. The packet may puff up a little as the steam expands.

Required Equipment:

Heavy-duty aluminum foil

Kimra Simmons, Abingdon, Maryland
Webelos Den Leader, Pack 936, Baltimore Area Council, Boy Scouts of America

Pine Cones

Servings: 1 / Multiply as Required | Challenge Level: Easy

Preparation at Camp:

1. To prevent flaming, quickly dip marshmallow in water.

2. Place marshmallow on a stick and toast over fire until golden brown.

3. Immediately roll hot marshmallow in chocolate syrup and then in coconut, cereal, nuts, or sprinkles.

Required Equipment:

Bowls for holding dipping ingredients
Roasting stick

1 large marshmallow

1 teaspoon chocolate syrup

1 teaspoon shredded coconut, Rice Krispies cereal, chopped nuts, or cookie sprinkles

Options: If no campfire is available for roasting your marshmallows, uncooked marshmallows can be rolled in melted chocolate or icing before dipping in other toppings.

Millie Hutchison, Pittsburgh, Pennsylvania
Girl Scout Trainer, Trillium Council, Girl Scouts of the USA

Bonfire Banana Boats

Servings: 1 / Multiply as Required | Challenge Level: Easy

"This is a great cookout dessert that even a Tiger Cub can help prepare!"

1 banana

3 tablespoons chocolate chips

3 tablespoons mini marshmallows

Preparation at Camp:

1. Sit the banana upright like a canoe. Peel one strip of skin from the top of the "boat" without removing the peel completely.

2. Scoop out about a third of the banana along its length. Go ahead and eat that part!

3. Pour chocolate chips and marshmallows into the scooped-out hollow of the banana.

4. Replace peel and wrap banana in heavy-duty aluminum foil.

5. Toss on hot coals for 5–10 minutes, just long enough to allow chocolate and marshmallows to melt.

6. Remove from fire. Carefully unwrap foil. Pull off the top strip of banana peel and serve.

Required Equipment:

Heavy-duty aluminum foil

Laura Vito, Allentown, Pennsylvania
Den Leader, Pack 22, Minsi Trails Council, Boy Scouts of America

Blennie's Hot Cinnamon Apples

Servings: 4 | Challenge Level: Easy

4 large baking apples (Pippins or Granny Smiths work well)

½ cup red hot cinnamon candies

4 caramel cubes

Preparation at Camp:

1. Core the apples, leaving a small amount of apple at bottom of each so that candies won't fall through.

2. Fill each cored apple with 2 tablespoons of cinnamon candies.

3. Place caramel cube in the top of each apple, molding it to create a seal.

4. Wrap each apple in two layers of heavy-duty aluminum foil.

5. Place on coals for about 15 minutes or until apple can be easily pierced with a fork.

6. Carefully remove from fire, and allow to cool before serving.

Required Equipment:

Heavy-duty aluminum foil

Tip: Use extra foil when wrapping apples to create a handle for easier extraction from the fire.

Blennie Danielson, Arcadia, California
Volunteer, Troop 111, Lucky Baldwin Council, Boy Scouts of America

Magic Wands

Servings: 1 / Multiply as Required | Challenge Level: Easy

1 miniature donut

1 marshmallow

Preparation at Camp:

1. Slide donut on a stick followed by the marshmallow on the end.

2. Toast over fire. Don't forget to say the magic words before you gobble them up!

Required Equipment:

Roasting stick

Millie Hutchison, Pittsburgh, Pennsylvania
Girl Scout Trainer, Trillium Council, Girl Scouts of the USA

Black Warrior Cannonballs

Servings: 4 | Challenge Level: Easy

Preparation at Camp:

1. Combine brown sugar, raisins, nuts, and cinnamon in a small bowl or plastic bag.

2. Wash and core the apples, leaving the bottom on the apples to retain juices. A small melon ball utensil can do the job more easily, neatly, and safely than a knife.

3. Place apples on individual sheets of heavy-duty aluminum foil. Spoon sugar mixture into the cored centers of each apple and set a piece of butter into top of mixture.

4. Wrap each apple tightly in foil. Place upright on coals and cook until tender, about 15 minutes.

Required Equipment:

Small-size bowl

Heavy-duty aluminum foil

Melon ball utensil (optional)

¼ cup light brown sugar

¼ cup raisins

2 tablespoons chopped pecans or walnuts

½ teaspoon ground cinnamon

4 large Granny Smith apples

2 tablespoons butter, cut into 4 pieces

Robert Rainwater, Brookwood, Alabama
Scoutmaster, Troop 3, Black Warrior Council, Boy Scouts of America

Twain's Twisters

Servings: 8 | Challenge Level: Easy

"We have a troop of developmentally disabled adults who love to cook and eat. They firmly believe the phrase 'a scout is hungry' is as much a part of scout law as 'a scout is loyal, thrifty, and brave.' We were determined to win the cooking contest last year, so we experimented with several different recipes, this being one. The crescent twists are a variation of the old bread-on-a-stick, but sweetened up and made a bit special."

½ cup granulated sugar

1 teaspoon ground cinnamon

1 (8-ounce, 8-count) container refrigerated crescent roll dough (such as Pillsbury)

¼ cup butter, melted

Preparation at Camp:

1. Combine sugar and cinnamon in a small paper bag.

2. Separate crescent dough into 8 separate rolls.

3. Wrap a dough triangle around each roasting stick, spiraling the rolls down the sticks.

4. Cook slowly over a wood fire or coals, turning frequently.

5. Once rolls are golden brown and no longer gooey, coat each with melted butter.

6. Immediately remove roll from the stick and place in the bag containing cinnamon and sugar. Shake well to coat.

7. Remove and serve.

Required Equipment:

Paper lunch bag
Roasting sticks

Albert Pabst, Hannibal, Missouri
Scoutmaster, Troop 594, Great River Council, Mark Twain District,
Boy Scouts of America

Joy Pabst, Hannibal, Missouri
Committee Chairman, Troop 594, Great River Council, Mark Twain District,
Boy Scouts of America

Kickin' Popcorn

Servings: 1 / Multiply as Required | Challenge Level: Easy

Preparation at Camp:

1. Cut a piece of heavy-duty aluminum foil into a sheet approximately 7x7-inches square.

2. Spread oil and popping corn in the center of foil sheet.

3. Take two opposite sides of the foil and bring them together, sealing them by rolling them together like the end of a tube of toothpaste. Now seal the two open ends, creating a pouch inside with plenty of room for the popcorn to expand.

4. Place camping fork prongs or a stick through the thick part of the rolled foil and hold over hot coals. Shake to avoid burning the kernels until the corn stops kickin'.

5. Salt to taste and serve.

Required Equipment:

Heavy-duty aluminum foil
Camping fork or stick

Tip: Using a high-heat oil, such as peanut, will help avoid smoking while the corn pops.

1 teaspoon peanut oil

1 tablespoon popping corn

Salt to taste

Millie Hutchison, Pittsburgh, Pennsylvania
Girl Scout Trainer, Trillium Council, Girl Scouts of the USA

Tanglewood Peach Pie

Servings: 4 | Challenge Level: Easy

"The following lyrics, sung to *The Addams Family* theme music, were written by Girl Scouts at Camp Tanglewood:

> We're hiking and we're cooking
> We're walking in the Brooking
> We're terribly good looking:
> The Girls of Tanglewood!
>
> We're playing in the sun
> We sing till day is done
> We're always having fun:
> The Girls of Tanglewood!
>
> The Food . . . The Crafts . . . The Bugs!"

2 (16.3-ounce, 8-count) container Pillsbury Grands! Homestyle Biscuits

1 fresh peach, sliced

4 teaspoons sugar

Options: If fresh peaches aren't available, canned sliced peaches work well. Also, try substituting chocolate and marshmallows for the peaches.

Preparation at Camp:

1. On each of four biscuits, lay one quarter of the peach slices.

2. Top peaches on each biscuit with one teaspoon sugar.

3. Cover each assembly with a second biscuit. Pinch biscuits together along the sides to seal in the peaches and sugar.

4. Wrap each biscuit ensemble in heavy-duty foil and lay on coals.

5. Heat for several minutes on each side until biscuits are cooked.

Required Equipment:

Heavy-duty aluminum foil

Donna Pettigrew, Anderson, Indiana
Tanglewood Day Camp Director and Master Trainer, Central Indiana Girl Scout Council, Girl Scouts of the USA

Camp Lachenwald Banana-Nut Kabobs

Servings: 4 | Challenge Level: Easy

"This recipe was adapted from a gourmet cooking class I took in Germany in 2002. Susi Edgar, an extremely talented writer and trainer, was our instructor. The recipe is named for Camp Lachenwald, the only American Girl Scout resident camp operating in Europe. The 100-acre camp is located on a wooded hillside, overlooking rolling meadows in the farming town of Hommertshausen, Germany."

Preparation at Camp:

1. Dip four banana quarters in melted butter.

2. Thread one banana piece onto a camping fork, followed by a cherry. Repeat sequence two more times, and follow up with the final banana piece. Repeat for each of the remaining three forks.

3. Roast over coals until warmed through.

4. Roll in chopped nuts and serve.

Required Equipment:

4 camping forks

4 bananas, each peeled and cut into 4 pieces

¼ cup (½ standard stick) butter, melted

12 maraschino cherries

½ cup chopped nuts (peanuts, walnuts, or pecans)

Options: "Fruit Kabobs" can be made using a similar method. Thread chunks of banana, pineapple, and cherries in between marshmallows. Toast over coals until marshmallows are golden brown then eat right off the skewer. The ingredients in this recipe can also be combined and cooked in aluminum foil over coals.

Katie Salyer Cox, Tucson, Arizona
Leader and Trainer, USA Girl Scouts Overseas and Sahuaro Council, Girl Scouts of the USA

Woofumms

Servings: 10 | Challenge Level: Moderate

"You'll understand this recipe's name the first time you make it: The kids woofumm down as fast as they can! This is a great campfire treat and beats marshmallows all to heck."

Nonstick vegetable spray (such as PAM)

2 (12-ounce, 10-count) containers refrigerated biscuit dough (such as Pillsbury)

3 (14-ounce, 4-pack) packages chocolate or vanilla pudding cups (such as Hunt's Snack Pack)

1 (7-ounce) can whipped topping (such as Reddi-wip)

Options: Biscuit bowls can also be filled with apple pie filling, chili, or just about anything you can imagine.

Preparation at Camp:

1. Lightly spray vegetable spray on the wooden end of your woofumm stick. Don't use too much or your biscuits will slide off.

2. Take one biscuit and wrap it over the end of the stick, shaping it into a bowl.

3. Hold biscuit over a bed of coals and toast until golden brown.

4. Fill your toasted biscuit bowl with chocolate or vanilla pudding. Top with whipped cream.

How to Make Reusable "Woofumm" Sticks:

Cut a 1-inch diameter closet rod into 2-inch long sections. Drill a small hole in the end of each dowel piece and firmly attach each to a 36-inch long, ⅛-inch diameter steel rod.

Don't have equipment and material handy to make a reusable stick? Try this handy suggestion from Katie Cox: Bunch a 12-inch square sheet of aluminum foil around the cooking end of a stick so that the foil makes a cylindrical wad about 1-inch in diameter. The foil wad should be about 3 to 4 inches in length along the stick once it's bunched up. Lightly spray Pam on the foil so the biscuit will easily slide off when it's finished cooking.

Required Equipment:

Reusable "woofumm" sticks (see instructions above for making)

Steven Boyack, Poway, California
Assistant District Commissioner / Former Scoutmaster, Imperial Council, Boy Scouts of America

Skidaway Banana Pudding

Servings: 2 / Multiply as Required | Challenge Level: Easy

"This recipe first appeared in our cookbook Lipsmackin' Vegetarian Backpackin'."

Preparation at Home:

1. In a bowl combine powdered milk with banana cream pudding mix.

2. Divide the mixture evenly into each of two quart-size ziplock bags.

3. Next, crush the vanilla wafers and banana chips into pieces, combine.

4. Divide wafer/banana pieces evenly into each of two separate ziplock bags. At this point you should have a total of four bags equivalent to two servings.

Preparation on Trail:

1. To produce one serving add one cup of cold filtered water to one bag of the pudding-milk mix. Shake vigorously for about one minute. The pudding will thicken within a couple of minutes.

2. Add the wafer/banana mix to the pudding bag and knead. Can be served straight from the bag.

⅔ cup non-fat powdered milk

1 (3.5-ounce) package banana cream instant pudding mix

20 vanilla wafers

1 cup banana chips

1 cup water per serving, added on the trail

Christine Conners, Statesboro, Georgia
Former Girl Scout, Hawaii Council, Girl Scouts of the USA

Tim Conners, Statesboro, Georgia
Former Leader, Coastal Empire Council, Boy Scouts of America

Miss Peggy's Car-Camping Ice Cream

Servings: 1 / Multiply as Required | Challenge Level: Easy

"I acquired this recipe from Miss Peggy, a teacher in the Agricultural Department at Morro Bay High School."

1 cup half-and-half

2 tablespoons granulated sugar

¼ teaspoon vanilla extract

2 cups crushed ice

¼ cup water

Chocolate or strawberry syrup (optional)

Preparation at Camp:

1. Combine half-and-half, sugar, and vanilla extract in a quart-size ziplock freezer bag. Remove as much air as possible and carefully zip shut. Use duct tape to double-seal the bag.

2. Place the quart-size bag inside a gallon-size ziplock freezer bag.

3. Add crushed ice, ¾ cup rock salt, and water to the gallon-size bag. Zip the bag closed and then add duct tape to double-seal it.

4. To protect your hands from the cold, wear heavy gloves or use a towel to gently massage the bag. Continue to knead the bag until the ice cream becomes frozen.

5. Cut and drain the gallon-size bag in a location where the salt water won't kill vegetation.

6. Remove and open the quart-size bag containing the ice cream. Spoon ice cream into a cup, adding any optional toppings.

Required Equipment:

Quart-size ziplock freezer bag
Gallon-size ziplock freezer bag
Duct tape
¾ cup rock salt
Heavy gloves or towel

George Brown, Los Osos, California
Former Scoutmaster, Troop 216, Los Padres Council, Boy Scouts of America

It Would'a Won!

Servings: 10 | Challenge Level: Easy

"This recipe would'a won the Sandia District Camporee dessert competition at Red Mountain Campground many years ago… if we hadn't been snowed out!"

Preparation at Camp:

1. In a gallon-size ziplock freezer bag, combine pudding and milk. Shake vigorously to remove any lumps and place in a cooler for 30 minutes to thicken.

2. Cut a small corner from the bag and squeeze pudding into each of the 10 cones.

3. Garnish with lots of sprinkles and banana slices.

Required Equipment:

Gallon-size ziplock freezer bag

Tip: Be sure to eat your cones quickly, otherwise they will become soggy.

2 (3.4-ounce) boxes Jell-O instant vanilla pudding mix

4 cups milk

10 flat-bottom ice cream cones

1 (2-ounce) jar cake sprinkles

2 bananas, sliced into thin circles

Vince Wahler, Albuquerque, New Mexico
Assistant Scoutmaster, Troop 395, Great Southwest Council, Boy Scouts of America

Jeepers Creepers Dirt Parfait

Servings: 6 | Challenge Level: Easy

1 (5.9-ounce) box Jello-O instant chocolate pudding mix

3 cups milk

1 (18-ounce) package Oreo cookies

1 (8-ounce) container whipped topping

1 (5-ounce) package gummy worms (or any other kind of creepy crawly gummy insects)

Options: To prepare Flippy Floppy Fish Parfait, use instant vanilla pudding and crushed creme-filled vanilla sandwich cookies instead of chocolate, and gummy fish instead of gummy worms!

Preparation at Camp:

1. Mix chocolate pudding with milk in a sealed gallon-size ziplock freezer bag. Carefully shake and knead until pudding becomes smooth.

2. Put cookies in a separate ziplock bag and smash into small pieces.

3. Cut small corner from bottom of pudding bag and squirt into each of six clear serving cups, reserving enough pudding for a second layer.

4. Top pudding with whipped topping and crushed cookies along with a gummy worm or two. Reserve enough cookies for a second layer.

5. Make a second layer of pudding and crushed cookies in each cup. Garnish with worms on top.

Required Equipment:

2 gallon-size ziplock freezer bags
Clear serving cups

Millie Hutchison, Pittsburgh, Pennsylvania
Girl Scout Trainer, Trillium Council, Girl Scouts of the USA

Lazy Days Lemonade Pie

Servings: 6–8 | Challenge Level: Easy

Preparation at Camp:

1. Mix whipped topping, frozen lemonade, and sweetened condensed milk in a medium-size bowl.

2. Spoon mixture into both pie shells.

3. Chill for at least 15 minutes in a cooler before serving.

Required Equipment:

Medium-size mixing bowl

1 (16-ounce) container whipped topping (such as Cool Whip)

1 (6-ounce) container frozen concentrated pink lemonade

1 (14-ounce) can sweetened condensed milk (such as Eagle Brand)

2 (6-ounce) shortbread pie shells (such as Keebler Ready Crust)

Ed Bedford, Chapel Hill, North Carolina
Scoutmaster, Troop 820, Occoneechee Council, Boy Scouts of America

Peach in a Cloud

Servings: 9 | Challenge Level: Easy

"This dish may be ugly, but it tastes incredible, just like a peach pie. Scouts love it because it's fun to make and looks really gross."

1 (29-ounce) can sliced peaches, drained

9 graham crackers (approximately 1 standard sleeve)

1 (12-ounce) container whipped topping (such as Cool Whip)

Preparation at Camp:

1. Place a few slices of peaches in each of the quart-size ziplock bags.

2. Add one graham cracker and a big spoonful of whipped topping to each of the bags.

3. Seal each bag, and mash until contents are smooth.

4. Cut a corner from bottom of each bag and suck out the contents.

Required Equipment:

9 one-quart-size ziplock bags

John Foster, Duchesne, Utah
Committee Chair / Cubmaster / Commissioner, Troop 268, Utah National Parks Council, Boy Scouts of America

Roger's Super-Duper Peanut Butter Ice Cream Sundaes

Servings: 8–10 | Challenge Level: Easy

"In remembrance of Roger Browne, Scouter forever!"

Preparation at Camp:

1. Stir peanut butter and corn syrup together in a medium-size bowl.

2. Add water until peanut butter mixture reaches a smooth consistency.

3. Scoop ice cream into cups or bowls and add peanut butter syrup to top.

4. Brandish bat to keep line in order when they demand seconds!

Required Equipment:

Medium-size mixing bowl

2 cups chunky peanut butter

¾ cup light corn syrup

3 tablespoons water

½ gallon vanilla ice cream

Steven Boyack, Poway, California
Assistant District Commissioner / Former Scoutmaster, Imperial Council, Boy Scouts of America

Venture Patrol Chocolate Pie

Servings: 5–6 | Challenge Level: Easy

"Having been prepared by the Venture Patrol on almost every campout since their creation, this recipe finally won the Dessert Award on the 2001 Carolina Beach State Park campout."

1 (5.9-ounce) package Jello-O instant chocolate pudding mix

3 cups cold milk

1 (6-ounce) premade graham cracker pie crust (such as Honey Maid)

1 (8-ounce) container whipped topping (such as Cool Whip)

Preparation at Camp:

1. In a gallon-size freezer bag, add pudding mix and cold milk. Seal and shake vigorously.

2. Pour pudding into graham crust. Chill in cooler for about 15 minutes.

3. Once set, top with whipped topping and serve.

Required Equipment:

1 gallon-size ziplock freezer bag

Ed Bedford, Chapel Hill, North Carolina
Scoutmaster, Troop 820, Occoneechee Council, Boy Scouts of America

"Better Than Scout Camp" Cake

Servings: 18–20 | Challenge Level: Easy

"Other recipes have used 'Better Than . . .' in their names and didn't live up to the billing. But I think this one does! The recipe cheats a bit because it is served, but not baked, in a Dutch oven. I prepare it at Courts-of-Honor and Merit Badge Powwows. The scouts go crazy over it!"

Preparation at Home:

1. Bake the two devil's food cakes according to package directions and bring to camp.

Preparation at Camp:

1. Crumple one of the premade devil's food cakes into large Dutch oven.

2. In medium-size bowl, prepare pudding with milk according to package directions.

3. Spoon chocolate pudding over the crumbled cake. Break Heath Bites or Bars into pieces and add them, along with the chopped Snickers, to the oven.

4. Crumble the second devil's food cake and layer it on top of the pudding, Snickers, and Heath pieces.

5. Spoon dollops of whipped topping in small mounds over the top. Sprinkle on toffee bits and pecans.

6. For the finishing touch, drizzle chocolate and caramel toppings in crisscross lines over the top.

Required Equipment:

Deep 14-inch Dutch oven

Tips: This recipe can be halved and prepared in a 12-inch Dutch oven, but there won't be enough because everybody always wants seconds! Toffee bits can be found in the baking section at the grocer.

---

2 (9-ounce) packages Jiffy devil's food cake mix and associated required ingredients

2 (5.9-ounce) packages Jello-O instant chocolate pudding mix

6 cups cold milk

4 (3.7-ounce) Snickers bars, chopped

1 (12-ounce) package Heath Bites, or 9 Heath Bars

1 (8-ounce) container whipped topping (such as Cool Whip)

4 ounces toffee bits

4 ounces chopped pecans

Chocolate syrup ice cream topping to taste

Caramel syrup ice cream topping to taste

John Foster, Duchesne, Utah
Committee Chair / Cubmaster / Commissioner, Troop 268, Utah National Parks Council, Boy Scouts of America

Kick-the-Can Ice Cream

Servings: 4 | Challenge Level: Moderate

"This recipe presents the traditional 'Kick-the-Can' method for making ice cream."

1 (3.4-ounce) package instant pudding (your choice of flavor)

1 quart half-and-half

5 cups ice (with extra for reserve)

Preparation at Camp:

1. Pour package of instant pudding into a small coffee can. Add half-and-half, leaving some room to the top of can.

2. Place lid on can and shake carefully until the pudding and half-and-half are well mixed.

3. Seal the small can with duct tape and place it inside the larger can.

4. Pack layers of ice and 1½ cups rock salt completely around the small can, filling the large can all the way to the top.

5. Place lid on the larger can, also sealing it securely with duct tape.

6. Have scouts gently roll and kick can back and forth.

7. After about 15 minutes, open the cans to check ice cream formation. Scrape the ice cream from the side of can and reseal, adding more ice and salt as needed.

8. Kick the can for another 15 minutes, then serve.

Required Equipment:

1 small (12-ounce) metal coffee can with lid
1 large (34½-ounce) metal coffee can with lid
1½ cups rock salt (with extra for reserve)
Duct tape

Zero Impact Tip: Dispose of salt water and ice in a location where it will not kill vegetation.

Tip: Equipment specially made for preparing ice cream outdoors can be found at retailers such as REI.

Georgia Bosse, Portland, Oregon
Leave No Trace Master Educator, Columbia River Girl Scout Council, Girl Scouts of the USA

Hikin' S'mores

Servings: 8–10 | Challenge Level: Easy

Preparation at Home:

1. Combine all ingredients in a large bowl.

2. Seal in serving-size ziplock bags for camp or hiking.

1 (13-ounce) box **Golden Grahams cereal**

1 (10½-ounce) bag **mini marshmallows**

1 (24-ounce) bag **chocolate chips**

Christine Conners, Statesboro, Georgia
Former Girl Scout, Hawaii Council, Girl Scouts of the USA

Thin Mint Backpacker's Pie

Servings: 6 | Challenge Level: Easy

1 (5.9-ounce) package Jello-O instant chocolate pudding mix

1 cup nonfat powdered milk

½ box Girl Scout Thin Mints cookies

3 cups cold water

Preparation at Home:

1. In a quart-size ziplock freezer bag, combine the dry pudding mix with the powdered milk. Seal bag and shake to mix.

2. Remove Thin Mint cookies from their pouch and place in a separate quart-size ziplock freezer bag.

Preparation on Trail:

1. Add cold water to bag of pudding mix. Seal, then shake and knead vigorously until thoroughly blended.

2. Cut a small opening in corner of pudding bag. Squeeze pudding into six separate cups.

3. Smash cookies in their ziplock bag. Pour crushed cookies on top of pudding in cups and serve.

Required Equipment:

6 small paper serving cups

Christine Conners, Statesboro, Georgia
Former Girl Scout, Hawaii Council, Girl Scouts of the USA

Lousy Lemonade

Servings: 6 | Challenge Level: Easy

"Lousy? Yep, because any lousy cook can make it!"

Preparation at Camp:

1. Combine water and sugar in a medium-size cook pot. Use low heat until sugar dissolves.

2. Stir in lemon juice and allow to cool. Serve over ice.

Required Equipment:

Medium-size cook pot

5 cups water

1 cup sugar

1½ cups fresh-squeezed lemon juice (from 15–20 lemons)

Tony Neubauer, Piscataway, New Jersey
Committee Chairperson, Troop 67, Central New Jersey Council, Boy Scouts of America

Rise and Rhorer Cocoa Mix

Servings: About 40 | Challenge Level: Easy

"Mr. Rhorer, our Scoutmaster, has always been the first person awake and semi-sociable on our campouts. Some of his words to the boys as they emerge, slow and sleepy, from their tents are, 'C'mon on over and warm yourself!' or 'Get 'cha something hot!' This cocoa lets them do just that. Even though he'd never touch the stuff (he's more the cowboy coffee type), he'd agree this cocoa gets 'em up and movin.'"

1 cup milk chocolate chips

1 cup powdered coffee creamer

1 cup powdered milk

1 cup powdered sugar

1 cup chocolate drink mix (such as Ovaltine or Nesquik)

Preparation at Home:

1. Combine all ingredients in a large bowl.

2. Pour into an airtight container or large ziplock freezer bag, and store in a cool place until ready for your outing.

Preparation at Camp:

1. Add 2 tablespoons cocoa mix to one cup hot water, heated in a cook pot.

2. Stir until completely dissolved. Use more or less cocoa mix depending on taste.

Required Equipment:

Large-size cook pot

Tip: If you don't like camp coffee that growls at you, a scoop of this cocoa in your cup of java will take the bite out of it.

Trish Day, Milford, Ohio
Relations / Advancement Committee Member, Troop 468, Blue Jacket Council, Boy Scouts of America

Sherpa's Climbing Tea

Servings: 1 / Multiply as Required | Challenge Level: Easy

"When I started climbing and snow-camping, I needed something that packed a lot of energy for its weight but was easy to prepare. I was bored with hot chocolate, and several other climbers mentioned Sherpa tea, a high-energy drink frequently used for climbing and other physically demanding activities. Everyone seemed to use a slightly different mix of ingredients, but all the recipes originated from one used traditionally by the Nepalese Sherpa. Many climbers have made it through bivouacs in very bad weather with this tea."

Preparation at Camp:

1. In a small-size cook pot, bring water to a boil and pour into a cup containing the tea bags.

2. Steep tea bags for about 4 minutes, then remove from water.

3. Add Nido powder, butter, honey, and spices. Stir and get ready to climb!

Required Equipment:

Small-size cook pot

8 ounces water

2 bags black tea

1 tablespoon Nestle Nido powdered milk

1 teaspoon butter

1 tablespoon honey

Ground cinnamon and nutmeg to taste

Option: Chai spice powder makes a great addition to this recipe.

Curt "The Titanium Chef" White, Forks, Washington
Scoutmaster, Troop 1467, Chief Seattle Council, Boy Scouts of America

Whoopee Ti-Yi-Yo
Git Along Little Dogies Hot Chocolate

Servings: 1 / Multiply as Required | Challenge Level: Easy

"Scouts will spontaneously break out in western folk song once they taste this drink!"

1 cup milk

3 bite-size pieces of chocolate

Preparation at Camp:

1. Heat milk in a small-size cook pot. Pour in cup.

2. Add chocolate pieces and stir until melted.

Required Equipment:

Small-size cook pot

Christine Conners, Statesboro, Georgia
Former Girl Scout, Hawaii Council, Girl Scouts of the USA

Fireside Punch

Servings: 14 | Challenge Level: Easy

1 (64-ounce) container cranberry juice cocktail

1 (46-ounce) can pineapple juice

1 teaspoon ground cinnamon

¼ teaspoon ground allspice

¼ teaspoon ground cloves

¼ teaspoon ground nutmeg

Sugar to taste (optional)

Preparation at Camp:

1. In a large-size pot, combine all ingredients and bring to a boil.

2. Reduce heat and simmer for 10 minutes. Serve warm in mugs.

Required Equipment:

Large-size cook pot

Tony Neubauer, Piscataway, New Jersey
Committee Chairperson, Troop 67, Central New Jersey Council, Boy Scouts of America

Crazy Ivan's Russian Tea

Servings: 20–30 | Challenge Level: Easy

"I adapted this recipe from one found in *Ray White's Canoe Guide for the Charles Sommers Canoe Base.* I got the idea for the name after watching *The Hunt for Red October,* referring to the wild and sudden maneuver performed in the movie by the Russian submarine commanders to determine if they were being trailed. We discovered that too much lemon or lime flavor in this recipe would produce a similarly wild and sudden maneuver…of the head and facial muscles!"

Preparation at Camp:

1. Mix all dry ingredients together.

2. Heat water in a large cook pot.

3. To make one serving, place 2 or 3 tablespoons of powder mix in a mug and add one cup of hot water. Stir and serve.

Required Equipment:

Large-size cook pot

2 cups powdered orange drink mix (such as Tang)

1 cup powdered lemonade drink mix

1 cup unsweetened and unflavored instant tea powder

1 tablespoon ground cinnamon

1 teaspoon ground cloves

1 cup hot water per serving

Options: For a very tangy drink with more Crazy Ivan kick, add a few drops of lemon or lime juice.

Curt "The Titanium Chef" White, Forks, Washington
Scoutmaster, Troop 1467, Chief Seattle Council, Boy Scouts of America

Fire Starter Cider

Servings: 8 | Challenge Level: Easy

64 ounces apple cider

½ cup red-hot cinnamon candies

Preparation at Camp:

1. Place cider and red-hots in a medium-size cook pot and bring to a boil.

2. Reduce heat then cover and simmer for 10 minutes. Serve warm.

Required Equipment:

Medium-size cook pot

Tony Neubauer, Piscataway, New Jersey
Committee Chairperson, Troop 67, Central New Jersey Council, Boy Scouts of America

Spiced Cow Juice

Servings: 1 / Multiply as Required | Challenge Level: Easy

"This recipe is adapted from the 1946 Girl Scout USA cookbook entitled *Cooking Out-Of-Doors*."

1 cup milk

¼ teaspoon ground cinnamon

¼ teaspoon nutmeg

1 teaspoon sugar

Preparation at Camp:

1. Scald milk in a small-size pot. Keep a close eye on the milk to prevent it from boiling over.

2. Stir in cinnamon, nutmeg, and sugar.

3. Pour in a cup and serve.

Required Equipment:

Small-size cook pot

Christine Conners, Statesboro, Georgia
Former Girl Scout, Hawaii Council, Girl Scouts of the USA

Marshmallowy Mountain Hot Cocoa

Servings: 1 / Multiply as Required | Challenge Level: Easy

Preparation at Camp:

1. Bring water to a boil in a small cook pot.

2. In a mug, combine powdered milk, sugar, cocoa powder, and marshmallows. Stir to blend.

3. Pour boiling water into mug and stir.

Required Equipment:

Small-size cook pot

1 cup water

⅓ cup powdered milk

1 tablespoon granulated sugar

2 teaspoons unsweetened cocoa powder

¼ cup miniature marshmallows

Option: Substitute one crushed peppermint candy for the marshmallows.

Tony Neubauer, Piscataway, New Jersey
Committee Chairperson, Troop 67, Central New Jersey Council, Boy Scouts of America

It's Orangealicious!

Servings: 8–10 | Challenge Level: Easy

"This is an adaptation of an old recipe from a booklet entitled Trail Cookery, distributed by the Kellogg's Company in 1942. Maria, our 8-year-old daughter (and scout recipe tester), spontaneously blurted out 'It's Orangealicious!' while sampling the drink. Sounded like a great recipe name to us!"

1 cup sugar

1 cup water

Rind from 1 orange

2 quarts water

Ice, if available

Preparation at Camp:

1. In a medium-size pot, bring sugar, one cup of water, and grated orange rind to a boil.

2. Remove from heat and add two quarts of cool water. Stir.

3. Serve with ice, if available.

Required Equipment:

Medium-size cook pot

Christine Conners, Statesboro, Georgia
Former Girl Scout, Hawaii Council, Girl Scouts of the USA

Razzle Dazzle

Servings: 8 | Challenge Level: Easy

Preparation at Camp:

1. Combine grape juice and raspberries in a medium-size cook pot or pan and bring to a boil.

2. Reduce heat, then cover and simmer for 10 minutes. Serve warm.

64 ounces white grape juice

1 (12-ounce) bag frozen raspberries

Required Equipment:

Medium-sized cook pot

Tony Neubauer, Piscataway, New Jersey
Committee Chairperson, Troop 67, Central New Jersey Council, Boy Scouts of America

Pickaxe Pete's Cowboy Coffee

Servings: 6 | Challenge Level: Easy

Author's Note: We don't make a habit of borrowing material from our other cookbooks. But good camp coffee is hard to find, and this recipe, lifted out of *Lipsmackin' Backpackin'*, is the best we've come across. It was given to us by our friend and former scouter, 'Pickaxe Pete' Fish. Retired from his job as a geologist in oil exploration, Pete is a hard-working volunteer crew leader who puts in amazingly long hours on his favorite footpath, the Pacific Crest Trail.

What does he do when he's not clearing brush? Well, from what we can gather, Pickaxe Pete's preferred pastime is precariously posing for pictures at the PCT's picturesque Pickhandle Point! Practice saying that fast while you're waiting for your coffee to brew. —Christine and Tim

½ cup coffee grounds

6 cups water

Option: Bring water to a boil, and add coffee grounds. Crack egg into coffee. Simmer 12 minutes. Settle grounds with a little cold water. The egg will collect the grounds, so dish it out and discard. Coffee is clear and great!

Preparation at Camp:

1. Over cold water in a pot, float enough coffee grounds to form a skim about ⅛ inch thick.

2. Bring water to a boil and remove from heat.

3. Add a splash of cold water to settle the grounds. Or for dramatic effect, use centrifugal force by slinging the pot around your head. (You'd better know what you're doing if you try the latter!)

4. One school says to drink immediately and never reboil coffee grounds. Another keeps adding grounds for the second and third pots, preserving the "mother liquid." Experiment!

Required Equipment:

Medium-size cook pot

Tip: To impress your high-society cowboy and cowgirl buddies, you'll want to remember these important coffee terms: "six-shooter" is a fine, strong cup of java; "black water" is coffee so weak that you'll need to pull yourself up by your stirrups and make a new batch before you go and embarrass yourself.

Pete "Pickaxe Pete" Fish, Ventura, California
Former Leader / Member–Order of the Arrow, Great Alaska Council, Boy Scouts of America

Sacagawea Sunshine Tea

Servings: 8 | Challenge Level: Easy

"I have many fond memories of my years as a Girl Scout Leader at Camp Sacagawea in Sparta, New Jersey. In my mind, I still can see that jar of sunshine tea glistening on our picnic table from morning until the sun went down."

Preparation at Camp:

1. Place tea bags in container filled with water. Seal tightly.

2. Set container outside in the sun for most of the day.

3. Tea should be ready to garnish with fresh raspberries by suppertime. Add sugar, if desired, then serve.

Required Equipment:

64-ounce clear container with lid

8 raspberry herbal tea bags

1 (64-ounce) container filled with fresh water

1 pint fresh raspberries

Sugar to taste (optional)

Options: Try other combinations, such as apple cinnamon tea, with a cinnamon stick stirrer, or lemon tea, with a wedge of lemon!

Kathleen Kirby, Milltown, New Jersey
Cooking Merit Badge Counselor, Troop 33, Central New Jersey Council, Boy Scouts of America
Former Leader, Troop 12, Delaware-Raritan Council, Girl Scouts of the USA

Juice from the Sun

Servings: 1 / Multiply as Required | Challenge Level: Easy

1 orange

1 cinnamon stick

Preparation at Camp:

1. To free the juice on the interior of the orange, roll it on a hard surface using firm pressure from your hands.

2. Poke a small hole through the peel and insert the cinnamon stick.

3. Drink the juice using the cinnamon stick as a straw.

Tips: The cinnamon stick can be gnawed on and enjoyed long after the juice is gone. And, of course, a straw can be used in lieu of the cinnamon stick, although you'll miss the spicy twang.

Christine Conners, Statesboro, Georgia
Former Girl Scout, Hawaii Council, Girl Scouts of the USA

Kittatinny Peach Smoothie

Servings: 4 | Challenge Level: Easy

"This recipe is named for a Boy Scout camp in New Jersey."

1 (12-ounce) can peach nectar, chilled

1 (15-ounce) can sliced peaches with juice

1 pint vanilla ice cream, softened

Preparation at Camp:

1. Seal all ingredients in a gallon-size ziplock freezer bag and mash by hand until smooth.

2. Cut a corner from the bottom of the bag and squeeze into four individual mugs.

Required Equipment:

1 gallon-size ziplock freezer bag

Tony Neubauer, Piscataway, New Jersey
Committee Chairperson, Troop 67, Central New Jersey Council, Boy Scouts of America

Citrus Surprise!

Servings: 12 | Challenge Level: Easy

Preparation at Camp:

1. Combine orange juice concentrate, limeade, and ginger ale in a large bowl.

2. Pour cherries into the punch. Add sherbet in large scoops. Serve.

Required Equipment:

Large-size mixing bowl

Tip: Sherbet doesn't need to be completely frozen for this recipe. It can be kept semi-frozen in a cooler prior to use.

1 (12-ounce) container frozen orange juice concentrate

1 (12-ounce) can limeade soda

1 (2-liter) bottle ginger ale

1 (10-ounce) jar maraschino cherries, drained

½ gallon rainbow sherbet

Julie Terranera, Port Orange, Florida
National Operational Volunteer / Instructor of Trainers / Lifetime Member, Citrus Council, Girl Scouts of the USA

Occoneechee Breakfast Mash

Servings: 2 / Multiply as Required | Challenge Level: Easy

1 banana or any non-citrus fruit

1 (6- or 8-ounce) container of yogurt (your choice)

1 cup fruit juice (your choice)

Option: This is a great recipe for using up extra fruit in the supplies.

Preparation at Camp:

1. Cut banana or other fruit into small pieces.

2. Place all ingredients in a medium-size bowl. Blend using a hand-cranked blender or masher.

3. Pour into individual mugs.

Required Equipment:

Medium-sized mixing bowl

Hand blender or masher

Stephen Hoyle, Chapel Hill, North Carolina
Assistant Scoutmaster / Leadership Patrol, Troop 820, Occoneechee Council, Boy Scouts of America

Radioactive Sludge

Servings: 8 | Challenge Level: Easy

"Remember scouts: always wear your biohazard suits whenever playing with radioactive material!"

1 (0.23-ounce) packet Kool-Aid Lemonade flavored drink mix

1 (0.22-ounce) packet Kool-Aid Berry Blue flavored drink mix

2 quarts water

1 cup sugar

Whipped topping (such as Cool Whip), to taste

Preparation at Camp:

1. In a medium-size bowl, combine Kool-Aid, water, and sugar. Mix thoroughly.

2. Swirl in a little whipped topping for extra sludge effect, and let if float on the top like toxic foam!

Required Equipment:

Medium-size mixing bowl

Christine Conners, Statesboro, Georgia
Former Girl Scout, Hawaii Council, Girl Scouts of the USA

Epilogue

Stone Soup

Once there was a great famine in Europe. So little food was available that people hoarded what they had, and they refused to share with others.

One day, a traveler came upon a small village and asked if anyone had anything to eat. The villagers swore not, and so the traveler said, "So be it. I will make stone soup."

The stranger filled a pot with water and placed a single stone in it. He began to heat it over a fire. Upon hearing that someone was preparing a special soup, the villagers began to gather around the man and his odd concoction.

"What are you cooking?" they asked. The stranger politely informed them, "Why, I am making stone soup." "But it does taste better with a little meat," he quickly added. "I have a bit of beef!" a villager announced, and she ran home to retrieve the meat she had stashed away.

"Stone soup is delicious with beef," the stranger commented to those who remained, "but it is even better with a few vegetables." "I have some cabbage!" a young boy said. "And I have a few carrots!" exclaimed another. "I have a potato and an onion!" announced a third. And the villagers ran off to bring their vegetables from where they were hidden.

"Stone soup is indeed wonderful with beef and vegetables," said the traveler to the few that were left standing, "but it is even better with a bit of seasoning." "I have some!" a woman exclaimed. And she ran off to retrieve what she had.

Together with the "magic" stone, and the small, but important, contributions of each of the villagers, the stranger was able to prepare a delicious soup that warmed the stomachs and hearts of a people who had long gone without a good meal.

Appendix A:

Measurement Conversions

Standard English–U.S. Conversions

3 teaspoons	1 tablespoon
48 teaspoons	1 cup
2 tablespoons	⅛ cup
4 tablespoons	¼ cup
5 tablespoons + 1 teaspoon	⅓ cup
8 tablespoons	½ cup
12 tablespoons	¾ cup
16 tablespoons	1 cup
1 ounce	2 tablespoons
4 ounces	½ cup
8 ounces	1 cup
⅝ cup	½ cup + 2 tablespoons
⅞ cup	¾ cup + 2 tablespoons
2 cups	1 pint
2 pints	1 quart
1 quart	4 cups
4 quarts	1 gallon
1 gallon	128 ounces
1 jigger	1½ fluid ounces
16 ounces water	1 pound
2 cups vegetable oil	1 pound
2 cups or 4 sticks butter	1 pound
2 cups granulated sugar	1 pound
3½ to 4 cups unsifted powdered sugar	1 pound
2¼ cups packed brown sugar	1 pound
4 cups sifted flour	1 pound
3½ cups unsifted whole wheat flour	1 pound
8–10 egg whites	1 cup
12–14 egg yolks	1 cup
1 whole lemon, squeezed	3 tablespoons juice
1 whole orange, squeezed	⅓ cup juice

Metric Conversions

Volume and Weight

English (U.S.)	Metric
¼ teaspoon	1.25 milliliters
½ teaspoon	2.50 milliliters
¾ teaspoon	3.75 milliliters
1 teaspoon	5 milliliters
1 tablespoon	15 milliliters
1 fluid ounce	30 milliliters
¼ cup	60 milliliters
½ cup	120 milliliters
¾ cup	180 milliliters
1 cup	240 milliliters
1 pint	0.48 liter
1 quart	0.95 liter
1 gallon	3.79 liters
1 ounce weight	28 grams
1 pound	0.45 kilogram

Temperature

English (degrees F)	Metric (degrees C)
175	80
200	95
225	105
250	120
275	135
300	150
325	165
350	175
375	190
400	205
425	220
450	230
475	245
500	260

Appendix B:

Cast-Iron Essentials

Cast iron makes for truly wonderful cookware, all the more so when you handle it like it was made to be treated: rough and wild. Don't waste your time babying the stuff because there's no need to. Just keep it away from soap. Avoid introducing hot cast iron to cold water. And don't drop it on your foot.

Heresy to some, but we spare our cupboards a beating by storing our heavy cast iron outside on the back porch. No warm, dry place for those bad boys. Covered only by an overhang of the roof, and just a few feet from direct exposure to the weather, our cookware sits all year long, getting covered in frost, splashed by rain, and coated in pine pollen.

When ready to use, we rinse out the occasional beetle and bits of bird food carried there by the squirrels. A light recoat of vegetable oil, and over the coals our cast iron goes. After the ovens and skillet have worked their magic, we scrub them with a plastic pad under plenty of plain water, and send them to bed with another quick swab of oil. And the cycle begins again.

Our cookware has been stored out in the elements for several years now, and it only gets better with time. Food refuses to stick, and rust has yet to rear its ugly head. Once you're familiar with cast iron, it becomes easy to see why our progeny will be using our cookware long after we're gone. With a little care, it can easily last hundreds of years. If only everything we owned had that kind of durability!

Taking Care of Cast Iron Cookware

According to Will Satak, Director of the Willamette Chapter of the International Dutch Oven Society, much of the cast iron used in scout cooking is improperly seasoned, as witnessed by the very rusty exteriors he often sees. Seasoning builds and strengthens the protective nonstick coating on the surface of the cookware. To form the initial protective base, cast iron must be properly conditioned before first use, if it hasn't already been seasoned at the factory.

It's not difficult to season cast iron. Once it's been performed properly on your cookware, it may never be necessary again, provided a few simple maintenance steps are observed. The following information, provided by Will, explains the seasoning process and provides additional tips for maintaining your cast iron.

Seasoning

1. Thoroughly wipe all surfaces of your cookware with a heavy layer of vegetable oil.

2. Turn the cookware upside down on the rack of a barbeque grill. Lean the cookware such that excess oil will drain from the surface.

3. Close the grill lid and bring heat to medium. The oil will smoke and may smell disagreeable. Bake until smoking completely abates, about 1 hour.

4. After baking, your cookware's new seasoned coating will be shiny brown or black in appearance. You may heat the metal for a longer period of time to deepen the color, but avoid overcooking. Otherwise the coating will eventually carbonize and flake off, requiring the process to be repeated.

If you don't have access to a grill suitable for the seasoning task, a kitchen oven can be used instead. Follow the cookware manufacturer's directions regarding oven temperature, typically 350 degrees F, and be prepared for smoke and odor in the kitchen. Be sure to use a sheet of aluminum foil on a lower oven rack for catching the sticky oil that drips from the cast iron while it bakes.

Maintenance

- Establishing the habit of rubbing a thin layer of oil on your cookware, both before using and after each cleaning, will help maintain and build the durability and effectiveness of the coating.
- Vegetable oil can be used to protect your cookware prior to short-term storage. But over long periods of time, the oil may turn rancid and sticky. For longer storage periods, a very thin coat of food-grade mineral oil is a better option. If mineral oil has been applied, wipe the surface of the cookware with a clean towel immediately prior to use.

- Do not use detergents or a dishwasher to clean cast iron. Doing so can remove so much coating that re-seasoning is required. The use of metal scouring pads will also destroy the coating. Properly seasoned cookware should require no more than a plastic scouring pad, plenty of water, a gentle scrubbing, and a dry towel to produce a thorough cleaning.

- Avoid placing very hot cast iron in water. Otherwise, the thermal shock may warp or crack the metal. Wait for your cookware to cool to the touch before cleaning.

Equipment for Dutch Oven Cooking

The term 'Dutch oven' broadly refers to a wide range of kettle-like cooking pots featuring thick walls and sturdy lids. Many Dutch oven designs have been created for the kitchen, but these are no more useful outdoors than a casserole bowl. However, the "camp Dutch oven" has been specifically designed for cooking with coals and is the type required for the outdoor recipes in this book. The camp Dutch oven features a flanged edge around the perimeter of the lid to contain briquettes and ash while cooking. It also sports short, sturdy legs to hold the bottom of the oven at some distance above hot coals.

The camp Dutch oven's legendary versatility results from the ability to finely tailor the heat distribution around its surface. With lid off and coals underneath, the camp oven makes a fine skillet for many foods. By adding the lid and distributing the coals so that most are on top, it becomes an outstanding baking device for cakes and breads. Distributing the coals more evenly between top and bottom provides an ideal cooking environment for dishes that contain or produce a lot of liquid, such as stews and roasts. And by using indirect heating by surrounding the base with an outer ring of coals, delicate dishes otherwise prone to burning can be prepared with ease. We have found the camp Dutch oven to be a truly remarkable, and forgiving, cooking device.

If you're new to Dutch oven cooking, you'll find that a camp oven with a lid diameter of 12 inches and an internal capacity of 6 quarts provides an excellent and versatile entry point. This is a very popular size, and most of our recipes that require a Dutch oven call for one of this capacity. The 12-inch/6-quart Dutch was the first piece of cast iron cookware that we ever purchased.

Before you prepare your mouth-watering debut recipe with your new oven, identify a cooking area free of ground vegetation and clear of surrounding combustibles. You'll also need to round up a few items for preparing a heat source and managing the oven once it's hot:

- Charcoal. Select a high-quality briquette of standard size. Extra large briquettes work fine in theory. However, their wide girth can make it difficult to achieve proper results when following a cookbook, like this one, that specifies coal counts based on the standard briquette size. Carry plenty of extra coal for contingency, especially when learning the number of recipes that can be prepared using a given brand and bag size.

- Coal Starter. There are several methods for creating hot coals, but one of the most popular, and the one we recommend, is the chimney starter. These are simple and inexpensive devices. Coals are loaded in the top of a cylindrical metal canister about one foot in length. A compartment underneath is used to burn a small amount of crumpled paper, and the rising flames ignite the briquettes in the upper portion of the chimney. Vents are designed to draw air into the cylinder, accelerating the heating of the coals. Once the briquettes are mostly ashed over, they are ready to be poured from the chimney by means of a handle on the side.

- Coal Tray. Some cooking areas are not conducive to pouring hot coals directly on the ground, either because of excessive soil moisture or because doing so can scar a sensitive brick or rock surface. In these cases, a metal pan or tray large enough to support the base of the oven can be used to preserve your briquettes and protect the cooking site.

- Tongs. Metal tongs are necessary for handling hot briquettes and for positioning them under, around, or on the oven. Sturdy tongs at least one foot in length are recommended.

- Heavy Gloves. Thick welder's-type gloves, made from leather or other insulating melt-resistant material, are required to protect your hands and forearms when handling coals, removing the lid, or transporting a hot Dutch oven by the bail handle.

- Lid Lifter. A lifter is a device used to firmly grip and remove the hot and heavy lid of a Dutch oven. These are available from vendors of outdoor cookware, and made especially for the purpose. They can also be crafted from an assortment of metal hand tools and hardware. Regardless of how you move and manage the lid, use caution. Keep in mind that the lid's weight makes it awkward to move; the loop handle can be searing hot; and the coals and gritty ash on the lid can't wait to fall into your food.

Camp Dutch ovens are substantial in size, and the use of dense cast iron in their manufacture makes their heft legendary. Some manufacturers offer Dutch ovens produced from anodized aluminum to reduce the weight of the cookware. This is a welcome option for those who might otherwise have trouble handling a fully loaded oven, or for when reduced weight is of the essence, such as when canoeing.

We didn't use aluminum Dutch ovens during testing for this book. Based on differences in performance when compared to cast iron, adjustments to coal counts and cooking times in our recipes will likely be necessary when using aluminum ovens. This is especially true when operating under non-ideal conditions, as aluminum absorbs and loses heat more rapidly than does cast iron and is more sensitive to the effects of wind and weather.

Regardless, camp cooking with aluminum Dutch ovens is akin to building your campfire out of wax logs from the hardware store. It may actually be a better option under some circumstances, but it just doesn't seem right! If oven weight isn't an issue for you, explore the world of cast iron and connect to the pioneering past. Discover why cast iron remains the most popular option in camp cookware.

Additional information on camp Dutch oven cooking can be found in the Recommendations and Tips chapter.

Appendix C:

Cooking in Cardboard

The box oven remains a popular cooking device for many scout troops. It can handily replace the Dutch oven for numerous baking jobs. And for baking large dishes, it may be your only option. If you can cook it at home in your kitchen oven, there is a very good chance you can bake it in a box.

Assistant Scoutmaster Chip Reinhardt, of Troop 451 in Durham, North Carolina, has been baking in boxes with his troop for many years now. The earliest reference to this method of cooking that Chip recalls comes from an article in a 1953 issue of *Boy's Life* magazine. He first witnessed it put to practice by another troop in the Durham area, but as Chip notes, "no scouter is ever above borrowing a great idea!"

There are many ways to build and assemble the components of a box oven. Chip provided us with the following method for creating a sturdy, professional looking unit along with tips for putting it to good use.

Required Materials and Tools

- 1 cardboard box, about the size that holds ten reams of copy paper
- 1 roll duct tape
- 1 roll heavy-duty aluminum foil
- 1 bottle contact cement
- 6 uncoated, bare metal coat hangers
- 1 shallow metal pan
- Utility knife for cutting cardboard
- Scissors for trimming aluminum foil
- Bolt-cutters or wire-cutters for sizing coat hangers
- Pliers for bending wire

343

Construction Details

1. Tape down all open box flaps using strips of duct tape applied only on the outside of the box. Use just enough tape to do the job. If the box has a lid, such as that used on a carton of copy paper, securely fasten it with duct tape applied to the outside of the box as well.

2. Cut a rectangular door panel in one of the longer sides of the box. Create slits for the vertical and bottom edges only, leaving about an inch of cardboard rim between the door slits and box edges. The door is to remain attached, hinging along the top edge of the box. Carefully fold the cardboard door along its top edge to help initiate the formation of the hinge line. Secure any loose cardboard flaps on the interior of the box using contact cement.

3. Through the door opening, fasten aluminum foil to the entire inside surface of the box using contact cement. Overlap the sheets of foil by at least 1 inch. Don't forget to attach foil to the inside surface of the door and the inner surface of the top hinge line. Ensure that the foil wraps over the cut edges of the door frame and the three edges of the door itself. Do not leave any cardboard exposed on the inside surface! If the aluminum foil tears while applying, cut additional patches of foil, and glue these over the torn areas. Apply cement sparingly, and be sure to follow any unique instructions or cautionary statements on the cement bottle's label. Allow cement to cure for at least 1 day before breaking the oven in with coals.

4. A more finished look can be obtained by using duct tape applied on the outside of the box to fasten down the edges of foil that have been wrapped around the door edges. Keep duct tape at least 1 inch from the door itself. Otherwise, the tape may melt from the escaping heat. If required, duct tape can also be applied at this time to reinforce outside corners and edges of the box.

5. Use bolt- or wire-cutters to remove the long straight wire section from six bare metal coat hangers. These will form the oven rack. Do not use coat hangers that are painted or coated in plastic! Before cutting, mark off lengths that will be adequate for the box you'll be using. If additional length is required, include a curved section of the coat hangar, straightening it with a pair of pliers before creating the rack. Batt insulation wire supports or metal racks from small ovens are other options that can be used to make box oven racks.

6. The rack should be positioned about halfway between the bottom and top surfaces of the box. With the tip of a knife blade, carefully create a row of six very small, equally spaced slits on either side of the box. The slits must all be of equal distance from the bottom of the box to ensure that the rods will be level once installed.

7. Using the slits as guides, push the straightened coat hanger wires through the outside wall of one side of the box, through the interior of the oven, and into and through the opposite side of the box. To prevent the rods from falling out, use pliers to bend the protruding edges down on either side of the box.

8. Place a shallow metal pan at the bottom of the oven for your heat source. The pan must rest on supports to prevent direct contact with, and potential burning of, the bottom surface of the oven. The supports can be made from several rolled balls of foil, small rocks, or other such fireproof devices that will provide a secure, insulating air gap between the pan and the bottom of the oven. If desired, line the pan with aluminum foil for easier cleaning.

9. Before baking food in your box oven for the first time, move it to a fire-safe area and break it in by setting a pan of ten hot briquettes in the oven. Close the door and allow the coals to expire on their own. Once the oven is cool, open the door for a short period of time to vent. Examine the box inside and out to ensure the rack remains secure and the oven wasn't burned or weakened during the check run. Correct any deficiencies before using the box oven in the field.

Using Your Box Oven in the Field

1. Start your coals using high-quality, standard-size briquettes. Do not take coals from a campfire, as they will smoke excessively and expire quickly. Do not start the coals inside the oven! Once the briquettes have completely ashed over, insert the coal pan into the oven using a pair of channel locks or welder's gloves. Ensure that the pan rests firmly on the supports.

2. The following temperature formula is useful as a starting point: One standard fresh briquette produces about 45 degrees F of temperature change. So for a recipe calling for a baking temperature of 450 degrees F, begin with ten briquettes. Your box oven's method of construction and size, as well as weather conditions, will likely require adjustment to this formula. Get to know your oven under different weather conditions by calibrating it using a cooking thermometer.

3. Keep the oven level while cooking. Position the box in a safe area on the ground or on a fireproof table where it will remain well out of the way of normal scout horseplay.

4. When baking, keep the door closed to prevent excessive heat from escaping. Some recipes create a lot of moisture. For these, the door may be left slightly ajar to permit steam to escape. A small vent door can also be cut into the top of the oven and opened and closed as necessary.

5. If you find the coals to be burning out before going completely to ash, the interior of the oven may be deprived of oxygen during baking. To remedy the situation, either leave the door slightly ajar or cut a few small vent holes around the base of the side walls and in the top surface of the oven.

Only thin layers of aluminum separate a box oven from a box oven on fire. Be certain that your oven is in good repair before using it in the field. Ensure that the oven is operated in a safe, protected area, and keep it away from low-hanging branches, fuel, and other combustibles. Imagine the box completely on fire, and build your fire-safe zone surrounding the oven accordingly. Have plenty of water on hand to douse flames should it become necessary.

Appendix D:

Low Impact Cooking

Low impact principles provide a method by which we learn to make informed decisions that respect and care for our wildlands, protect limited resources, and preserve opportunities for future outdoor recreation. When following low impact principles, we minimize our impact to our surroundings and others, especially when hiking and camping.

The Leave No Trace organization teaches us seven principles for low impact outdoor recreation:

1. Plan ahead and prepare

2. Travel and camp on durable surfaces

3. Dispose of waste properly

4. Leave what you find

5. Minimize campfire impacts

6. Respect wildlife

7. Be considerate of other people

Georgia Bosse, Leave No Trace Master Educator for the Columbia River Council of the Girl Scouts of the USA, provided the following information on low impact principles applied specifically to outdoor food preparation.

Careful planning is critical to successfully following low impact principles, most of which are touched on even before arriving at the trail or camp. Consider the following list of planning and application points when discussing food options with your troop. They can help you make wise decisions that protect and preserve our wild places.

Decide how you'll prepare your food.

Some methods of cooking create less impact than others. You can plan a menu that requires fewer cooked meals or no heat source at all. Gas stoves and grills also minimize impact. Follow local fire restrictions regarding open fires and wood fuel, and use an established fire ring instead of creating a new one whenever possible. Collect wood from the ground rather than from standing trees. To avoid creating barren earth, find wood farther away from camp. If you bring wood with you, make sure it doesn't harbor insects or disease. Select smaller pieces of wood, and burn them completely to ash. Afterwards, make sure the fire is completely out, then scatter the cool ashes. Learn how to use a fire pan or build a mound fire to prevent scorching the ground and blackening rocks.

Carefully select and repackage your food to minimize trash.

Reduce your pack load and trash by repackaging and combining foods whenever possible. Measure salt, seasonings, rice, and other dry ingredients into the same bag if they will be cooked together. Pack every bag necessary for a meal in a single, larger bag and use that same bag to pack out the trash from the meal. Before packing your food for trail use, trim away peelings, carrot tops, green pepper cores, and anything else you won't eat or need.

Small pieces of micro-trash can easily become litter. Avoid bringing hard candies, chocolates, or other individually packaged small items unless you can contain the wrappers. Twist ties or bread clips are easily lost when dropped. Repackage such foods into ziplock bags or use knots to seal.

Metal containers and their lids can easily cut or puncture trash sacks. Crushed beverage cans and broken glass are even worse. Wrap them carefully before placing them in your trash. Better yet, avoid bringing canned foods and canned or bottled beverages on a trail, and minimize glass use in more formal camp sites.

Determine the amount of food needed to minimize wasted leftovers.

Do not cook more than you can eat. Leftover foods make for messy trash that is heavy and difficult to pack out, especially when on a trail. If poured on the ground, leftovers are unsightly and unsanitary. And if buried, animals will dig them up. Leftovers encourage problem animals to come into camp. Share leftovers with others or set aside in a protected place to eat at a later meal.

Plan to protect your food, trash, and other odorous items from animals.

Consider avoiding the use of very aromatic foods that can attract animals. Store food, trash, and other odorous items where animals won't be able to get to them. Besides being potentially dangerous to the animal, and inconvenient for the hiker or camper, trash is often spread over a large area once the animal gains access. Understand and follow local regulations regarding proper food storage.

Decide whether to avoid collecting wild foods.

Avoid harvesting wild foods, such as berries, if these foods are not plentiful in the area you're visiting. Such foods may be a key component of the local ecosystem, especially if scarce.

These are just a few of the practical considerations and potential applications of zero impact principles. Visit www.LNT.org for additional information provided by the Leave No Trace Center for Outdoor Ethics.

Appendix E:

Find Your Path on the National Trails

Is your path in life becoming too familiar or boring? Are you looking for a place where you can apply your scouting skills and at the same time challenge your physical and mental strengths? Are you interested in our country's rich and amazing history? As you contemplate the many paths in life, consider those offered within the National Trails System.

A masterpiece of 25 unique trails that crisscross the United States, the National Trails System was created by Congress in 1968 to specifically set aside and protect paths of high scenic and historic interest. Whether you set out on foot, horseback, watercraft, or motorized vehicle, you will find some of our nation's most beautiful, challenging, and thought-provoking places along these very trails.

Appalachian, Pacific Crest, and Continental Divide are probably the most well-known of the National Scenic Trails, but they are only three of our country's eight. Together covering more than 15,000 miles, and spanning most states in the Union, these footpaths have been created to give you ultimate access to the country's most awesome wild areas. Each trail presents a challenge like no other.

Pony Express, Lewis and Clark, and Oregon Trail are names from the past, but did you know these trails still exist? And they are just a few of those being preserved for our country's posterity. Collectively, the National Historic Trails span over 28,000 miles, all of them weaving together the fabric of America's past. You too can explore the same paths traveled by many of the people you've read about in your American history books.

So where is your path heading?

Visit www.nationaltrailspartnership.org to learn more about exploring and protecting these national treasures.

Index

About the Authors

Tim took the phone call while out West on business. On the other end of the line, Christine was breathless. "You have to see this place! It has a great fire pit out back for the Dutch ovens!" her first words describing what would ultimately become their country home in southeast Georgia. Most people probably wouldn't rank the fire pit high on the list of important features for a new house. But the Conners do, and it underscores their long fascination with the challenges presented by outdoor cooking.

Christine is a former Girl Scout from her home state of Hawaii. Tim was a Cub Scout during his youth in Ohio and, as an adult, has served as Den Leader and Assistant Cubmaster in Georgia's Coastal Empire Council. At the invitation

of the Boy Scouts of America, the Conners recently served as judges for *Scouting* magazine's prestigious national camp food cooking contest, a watershed moment that ultimately led to the creation of this book.

Experienced backpackers, Christine and Tim are the authors of *Lipsmackin' Backpackin'* and *Lipsmackin' Vegetarian Backpackin'*, two of the most popular trail cooking books of the past decade. They are active supporters of volunteer-based organizations that preserve and protect the nation's national scenic and historic trails. Christine is also a part-time college instructor of psychology as well as the author of *From High Heels to Bunny Slippers: Surviving the Transition from Career to Home*. By day, Tim is an aerospace engineer specializing in propulsion system design for supersonic aircraft.

Tim and Christine have been testing outdoor foods practically nonstop for over ten years now. They are grateful that their children, James, Michael, Maria, and David, are wonderfully accustomed to, and generally entertained by, the enormous range of outdoor culinary eccentricities that their parents have brought into the kitchen from the backyard.

The Conners family lives near Statesboro, Georgia, where a Dutch oven can often be found warming over coals in the fire pit.